Praise for

Up Tunket R

"Anyone who has heard Philip speak, seen his garden and home, or watched him teach about heritage breeds and heirloom seeds, knows that there is magic in this man. Now we are blessed with a story of his homestead that not only honors the past, but builds toward a healthier, richer future. Join in the magic!"

GARY PAUL NABHAN, author of *Where Our Food Comes From* and *Coming Home to Eat*, and editor of *Renewing America's Food Traditions*

"Anyone seeking a life characterized by noble intent will find this elegantly portrayed journey up Tunket Road both challenging and heartwarming. Philip Ackerman-Leist masterfully wrestles with homesteading tensions like independence versus community and ecological economy versus efficiency. I couldn't put it down."

JOEL SALATIN, founder of Polyface Farm and author of *Everything I Want to Do Is Illegal*

"Philip Ackerman-Leist's book, *Up Tunket Road*, combines highly literary writing with hard-nosed, down-home practicality about his homesteading ventures, all delivered with gentle good humor and an unerring eye for important details often left out of books like this. In the process, the author lays the groundwork for a definitive new approach to the classic back-to-the-land philosophy. A great book for thinkers and doers alike."

GENE LOGSDON, author of *Small-Scale Grain Raising* and *Living at Nature's Pace*

"There's something to learn on every page of this fertile and powerful book. One will find not simply good information, but also a fine and well-honed wisdom. In a voice that manages to be both teacher and student, Ackerman-Leist joins the literary tradition of Thoreau, the Nearings, and Harlan Hubbard. This is an honest and uplifting look at modern homesteading. What a delight to read this hopeful and iconic account of a sensible, accountable, and richly lived life. Now more than ever, we desperately need what this book offers."

JANISSE RAY, author of *Ecology of a Cracker Childhood*

"*Up Tunket Road* makes a delightful addition to the literature of homesteading. As persuasive and current as this book is about such subjects as grass-farming, composting toilets, and on-site generation of power, its strongest appeal to me is as the story of one intrepid family putting down roots in Vermont with the help of a generous, if highly eccentric, cast of mentors. Ackerman-Leist's deft use of dialogue, and his inclination to view even disasters humorously, also let him escape completely from the self-righteous tone that has sometimes marred America's literature of self-sufficiency. As a memoir, a piece of social history, and a reflection on farming and food at the cusp of the twenty-first century, this is a timely and valuable work."

JOHN ELDER, author of *Reading the Mountains of Home* and *The Frog Run*

"Having walked up the real Tunket Road many times over the past ten years to visit Philip and Erin, I have seen firsthand how they have transformed not only the landscape, but themselves and their lives. It is a model for us all to follow, rural or urban."

SHEPHERD OGDEN, editor of GreenRFD.com

"Philip Ackerman-Leist passionately describes homesteading not so much as a back-to-the-land form of self-reliance, but rather as a Zen-like practice of conscious decision making and being in right relationship. With this new understanding, creating a homestead is something any reflective practitioner can accomplish."

TOM WESSELS, author of *The Myth of Progress* and *Reading the Forested Landscape*

"*Up Tunket Road* captures the heart of homesteading by exploring its many tensions: romanticism versus pragmatism, humility versus bold determination, interdependence versus self-reliance, and vulnerability versus fortitude. Any thoughtful homesteader will find their perspective challenged and broadened by the anecdotes and reflections in these pages."

ABIGAIL R. GEHRING, editor of *Back to Basics* and *Homesteading*

UP TUNKET ROAD

UP TUNKET ROAD

the education of a
modern homesteader

PHILIP ACKERMAN-LEIST

Illustrations by
ERIN ACKERMAN-LEIST

CHELSEA GREEN PUBLISHING
WHITE RIVER JUNCTION, VERMONT

Project Manager: Patricia Stone
Developmental Editor: Benjamin Watson
Copy Editor: Laura Jorstad
Proofreader: Helen Walden
Designer: Peter Holm, Sterling Hill Productions

Printed in the United States of America
First printing May, 2010
10 9 8 7 6 5 4 3 2 1   10 11 12 13

Our Commitment to Green Publishing
Chelsea Green sees publishing as a tool for cultural change and ecological stewardship. We strive to align our book manufacturing practices with our editorial mission and to reduce the impact of our business enterprise on the environment. We print our books and catalogs on chlorine-free recycled paper, using vegetable-based inks whenever possible. This book may cost slightly more because we use recycled paper, and we hope you'll agree that it's worth it. Chelsea Green is a member of the Green Press Initiative (www .greenpressinitiative.org), a nonprofit coalition of publishers, manufacturers, and authors working to protect the world's endangered forests and conserve natural resources.

    Up Tunket Road was printed on Natures Book Natural, a 30-percent postconsumer recycled paper supplied by Thomson-Shore.

Library of Congress Cataloging-in-Publication Data
Ackerman-Leist, Philip, 1963-
  Up Tunket Road : the education of a modern homesteader / Philip
Ackerman-Leist ; illustrations by Erin Ackerman-Leist.
    p. cm.
  Includes bibliographical references and index.
  ISBN 978-1-60358-033-5
  1. Farm life--Vermont--Pawlet. 2. Family farms--Vermont--Pawlet. 3.
Sustainable living--Vermont--Pawlet. 4. Ackerman-Leist, Philip,
1963---Homes and haunts. 5. Ackerman-Leist, Erin--Homes and haunts. I.
Title.

  S521.5.V5A285 2010
  630.9743--dc22

2010010722

Chelsea Green Publishing Company
Post Office Box 428
White River Junction, VT 05001
(802) 295-6300
www.chelseagreen.com

To Bill & JoAnn Leist and Maggie & Daryl Ackerman,
for their love and support;

To Addy, Ethan, and Asa, who will follow Tunket Road,
wherever it might lead;

And to Erin, naturally, with love.

CONTENTS

Prologue . . . But Not Clear-Cut, ix

1. Once Upon a Tunket Time, 1
2. Learning One's Place, 18
3. When Time Was Made of Trees, 37
4. *Oikos:* A Household Economy and Ecology, 53
5. Looking Forward to Yesterday: Weaving Chronologies for the Future, 70
6. The Simple Life: An Ecological Misnomer, 102
7. Framing a Life, 119
8. Of Scale and Skill: Homestead or Farm?, 133
9. The End of Petrol, 143
10. Plowshares into Swards: Grass Farming, 152
11. The Smallholder as Placeholder, 163
12. Building a Future, 181
13. Crafting a Croft, 191
14. Technological Cascade, 213
15. The Clock, the Wallet, and the Hand, 236
16. Rewired Rewards, 250
17. To Gather Together, 263

Epi+log, 275

Acknowledgments, 277

Endnotes, 279

About the Author, 285

PROLOGUE . . . BUT NOT CLEAR-CUT

———

"You're gonna teach a course *on what?*" my friend Jim asked.

"Homesteading," I replied blithely, trying hard to counter his exaggerated disbelief with as much matter-of-factness as I could muster. "What's wrong with that?"

"*Homesteading?* Philip, this is a *college*—not a kids' survival camp or a retreat center for crystal-totin' barefoot Buddhists who want to live in the woods and poop in a bucket like you do!"

It was pretty much the response that I'd expected from Jim, a colleague known for his hyperbolic knee-jerk reactions to most anything outside his urbanized comfort zone. However, I suspect there were other colleagues who were just as skeptical of such a course, despite the fact that our college is known for breaking down a lot of traditional barriers in higher education. I couldn't really blame them.

After all, it was only after two decades of feeling the tug between the worlds of homesteading and academia that I myself was beginning to deeply appreciate the fact that homesteading is as much about values as it is about skills—in other words, just as much "why to" as "how to." Initially, I'd been more interested in how to sharpen chisels and scythes than I had been in articulating well-honed reasons for choosing and shaping an alternative lifestyle. Yet as the years went by, the rich history of life choices and the cultural heritage of the "how-tos" led me to believe that homesteading does in fact have a home within a progressive liberal arts education. After all, where else do theory, praxis, and notions of sustainability come together in a more palpable form than on a homestead?

Jim was clearly less convinced than I was of homesteading's relevance to any kind of academic inquiry. "You think the distance between your cabin and your outhouse is a path to enlightenment," he chided. "So why don't we all just trade our caps and gowns for coonskin hats and buckskin jackets?" He pretended to don and adjust a cap with what was obviously a long tail before starting to whistle a Daniel Boone tune for the march back to his office.

"Go back to your box, Jim, while the rest of us are working our way out of it. Maybe you're just jealous!"

Halting his one-man parade long enough to get in the last jab, he turned abruptly on his heel and gave me an exasperated look. "Oh yeah, and I go home and cry myself to sleep every night because I don't get to see the stars whenever I've gotta get up in the middle of the night and take a leak. . . ."

I began offering my new course, A Homesteader's Ecology, in spring 2005. Late in the semester, I was packing up after teaching class, putting my notes that had guided our discussion that day back in order, and tucking Scott Savage's *The Plain Reader* and Eric Brende's *Better Off: Flipping the Switch on Technology* back into my bag. I'd wondered how the discussion was going to go, since we were tackling homesteading from more of a philosophical approach that day—more why than how. But the students had found the readings engaging, as well as a bit controversial, so not only had they taken my questions seriously, but they'd come to class with plenty of their own. It had actually turned out to be one of the best classes of the semester.

Nonetheless, it was a glorious April day, and most of them made a beeline for the outside door as soon as we'd wrapped up the discussion and I'd given them a sense of my expectations for their final projects. No one had seemed completely confident about how to turn a homesteading project into an academic presentation. In fact, I was still working through that concept myself.

Aviva was casually packing up her belongings, screwing the lid back on her Mason jar that had been holding some hot-brewed concoction—now tinted green but probably not even lukewarm after a three-hour class. I think she was actually discreetly waiting to see if I needed any help carrying my bags. I was still on crutches after having my leg broken by a cow, ready to hurriedly hobble home to try and help my wife, Erin, juggle dinner while caring for two-year-old Asa and our new son Ethan, who was barely a month old.

I was still struggling with the dramatic shift in my reality—going from an independent do-it-myselfer to a high-maintenance encumbrance, particularly for Erin. Nowhere was the irony and the struggle more apparent to me or anyone else than in this class.

I stood up with the help of my crutches, then hoisted my backpack and struggled to get my arms through the straps, with one crutch falling against the whiteboard and then to the floor with an aluminum clatter. Aviva quickly grabbed the fallen crutch and got my second bag for me. She'd been kind enough to come up to our homestead with several students a few nights earlier to check on me and to help Erin with chores. In fact, we'd been barraged with help and food from the entire college community for several weeks, and I was trying to reconcile my long-cherished desire for independence and self-sufficiency with the reality of our reliance on others to get us through a particularly difficult predicament.

I hit the classroom light switch with my crutch, and we walked down the hall together, heading out the back door of the library basement to avoid the treacherously narrow staircase back up to the main exit. As I clumsily made my way through the heavy metal door to get to the parking lot, I thanked Aviva for the help and the food that she and the other students had provided. "I don't know what we would've done without everyone's help these last few weeks," I added.

"You would have managed, I guess, but I doubt it would be much fun." Understatement was one charming part of Aviva's contagious calm.

As we walked toward the parking lot, Aviva caught me off-guard. "You know, I don't think I'm so interested in this version of homesteading where you head for the hills and give up phone and e-mail access. I mean, I like staying connected—to friends, family . . . the world really. I don't need a lot of stuff. But I do need to feel a part of a community. I'm not even sure about the whole rural thing."

I took Aviva's response to heart. Besides the fact that she was an excellent student, she had come to the college a well-seasoned traveler and a quiet but articulate community activist. Not only had she worked on a kibbutz in Israel, but she had also volunteered for The Food Project in inner-city Boston, an extraordinary organization dedicated to building healthy urban communities through the skills passed on in community garden projects—in places where homesteading in its traditional rural American form probably seems like a far-fetched luxury.

I found myself coming back to her comment several times over the next few days. If someone like Aviva embraced so many of the ideals of the American homesteading vein but felt slightly disenfranchised from it because of the rural, back-to-the-land nature of its history, did it still make sense? Was there still something inherent in the homesteading tradition that made sense in our contemporary, high-tech, and increasingly urbanized world?

The students' presentations in the next two classes only pushed me farther in this line of thinking about homesteading's relevance to our contemporary world. Chris tackled the technology and communications issue head-on, journaling about his efforts to avoid using any electricity, telecommunications devices, and computers in his on-campus life for a week, despite living in a residence hall—wondering aloud if one could actually find a way to "homestead" on a college campus, even at a progressive college like ours. Ross designed a compact "sustainable" camper for leading a mobile lifestyle as a cross-country "nomadic homesteader." Morgan developed a full-fledged square-foot schematic for turning his entire suburban lot in Rhode Island into an edible landscape, dubbing it the "back-to-the-yard movement," a passion that eventually landed him in the Rhode Island School of Design to study landscape architecture.

They were all testing the homesteading definition, questioning its traditional rural context, and debating its place in the Information Age—just what young people are supposed to do . . . and precisely what a college education should foster. And yet they were still gravitating toward the ideals of minimized consumption, skills for self-reliance, and the search for meaning in the mundane.

In a way, they were thinking ecologically, recognizing that individuals and households are not autonomous units, segregated from ecological or social realities by distance, location, or ideals. They were, in fact, recognizing their place in the scheme of things, and instead of wanting to rebel by retreating, they were searching for new forms of "radical engagement."

As this next generation pushes the boundaries of homesteading, I've been fascinated with trying to understand what common elements in their new approaches constitute what we might call homesteading, especially when it's clear that the rural setting is no longer a prerequisite for one to be considered a homesteader.

The first assignment that I generally give in the course is to ask the students to define *homesteading* on blank pieces of paper—an exercise that I often repeat at the end of the course so that the students can see the progression of their thoughts. Initially, their expressions are about as blank as their sheets of paper. Then I see several slight smiles emerging, along with plenty of furrowed brows and a few continued puzzled expressions. A few students then start to whip out words with obvious confidence. Others begin writing reluctantly, their faces pensive and uncertain as they look between the ceiling and the paper for inspiration. Inevitably, the students' definitions orbit a few common themes. As the students share their definitions, their notions begin to overlap until the definitions start to sound repetitive. Despite the fact that many of them will soon veer away from their culturally instilled definition, nearly all gravitate toward a shared view of homesteading as *finding a piece of land in a rural setting to live a life of self-reliance.*

This book is as much a story about the evolution of a homesteader's assumptions and beliefs as it is a story about creating a back-to-the-land homestead. It is in part the story of living nearly eight years without electricity or running water in a small cabin before designing, building, and moving into a comfortable off-grid home built for a growing family and an expanding farm. But at its core, it is a book about the education of a homesteader . . . who just so happens to be an educator.

There are two obvious ironies that pervade the book. First, although the book is written by a college professor, it is clear that much of the learning I have most needed and cherished has either happened far outside any institutional bounds or has in fact been a direct result of questions and challenges raised by my students. The other irony is that living the back-to-the-land lifestyle in the midst of all of the ecological and social challenges of the early twenty-first century has forced me to question many of the inherited assumptions of the back-to-the-land tradition that I have for so long embraced.

This narrative is not about how to build a perfect homestead in the woods, although I would hope that an attentive reader would mine the ensuing adventures and misadventures for nuggets of wisdom. Rather, it is about choices, compromises, and realizations in the pursuit of evolving ideals. Our family's experience in contrasting much of the traditional homesteading literature with the realities of actually creating a rural homestead suggests that humility and honesty about the difficult individual choices and compromises are lacking in some of the accounts. Furthermore, the ecological constraints of our planet are clearer today than they have ever been, and we back-to-the-land homesteaders can no longer assume that our lives are quite as environmentally benign as we once thought them to be.

Like many back-to-the-landers, Erin and I began homesteading with the culturally inherited influences of Thoreau, the Nearings, John

Seymour, and a host of others. We inherited a rich cultural tradition of back-to-the-land values and approaches. However, the seeming cultural consensus—that homesteading should generally involve *finding a piece of land in a rural setting to live a life of self-reliance*—now strikes me as problematic at this point in human history.

It's not that such a view doesn't work—but I am not convinced that such a narrow definition adequately fits our contemporary realities. Thoreau's Walden Pond is now surrounded by a highly urbanized culture. We've traded a wild world for a wired world, and the homesteader's quest for answers to burning philosophical questions is now more a search for responses to a warming planet suffering from overconsumption, biodiversity losses, increasing population pressures, and continuing poverty.

Nonetheless, if ever homesteading could be relevant, it is now. After all, so much of what homesteading can engender—sustainability values, practical living skills, and appropriate technologies—is critically important in helping to work our way through many of our current ecological and cultural problems. Ultimately, what is not pioneered and adopted in our own households is unlikely to become either a cultural norm or sound public policy.

However, homesteading will not be relevant if we continue to define it in the same way that we have in the United States for nearly two centuries. In my view, there are three basic misconceptions in our inherited cultural understanding of homesteading as *finding a piece of land in a rural setting to live a life of self-reliance*.

Misconception #1: "finding a piece of land"
Unfortunately, our culture tends to assume that homesteading, however you choose to define it, is an act that begins with finding a piece of land. Yet with the advantage of hindsight after years of homesteading, I think homesteading starts well before there's a place involved. It involves a kind of learning generally not embraced by our educational system or our culture of instantaneous information.

I believe that homesteading begins first by questioning the status quo. Sometimes the questions are ecological in nature, but they may just as often be related to personal health, spiritual quests, cultural morals, or technological concerns. This questioning of the status quo is generally followed by listening, observing, apprenticing, and experimenting, often for many years before there is ever a piece of property—or an apartment or an anchorage—where one decides to put down roots. In fact, there doesn't even have to be a place associated with homesteading: It can be a state of mind instead of a state of residence.

Sadly, many of us now have to relearn how to homestead because so many of the necessary skills that were once considered an ordinary part of life were traded in for a manufactured life of relative ease and convenience over the course of just a few generations. Those all-too-rare people who can teach us *how* to homestead can also teach us *why* to homestead. Knowing why keeps us doing it on the days when it's not as simple as we thought when we first started . . . and it reminds us where we were headed when we waved good-bye to a more familiar life and struck out for unfamiliar territory—even if that new territory was mostly just the uncharted terrain of our own minds.

Misconception #2: "in a rural setting"
For some of us, perhaps. However, homesteading, as our culture typically portrays it, has been predominantly a monochrome and middle- to upper-class phenomenon over the years, following bucolic footsteps into pastoral and forested settings . . . and that's not where most of the world is headed. We just recently crested the global demographic wave at which point more humans now live in cities than elsewhere.

If we believe that homesteading values, skills, and technologies are relevant in their utility for persons of all places and persuasions, and that the homesteading "movement" can benefit from a diversity of perspectives and approaches, then it's high time for us to shed the notion that homesteading is exclusively a rural, back-to-the-land phenomenon, reserved only for those financially comfortable enough to make the deliberate choice to explore the flip side of the contemporary American dream, swapping comfort for vulnerability, convenience for complexity, and paved routes for country roots. And if homesteaders are indeed pioneers in the search for more appropriate values and lifestyles, then the true frontiers for such collaborative exploration include urban areas, suburbs, and crumbling rural communities—not just the old *Mother Earth News* backwoods dream.

Lest I be accused of hypocrisy, for I have certainly followed the trajectory of the homesteading tradition into the forests and fields of several mountain cultures, I should make it clear that I simply believe that we all have preferences for certain environments, places that we call home and make home. Homesteading, at its best, is a way of transforming skills and values into a lifestyle, no matter where one feels most at home.

I confess to being of a back-to-the-land persuasion—deeply influenced by the rich literary tradition of a host of rural homesteaders and agrarians—but as I explore the concept of homesteading with students from urban and suburban backgrounds, as well as from other countries, it is clear to me that it makes little sense to encourage the next generation of homesteaders to carve up the remainder of our relatively intact natural ecosystems simply for the sake of well-intentioned homesteading experiments, particularly when the transformation of our suburban, urban, and rural neighborhoods and ecosystems is so critical.

Finally, while this next generation seems to find homesteading values, skills, and technologies appealing, many of them are not so excited about the prospects of giving up the urban and suburban environments that they consider home. If the homesteading movement can build upon coming generations' sense of belonging in more densely populated areas than we have traditionally considered to be homesteading territory, then homesteading might move closer to the core of our culture, accompanied by revisited homesteading values, skills, and technologies that fit those environments.

Misconception #3: "to live a life of self-reliance"

The icons of the homesteading movement, unfortunately, have portrayed themselves (or have been portrayed by others) as virtually self-reliant individuals who retreated from society in order to live lives of utter independence. Our cultural images and casual interpretations don't tell the whole story—of Thoreau's trips to town for meals and supplies during his relatively short two-year stint portrayed in *Walden,* of the Nearings' dependence upon visitors and apprentices for labor, of the Mother Earth back-to-the-landers who would have failed or in some cases perished were it not for the native pragmatism of their farmer neighbors. We need to recognize that homesteading is as much about recognizing interdependence as it is about seeking isolation and independence. It is also about letting go of ego. The more serious we get about ecology, the clearer it should become that a search for complete autonomy is neither laudable nor realistic.

To whatever degree *interdependence* was once a more accurate description of homesteading than utter *independence,* it is increasingly true today. We are trading our wild world for a wired world and creating a world of unprecedented "connectivity." Meanwhile, the ecological and social challenges that we currently face make any call to disengage from society seem selfish and shortsighted, particularly if the values, skills, and ecological understandings shared by most homesteaders are considered valuable and worth passing on to others.

If there is any misperception about homesteading that needs to be corrected, it is that homesteading is ultimately a quest for total independence. While it may be true that many of us are searching for a certain control over our lives, we need to recognize the painful irony that we are in our current national predicament because we have been living atomistic lives of wild abandon—ignoring the sum total of our individual frenzies. We now have the chance to get a hold on our households and collectively rekindle common purposes that are bigger than any one of us.

Homesteaders cannot afford to try to completely retreat from society with what are hopefully well-considered values and reasonably sophisticated ecological understandings—particularly not in a time of ecological and human peril. We need to jettison our cultural belief that homesteading must involve ascetic self-righteousness in our rural retreats and instead embrace the belief that we are collectively in search of a carefully crafted interdependence. And while this interdependence should perhaps most often be locally rooted, it must also be global in scope.

Distance, in and of itself, is not our enemy; distance is not inherently evil. Our concern should be less about distance than it is about the lack of relationships that underlie our mutual interdependence. The key is to trade anonymity and ignorance for intimacy and understanding. Distance is an ecological concern, not a moral one.

One of the best things about teaching—in fact, its greatest privilege—is learning with and from one's students. I've been fortunate enough to think and read a lot about homesteading over the past few years, while also visiting a number of homesteads with my students, sometimes as field trips and at other times vicariously, by way of student papers and projects describing homesteads that they are required to visit on their own. My students, fellow homesteaders, and a host of authors, bloggers, and videographers have pushed me to think not just about what homesteading is and has been, but also about what it can be.

I confess that I am hesitant to try to define homesteading, partly because it seems perilous to define something that is constantly changing, perhaps now more than ever before. Furthermore, so much of the American homesteading tradition involves trying to break down definitions, stereotypes, and cultural behaviors. Trying to create a staid and enduring definition of homesteading would be at best to circumscribe the possibilities and at worst to deny the inclusion of a diversity of approaches.

However, I am willing to propose a spirit of intent for homesteading in the twenty-first century. It is what I would call "a homesteader's ecology"—a way of thinking that can inform many ways of living.

Developing a homesteader's ecology involves first trying to understand one's place in a vast ecological web and then creating a life that aims to address the scientifically documented constraints of our planet. The challenges are daunting: dwindling resources stretched further by exploding consumption, dramatic increases in human population matched by unprecedented population losses in other species, and climate change magnified by the status quo. Ultimately, a homesteader's ecology is a never-ending experiment in minimizing our individual and collective consumption of resources, a modest exercise in determined optimism.

Consumption in and of itself is an ecological process, not an abstract evil. Overconsumption is the issue—creating social inequities, species imbalances, and out-of-kilter ecosystems. A homesteader's ecology is not about dancing around the edges of the conundrum of overconsumption. Rather, it is about consciously habiting the center of these questions, all the while contemplating and calibrating our individual and collective scales of expectation. The household is the starting point for these questions, and any household that constantly pries apart the questions and then tests the potential answers on a daily basis is a homestead, whether it is in a rural, suburban, or urban area.

While homesteading has traditionally involved a rejection of the status quo, the notion of homesteading as an act of social disengagement is probably too selfish in our current era. If a homesteader is by nature an ecologist, then he or she must recognize that we are all connected, no matter how distant. And in a world in peril—be the dangers ecological, economic, social, or cultural—it makes no sense to feign autonomy. Checking out is, in most ways, an artificial exercise. It does little to solve our collective quandary.

We share the dilemmas, but if we don't work to share the solutions, then we probably won't get too far—and certainly not fast enough. Homesteading can be a relatively passive and isolated life of inquiry, or it can be an engaging means of bringing the questions to life . . . and then sharing not only the answers but also the lingering uncertainties.

The magnitude of the challenges we face is surpassed only by their impending velocity, not to mention their snowballing interrelatedness. Pondered for any length of time, it can all seem overwhelming. As a result, we can wallow in despair and apathy.

Or we can celebrate the reinventing of the world.

The adventure begins at home.

ONE

Once Upon a Tunket Time

I've envisioned a lot of ways that I don't want to die, and it was in part the fear of becoming a casualty of a "hippie burner"—a 55-gallon drum converted into a woodstove—that drove me to strike out one morning in fall 1996 to find our "grubstake," an affordable place that we would probably need to make into a home before calling it home. At the time, my wife Erin and I were "island-sitting" as summer caretakers on Neshobe Island in the middle of Lake Bomoseen in western Vermont. That's when I decided that, no matter how nice or how free the digs were, we needed a home and a safer source of heat than a woodstove that might incinerate us, leaving nothing behind but two charred pairs of Birkenstocks. And getting to and from our island home by means of "The Frog"—the avocado-green boat that shuttled us back and forth—was beginning to lose its romanticism as autumn weather set in.

A few days earlier, our landlord Mr. Chandler had told us the story of hanging out on the island too late one fall day while working on the furnace, only to see the ice begin to skim across the lake. His depiction of the event was enough to make me feel like a bear getting an urge to settle into a den while his belly was still full and the air not utterly frigid. Apparently, Mr. Chandler and his friend had learned how quickly skim ice can become real ice, and they had to use the bow of the boat to break through the thickening surface to get from the island back to shore—an idea that worked fine, until a piece of ice pierced the bow, and Mr. Chandler had to spend the rest of the ride keeping his foot and a towel in the hole, with both he and his friend frantically baling while navigating through and even over the growing ice. I wasn't quite sure what to expect of our first Vermont winter, but I was pretty sure it didn't make sense to spend it on an island.

So I left Erin and Maggie, her mom, basking in the sun on this spectacular fall day and promised to be back before too long with The Frog, in case they wanted to go somewhere that evening. I shot across the half mile of slate-gray water with that chortling throttle noise that was half gurgle and half whine—the blue sky beckoning and the brisk air reminding me why I was headed out with a certain urgency, but with not a clue as to where. It just seemed like a good day to find home.

I'd been a vagabond for the decade prior, always coming back to farming and carpentry as my two insatiable passions. *What* I did was more important to me than where I did it, although everywhere I ended up was always pretty much where I wanted to be at the time. Three of those years, from 1991 to 1994, were spent in the Alps of the South Tirol, living and working at Brunnenburg Castle—a farm, an agricultural museum, an international study center, and home to the family of American poet Ezra Pound. I'd been a student there in 1983 and returned as an instructor for a semester in 1988, and I just couldn't get enough, so an invitation from the family to return there to farm and to teach for several years was a good way to get distance from a failed first marriage.

Not a bad place to end up—and a pretty idyllic place to meet Erin, the beautiful, long-haired, hardy artist type that I'd always hoped to meet. Not every guy gets to meet his dream in a castle. But I had also fallen in love with a culture that enraptured me—and one that was just as adept as Erin at playing hard to get—that of the South Tirolean *Bergbauern,* or "mountain farmers."

The American suburbs were, for me (and as it turned out, for Erin, too) a place of ennui and overdone comfort. The La-Z-Boy rocker and the challenge of maintaining impossibly perfect, ego-laden lawns were, to us, the symbols of good intentions gone awry. Life on the steep slopes with mountain farmers was far different. These were people who were "made of home," native to a place in a way that I'd never seen before but living a life that I had always wanted. Leaving that culture after three years was the hardest decision I've ever made, but it didn't seem likely that I would ever be able to afford a piece of land there, and my yearning for a place that offered wildness as well as a rich farming tradition meant that the United States was probably a better choice to build the life that Erin and I both seemed to want. The Tiroleans have a topographically intense life, but they don't have much in the way of expansive wilderness, as we do. In fact, many of my friends there dream of coming to the US or Canada to live "the trapper's life," a romanticized version of what our culture has fled from. I shared some of their sentiments and felt like I was embarking on a similar quest for solace and a simpler life.

The Frog eased up to the dock, with an inevitable bump signaling the end of the ride and a certain transition to normalcy. Tying the boat to the cleats was always an acknowledgment that we were again trading our relative solitude for the usual ways of the world. That said, coming back to the dock later in the day and unleashing ourselves with a quick flick of braided rope meant that we could make a conscious choice to "check out" from a world that we found too fast and materialistic. On this particular day, I was especially curious as to what I might find in the short time between mooring and unmooring.

Although eager to see what kind of land options might be out there, I didn't expect to come back to Erin and Maggie with much more news than the details of a beautiful drive. It wasn't as if I was heading out with any substantial financial reserves, or even a lucrative or stable job—we were living well below the poverty line at that time. We'd recently come to Vermont, where I was offered a job teaching English to international students at Green Mountain College, a school that had recently adopted an innovative "environmental liberal arts" program in which all students take the standard array of liberal arts requirements, but through a suite of courses that have the environment as a central theme. My ultimate intention was to start a college farm on campus, but at the time more people seemed opposed to the idea than for it, including several key members of the board of trustees. I never suspected that starting a garden would be such a controversial act, and it wasn't entirely clear at that point in time that I was going to survive at the college, either. Whatever place we found had to be the right spot, a place where we wanted to stay, regardless of my employment situation.

I got The Frog tied off on the proper side of the dock, given the prevailing winds. We had sunk it twice already, right to the end of its mooring ropes, due to the fact that a northwest wind would sometimes sneak up on the far end of the lake and bring waves up and over the stern, filling the boat to its brim and swamping it. Believe me, it is quite disconcerting to come back to a dock and find your boat missing, with nothing but the ropes as evidence of its watery resting place. Outboard motors may have their ecological shortcomings, but they are particularly inefficient after being submerged.

I jumped in our red Nissan four-wheel-drive truck, fresh from my home state of North Carolina and ready for Vermont. I hadn't yet learned that four-wheel drive is simply an excuse for my employer to expect me to make it to work in most any weather and for me to get stuck deeper, worse, and faster.

I went less than a mile down the road and grabbed the local real estate guide from a nearby convenience store. I perused it with a cup of coffee in my hand, circling a few listings that seemed somewhat interesting. Actually, our price range—as close to zero as possible—meant that most of the interesting options never got to the point of being considered. "Old farmhouse and barn with outbuildings, set on 50 acres of land with south-facing slopes and ample water—mix of pastures and forest-land" was clearly the out-of-reach ideal, but seclusion and the right price came in a close second. If the South Tirolean Bergbauern had taught me anything, it was that one can make do, get by, and be happy with steep slopes, constrained soils, and minimal access. Of course, they'd generally had anywhere between ten and thirty generations of large farm families to get the farms in order, but Erin and I had time, patience, and obstinacy on our side. It also seemed like one more argument for the practice of procreation.

As I worked my way through the real estate ads, I noted one that said:

> **VERMONT AT ITS BEST.** An old stagecoach road leads to this beautiful 25-acre parcel of vintage Vermont Americana. The land is gently sloping back through some gorgeous hard-woods with a magnificent meadow in front. An old 2-room cabin sits atop the meadow with beautiful long-range views down the Mettowee Valley! The setting and ambiance has to be seen—truly Vermont at its best. **Offered exclusively at $39,900 with possible owner financing.**

It stood out, both for its isolation and its price. It would be my orbit for the day. I would check out a few other properties on the way and then zero in on that one. I began by driving past one of the listed properties, but it had little visual appeal. I've always trusted my gut and my sense of visual imagination in such matters, so when my imagination wasn't sparked by the lay of the land, I kept driving. The next parcel had a bit more appeal. It was sloped toward the south and east, and it had several old apple trees scattered about. Water, however, seemed marginal, and it was in a spot prime to become part of a bedroom community for the nearby city of Rutland.

I headed on to the village of Pawlet to find the Realty office that was listing the property on "an old stagecoach road." Nearing the hamlet, I was immediately drawn to the surrounding landscape of the Mettowee Valley, and I could feel a sense of community that seemed to fit the bottomland farms lining the southbound valley. As I traveled south, the valley floor broadened while the flanking hills grew in elevation. I could see the faint etching of gravel roads darting east and west into the burnished hills. The patchwork of pastures and cornfields hugged the valley floor rather tightly for the most part, with a few slipping up into the hills, often bordering brook-fed ravines.

I followed the southward swoop of Route 30 in its last sweeping curve before entering the hill-tucked hamlet of Pawlet. I felt my body pulled left by the tug of the tilting truck, but my eyes were drawn to the right, smitten by the sight of farm fields hugging the Mettowee River before surrendering to the wooded edge of the village center. As I slowed to pass the post office and millpond on my left, I realized that this big curve in the road—built over the fast-charging waters of Flower Brook—was in fact the center of Pawlet. Like so many Vermont villages, the confluence of waterways was also the confluence of commerce. Sure enough, I could see the blocky, black-stenciled lettering for Mach's General Store on the white facade of the building that actually straddled the two sides of Flower Brook, on the opposite side of the road from the mill pond.

I could smell the wood smoke I saw rising from a little building attached to the road side of the general store, and I saw a sign for Mach's Brick Oven, with handwritten pizza-box ads for fresh bread and wood-fired pizza taped to the windows. I turned off Route 30 and parked right in front of the general store, in the company of an assortment of pickups. The scent of wood smoke, bread, and pizza from a wood-fired oven, the muffled cascade of water, a general store, well-tended dairy farms—it was as close as I'd gotten to the Alps since I'd left them.

Ducking into the store to get some juice and a snack, I opened the door and was greeted—with muted nods—by a gathering of locals perched around the coffeepot, all of them trading gentle jabs with the woman behind the deli counter. She was lobbing back one-liners that made it clear just how consistent and practiced the gathering was—and who was in charge. I smiled, nodded back to the few who'd tipped their heads my way, and headed for the beverage cooler that I could see in the rear of the store.

Walking to the back, I heard the rushing of water. I looked to see if someone had opened a nearby door to the outside, but it sounded like the murmur was coming from the middle of the store. The worn, wooden floors squeaked as I continued to walk back to the cooler, with the sound amplifying in volume. As I neared the cooler, I saw what looked to be a large wooden box rising up out of the floor, with a decorative metal heating register fastened to its top. I could smell water. To my complete shock, I looked down through the ornate register and into what was in fact an open shaft above the roiling waters of Flower Brook, with a good portion of the brook's flow snared and twisted in whirlpools by giant, sculpted bowls in the solid rock below. I immediately started to hope that the stagecoach road might have as much appeal as the village of Pawlet.

I walked out of the store and, surprisingly, the sign for McChesney Real Estate was directly across the street. I'd parked in just the right spot. Nonetheless, I was quite nervous walking into the brick real estate building perched in the center of the village. I didn't have any business looking for land.

I had a tenuous, low-paying job that seemed only as certain as my own bullheadedness. We had a few thousand dollars to use as a down payment toward the purchase of our "farm in the mountains," a phrase that I'd slipped into Erin's copy of our wedding vows that I had written for us and that we'd practiced a few times. Once I saw that she was going to need a cheat-sheet, I saw the opportunity to help fulfill my lifelong dream, so I recopied the vows and stuck in the sentence, "I also promise to buy you a farm in the mountains." I didn't insert any requirements as to when or where, but I did need some verbal buy-in for the concept, preferably stated in public. It worked.

I walked into the real estate office, expecting to deal with either a skeptical, spectacled old Vermonter or a grease-your-palm slippery character just waiting for a fool like me. What I found instead was a young fellow about my age and with most of my aspirations. Scott McChesney was stepping into his father's shoes, learning the real estate business while building his own house. He had a work ethic that I immediately liked, and he didn't laugh me out of the office, as he should have, especially for the inevitably paltry commission he'd earn on a high-risk candidate like me. Before I knew it, I'd laid my heart out on the table, and he had given me directions to find the property on Tunket Road, the old stagecoach road mentioned in the ad.

"You won't believe this," Scott said, "but I even named my dog Tunket—just because I love that place so much." Even though I'd already gotten to the point of really liking Scott, I couldn't help but think that this had to be the oldest trick in the shadowy book of the real estate world—and I wasn't going to be a sucker. I wouldn't believe it until I heard him call the dog by name and saw the pooch come to him.

Sure enough, as soon as I got the hand-drawn map from Scott and went to head out the door, I heard him say, "C'mere, Tunket, let's go home!" A big yellow Lab bounded up from a nap in the corner, his oversized feet slipping into second gear on the hardwood floor.

Hmm, maybe this all does make sense in some weird way, I thought as I headed out the door and into the truck. I drove more on adrenaline than gas, I think.

The property on Tunket Road was accessed by a long-standing right-of-way through Tunket Meadows, otherwise known as "Donald Waite's farm." Scott had told me to park at the bottom of the hill, out of the way of the farm access roads, and head up the hill. If I met any of the Waite family, he said that I should simply tell them that I was going to look at "Ruth and Tom's property" up the hill. My uncle, a savvy real estate investor, once told me to avoid properties with rights-of-way, but I couldn't help but imagine how I was going to get "way back in" without having to cross someone's land.

I jumped out of the truck with my parcel map, most of it drawn in by a surveyor, but with a 3-acre portion of it sketched in by a Realtor's untrained hand.

"That's the 3 acres across the road that makes this a 25-acre parcel," Scott noted as he had handed me the map. "Twenty-five acres gives you enough to build on in that zone, and it means you can put the land in Current Use—the forestry management program that helps keep your taxes down if you agree to log it. Tom and Ruth have just used it as a summer getaway. He's a Unitarian minister from Rhode Island, and this is where he came to regroup. It's pretty primitive, but see what you think. Be careful not to fall through the porch—it's got some rotten spots!"

The day was getting later than I'd planned. *Tunket Road,* as it turned out, was a bit of a misnomer. It was definitely more than a path, but its northern trajectory from the base of the hill adjacent to the Waites' farm was more an invitation to a hiker than an enticement to a driver of anything that needed an intact exhaust system, much less an oil pan. The early-autumn light streaming in from the west pushed its way through the leaves on the left-hand side of the road, turning the walk into a tunnel of greens and anxious yellows.

I went uphill, just as Scott said, but I wasn't prepared for the vista from the meadow at the top of the hill, the point at which the old road emerged from the tunnel of tree-filtered light. As soon as I crested the hill, Haystack Mountain leapt up in the western sky—not with the drama of the Alps, but with all of the gentle beauty that makes Vermonters stay despite mud season (both the fall and the spring versions), the bitter cold (sometimes in January and occasionally in July), or the annual invasion of those who want to know what all of the fuss is about in autumn (but aren't always sure when it occurs). Haystack's southern flank fell sharply, with stone-honed edges that are reminders of an ancient glacier's game of plucking off the southern ends of north–south mountain chains in our hemisphere.

Behind Haystack rose Middle Mountain, a slightly bigger sister but with rounder form and not quite the height of the third sibling, Bald Mountain. "Baldy" was the broody one in the bunch, hovering knowingly from a distance, not quite sure what to think of Haystack's more juvenile form—cleavage showing and open top, beckoning to anyone in a playful mood to swing by for a jaunt.

The road flattened, as if in sync with a hiker's need to bask in the vista for a while, before entering another arbor-arcade and twisting gently uphill. At this point, I couldn't help but think that the property must be nearby. I kept looking for fences and red-tipped corner posts, but the road kept winding through the trees. After about a quarter of a mile, I came to a point where the light ahead and to the right seemed to intensify . . . a clearing, of sorts—if brambles 5 feet high warrant the word *clearing*. With enough imagination and an appreciation for the seeming spontaneity of late-hanging berries, such a clearing can feel like paradise.

Erin and I had built a log cabin on my grandparents' farm in North Carolina during the months prior to moving to Vermont. We thought that we might live in it if we could adapt to eastern North Carolina. However, the heat and topographically monotonous landscape were too much of a contrast with life in the Alps. Yearnings for a more captivating landscape often left me melancholic, and Erin had never been comfortable with the idea of living anywhere south of her home state of

Pennsylvania. Nonetheless, we thought that investing ourselves in the construction of a cabin might somehow foster our sense of belonging to the somewhat austere eastern North Carolina landscape. We cleared an area just big enough for the cabin next to the pond, only to discover that we had the perfect vantage point for watching water moccasins that rivaled my wiry 6-foot length swim across the pond—an unsettling sight for anyone thinking of settling down.

Keeping an eye out for snakes, poison ivy, and black widow spiders, I took down the trees for the cabin with an ax. We cleaned them with drawknives and carved the saddle notches with a chainsaw and hand tools. The trees surrounding the cabin weren't large enough to harvest for construction, so we left the forest intact—except for the footprint of the cabin—and took down some of the yellow pines planted elsewhere on the farm by my grandfather in order to halt the rampant erosion he'd found when he had purchased the land twenty-five years before.

There were ample fields and orchards on the rest of the farm. In fact, we'd chosen the cabin site in an effort to have some shelter from the openness of the eastern North Carolina landscape, to have a hovel that contrasted with the daily farmwork in the open fields and peach orchards. Creating a forest retreat, instead of retreating from the forest, was an idea that stood in stark contrast with the prevailing tendencies in Europe and America. Generally, the move from forest to clearing has been considered in our cultures to be a shift from savagery, vagary, and mere subsistence to civilization, certainty, and a profitable life.

The eighteenth-century Italian philosopher Vico maintained that civilization is born out of a clearing, the opening or "eye" of the forest. There is a long European history of fearing the entropy of the forest, and it has persisted in the American mind-set in many regards. While I have never wanted to subscribe even to an informal doctrine that sees order in humans and chaos in nature—as opposed to the reverse—I do confess to a persistent yearning to circumscribe and set boundaries, to carve meaning out of the landscape in an effort to link subsistence with everyday life.

A clearing in the midst of the woods has always appealed to me—the joy of having it both ways, "letting go" in the forest and giving form to a well-ordered farm in the clearing. A homestead, for me, was countercultural in that it seemed to involve leading a carefully considered life. Crafting a life of intentionality, one that is neither narcissistic nor nihilistic, is certainly a cultural challenge for those of us Americans of moderate or ample means. But it's hard to be narcissistic or nihilistic when wielding a hoe, especially when facing a forest's edge.

"Wild" apple trees served as the intermediaries between the forest and this clearing a mile up Tunket Road. They were the sentinels of change in this clearing's ambiguous identity—neither field nor forest. Some of the apple trees swept up large portions of sky in their arcing branches, while others drooped with the weight of time and the encroaching shadows from the woods' edge. As I walked, I started sampling the balance of apples remaining after the early-autumn winds and chattering squirrels had gleaned their fair share during the previous weeks. Tart, sweet, tangy, bitter—the tastes were as varied as the appearances—red, green, yellow, russet; mottled, spotted, round, and cat-faced.

I'd seen colored plates in old books that depicted some of the apple diversity surrounding me in this field, but now I was coloring my palate with unexpected shades of taste. I'd only gotten a taste of Tunket, and I could barely make out the faint outline of a cabin roof emerging from the brambles just uphill, but I'd tasted enough to sense that I'd come home to a place of magic that had been priced at $39,900 because of its isolation—precisely what we were in the market for! Someone long ago had lived here year-round—that was evident from the number of apple trees and stone walls. Perhaps we could reclaim instead of invade.

I worked my way through the brambles as the sun leveled out and neared Haystack's silhouette. The cabin was small, 12' × 28', but it was simple and cozy. I looked in the windows, and the selection of books confirmed my hunch that this was the place to be. I just hoped they would throw the books into the deal—an eclectic mix of nature writing, religious works, and how-to texts that all fit the spirit of the place. I didn't plan on entering the cabin, but someone had broken the padlock on the door at some point, so it was easy to open. I stepped inside, struck first by the earthy smell of several species of rodents—from deer mice to flying squirrels. The mattress was a mess—apparently used by hunters or hikers in rut and subsequently by rodents in jubilee mode. A marble slab on the floor and a dangling stovepipe marked the nearly haunting absence of a woodstove. The cabin comprised two abutting rooms, one apparently built after the other. As I stepped from one to the other, I had the sensation of being in the fun house at a county fair, with rooms slightly askew and the door oddly ajar. I looked up and noticed that the roof of the second, smaller addition had pulled away from the main room, with water stains on the inside wall marking the gap.

I went outside to investigate the problem, nearly falling through a rotten section of the porch. Prolific rosebushes, bearing the biggest rose hips I'd ever seen, skirted the edges of the porch. I painfully made my way to the edge of the cabin and peeked under to check out the foundation. Each part of the cabin had been built on cinder-block pillars that had sunk and pitched, leaving the cabin's two rooms sitting on the ground and stretching apart, with some of the sills and joists rotting in the wet humus and rich mud of the gently sloping hill. It didn't look like anything I couldn't fix, based on the several years of carpentry experience that I'd gained after getting a college degree in philosophy.

My heart raced as fast as my mind as I went back up to the cabin for a final peek. I noticed several identical bumper stickers on a shelf that said I'D RATHER BE STARGAZING, with a telescope pointing up. Maybe Unitarians and Vico had something in common. Part of the reason Vico believed clearings to be so important in creating civilizations was because the "eye" of the clearing allowed humans to forge a celestial connection that lent itself to spiritual understanding.[1] Regardless, I didn't need philosophical or spiritual rationalizations for being smitten with the landscape up Tunket Road—I'd tasted the apples.

But I still needed to see at least a representative sample of the rest of the property. From the vantage point of the cabin, I could see that the clearing was fringed with white pines, which were in turn bounded by mixed hardwoods. The reason for these concentric rings of vegetation—old field to white pine to hardwoods—would become clearer with time and inquiry, thanks to our farmer neighbors and my graduate school professors. I set out uphill and east behind the cabin, moving from a carpet of pine needles, interspersed with apple drops, and to a rich hardwood duff, potent with the scent of fungal decomposition.

The hardwoods appeared almost as suddenly as did the tumbledown stone wall running north–south across the property, nearly paralleling Tunket Road. The hardwoods continued from the stone wall nearly to the top of the hill, a promontory that I later learned was called Fox Cobble. That was the point at which the hardwood forest transitioned almost immediately to a landscape reminiscent of the Southern Appalachians: hop hornbeam, hickory, red oak, and even a few scattered white oaks predominated, all set within a park-like landscape of grasses draping all but the sharpest rock outcrops. None of what I noticed turned out to be sheer coincidence, but it took years of study and questions at our neighbors' dinner table to decipher much of what had happened here. What I didn't know at the time was that the landscape that stirred my visual imagination had already aroused the ecological imaginations of the staff at the Vermont chapter of The Nature Conservancy.

Just the rich store of untouched maples, oak, and ash in the ledge-encompassed bowl on the eastern half of the property seemed to be worth $39,900 to me—certainly so when combined with the view to the west from the uphill lip of the semicircular ledge that wrapped around the parcel as if it were an arm of the earth, protecting this little hardwood haven from the ravages of the cut-and-run logging operation that I had noted on the opposite side of Tunket Road. Regardless of whether we thought the cabin could serve as a long-term residence for us, the clearing, the hardwoods, and the ample number of springs working their way downhill from the ledge-lined basin all made it seem to me that the marriage vows were perhaps nearly complete.

The next step was to see what Erin thought. I wasn't sure if she would be smitten quite as quickly as I was. She had always been the realist who saw things at face value, whereas I was generally more optimistic and willing to look for potential—whether in land, houses, or people. Both perspectives had their merit: she saw the realities, and I conjured the dreams. In sum, I tend to be the one more likely to get burned. It was time to head back to the island and confer with my reality check.

I made my way back downhill to the edge of the clearing. I got my bearings as I aimed toward Haystack, slightly obscured by the several white pines that were the harbingers of the return of the forest. I crushed my way through the brambles again, paying close attention to the more heavily barbed blackberries, opting instead to part my way through the waxy purple raspberry stems, their raspy arms better at tangling than piercing. I bade farewell to a view I hoped we might call home.

I've always felt nestled by mountains and vulnerable in openness. I don't need to be coddled, but I do need to be cradled—and mountains ensure both, no matter how high or steep. I knew I could trade the severity and the drama of the Alps for the wildness and the isolation of Tunket Road, especially if it meant sharing the experience of building a homestead with Erin.

I took one more look at the cabin, barely visible among the vertical stubbornness of the New England forest. The last three centuries in Vermont have been a shifting tide of clearings and forest, with surges emanating from demographic pressures to settle every nook and cranny and subsequent tugs stemming from cultural trends to move elsewhere or to trade fields and pastures for easier, better-paying jobs. In fact, ecologists call the shift from open land to forest a "release." Nature is once again unfettered by the demands and constraints of our need and desire to raise food and fiber, and, in Vermont, nature released is like a freed captive, sprinting for somewhere as distant as possible from current reality.

As I headed back down Tunket Road with light feet and racing thoughts, I took closer note of the route down. Locust posts held fast to strings of barbed wire along the eastern flank of the road, and the old field with the spectacular views of Haystack boasted of its history with three huge sugar maples along the roadside, all more heavily branched on the open western sides in an effort to capture as much sun as possible. All three bore the Vermont trademark—rings of now barely visible tap holes circling each tree's girth from waist to breast height.

The stone walls that flanked both sides of the road on its downhill trajectory were diminished from their original 4-foot-plus stature by frost-heaves, forest duff, accumulated road gravel, and the collapse of neighboring trees. Nonetheless, the careful placement of the remaining stones and their long-established colonies of lichens were reminders that someone long ago had chosen this spot quite intentionally.

It would be a few years before I discovered a reference to *Tunket* in a history of Vermont place-names, in which *Tunket* is described as a possible derivation of the Abenaki word *k't-hunk,* meaning "a large, swift stream." The entry goes on, however, to describe *Tunket* as a mild curse—an epithet for "hell"—then citing a possible example of its use:

"Why in the Tunket would he want to live there?"[2]

As I got back down to the Waite farm, I was nervous that I might run into some member of the family who would want to know what I was doing "up Tunket." I was pretty sure that if I responded that I was looking at Ruth and Tom's place, the scowling inquiry would be truncated in true Vermont farmer parlance, going something like: "Why in the hell would you even want to think about living there?"

It was a question that I feared Erin might ask, too.

• • •

I got back to the island just in time for dinner. Erin and her mom took my late return in stride. They knew that if I'm not late, I'm not on time. "How'd it go?" Maggie asked, a twinkle in her eye.

"Well, I think I found our new home," I replied somewhat mutedly, not wanting to panic Erin with an excessive enthusiasm that she felt she might have to damp down later.

"Oh—did you find an apartment or something?" Maggie knew that we needed somewhere to live right away.

"Um, nope, not exactly—actually, I found an incredible 25-acre parcel with a cabin that I think we can make livable, but probably not until spring. It's *so* gorgeous that you can't even imagine it. It's down in Pawlet, just south of the college about twenty or twenty-five minutes. Cheap, too: $39,900—just about our price range!"

Maggie is far too kind to give anyone a demeaning or suspicious look, but she didn't look at all convinced of my real estate savvy.

It was obvious that I needed to do a little more to reassure her. "And I met this really cool Realtor who's about my own age, newly married like us, and building his own house! The land is way off the beaten track—about a mile in. I'm sure that's why it's so cheap. They're not thinking that there are crazies like us who are willing to live in a place like that year-round."

Erin had remained quiet up to this point, but she finally weighed in. "I'm not so sure how crazy I want to be."

"But it might be that 'farm in the mountains' that you promised me!"

Half-humored, Maggie smiled with a faint hint of concern. It can't be easy seeing your children realize that dreams usually don't just come true—they have to be built.

Erin and I headed out the next day. My excitement clearly made her nervous. I tried to subdue it, since I wanted it to be her decision, too. She had to be invested in the investment. Opting to live in a place like Tunket was only going to work if we both wanted to be there, since the sacrifices and hard work were going to take their toll on both of us in different ways at different times—but hopefully not on the marriage. I trusted that the Bergbauern image would stick in her head, too.

A life up Tunket Road might not be easy, but the prospects didn't surpass much of what we'd seen in the South Tirol. In fact, it seemed a place that might help us recapture some of what we'd loved about our experiences there. Coming back to a world of ease and comfort and unchallenging topography had not been easy for either one of us. The sense of work, craft, and simple pleasures that we'd found in South Tirol had been hard to find in the United States. Vermont seemed to be a place where, if we couldn't find it, at least we could make it.

It's not that cultures in the Alps weren't shifting to an easier, more sedentary and consumerist lifestyle—they were. And we were acutely aware of the shift in large part because I had been working on a farm and in an agricultural museum that were both dedicated to preserving the traditions of the South Tirolean Bergbauern. My boss, Siegfried de Rachewiltz, or "Sizzo," as he is generally called, is the grandson of American poet Ezra Pound. Sizzo, like his grandfather, is at ease in several languages and at his best when he is steeped in their nuances. As he saw the modern world slipping in and eroding the isolation and the fastidious nature of the Bergbauern, he began going from valley to valley collecting endangered words—yes, words—that were used in specific, relatively isolated valleys to denote agricultural tools and traditions. As he collected the reminiscences of farmers, he also ended up collecting the tools themselves. The tools soon became more voluminous than the words, so he ended up displaying the tools in his family's home, Brunnenburg Castle, until the collection became a museum that continues to grow to this day.

One of the exhibitions at the museum during my time there was a collection of photographs by Dr. Erika Hubatschek. A high school geography teacher in Innsbruck, Austria, Erika began taking photographs of the Bergbauern in the 1930s during her constant hikes in the Alps. Originally outfitted only with the simplest of cameras, she began documenting a world that would begin disappearing rapidly in the last quarter of the twentieth century. Erin and I became fast friends with Erika and her daughter Irmtraud, who has maintained and expanded upon her mother's tradition of documenting disappearing tools, techniques, traditions, and accumulated "generational knowledge."

Working with these dynamic archivists and others—people who recognize the links among land, work, tradition, and ecological knowledge—had a lasting impact on how Erin and I viewed our own future. We had no illusions of transporting a bygone era from a distant culture into a kitschy lifestyle. We did, however, take to heart the lessons of a culture that was tried and true, a culture in transition. The deep sense of place in the Alps couldn't be replicated in an unadulterated way, but some of the basic tenets could be emulated, although only in a manner that fit our own culture, landscape, and ecological understanding.

Erin and I parked at the intersection of the gravel town road and Tunket Road and began our hike uphill. I was chatty and nervous; Erin was quiet and unsure. It didn't take long for the beauty of the hike to put her at ease, but she clearly didn't want to squander our meager land fund or to squelch my uneasy excitement. Silence seemed to be the best way for her to let the place and the choices soak in. The view of Haystack at the top of the hill definitely caught her attention, but it was also at this point that she began to realize the distance from the town road below to the cabin site, which was still about half a mile farther in. The walk seemed longer to me than it had the last time, since I was bearing the burden of Erin's questions and concerns, as well as my own.

I'm still not quite sure what her initial impression was of the clearing and the obscured cabin, but it wasn't immediate enthusiasm. (She says now that she was most impressed by the smell of the apple mint among all of the goldenrod and brambles surrounding the cabin.) There was no water, no power, no road to speak of—no real certainty in much of anything except each other . . . not even a secure job. I was becoming more and more an emblem of change at the college, and, therefore, an increasingly prominent target of some ill will, particularly as I laid plans for the new college farm, even though the concept was no more threatening initially than that of a garden. But even a garden, in certain contexts, can be seen as an overt political act, a shift in values and lifestyle.

We parted our way through the brambles and up to the cabin. It seemed best to avoid the skewed steps up to the porch, and if the front door hadn't been accessible only via the porch, it would have been better to avoid the porch entirely. Once again, I had a foot break through a board on the porch, so we made our way to the door and opened it with some trepidation. Erin liked the cabin—not so much as it was, but for its potential. The foundation problems were of some concern to her, but she could see it was a much better fit for us than a room in a college residence hall, which we'd lived in for a few weeks before getting on the island and were likely to do again before we had a secure home, here or elsewhere.

Erin made a few casual observations, still conveying a noncommittal attitude that kept me relatively quiet, inserting a few optimistic notes of potential here and there. I was settled on settling here, but only if she came away persuaded. We looked the cabin over thoroughly, she doing what I have seen her do so well through the years—envisioning a space to its point of highest possible potential for utility. By the time we walked out of the cabin to wander the woods, she had decided that the current two-room layout of bedroom and kitchen needed to be switched.

What she decided in a few minutes ended up working for eight years . . . even though I stated repeatedly at the time that we would need to live in the cabin only for two or three years before building another, better-designed house. I steadfastly stuck by my assertion until the three-year time period was up, at which point it all evolved into a long-standing joke (and occasional prod) that will probably follow me to the grave. I hope I'm slow in getting there, too. My best chance at delay is probably to build my own casket.

We stepped out of the chilly, uninsulated cabin and into the partial sun seeping in through the pines. As we walked through the woods and up to the ledges forming the hardwood basin, Erin was just as taken by the hardwoods and the abundance of scattered wild apples as I was . . . but she was still not ready to give in. It took the view of Haystack from up on the Fox Cobble for me to see her uncertainty give way to the notion of possibility. Her decisions need to be slow and deliberate, so I knew better than to push her. She needed time to let the thoughts and ideas ferment, with the yeasts of the decision consuming all of their illusory sweetness until only the hard possibility was palatable.

It was a pretty quiet walk down the hill. It wasn't me that had to win her over. It was Tunket.

A few days later, we were sitting in Scott McChesney's real estate office, asking him to negotiate not on price but on whether the sellers would be willing to take a modest down payment and finance the purchase themselves. After some hemming and hawing—and a gut-wrenching moment when they almost pulled the land off the market because their daughter didn't want them to sell—they conceded.

With more hope than dollars and more notions than sense, we committed. We were headed up Tunket, with a pretty good idea why in the hell we wanted to live up there . . . but not quite how.

TWO

Learning One's Place

In deed, we had land. But Erin and I still didn't have a habitable abode in which to spend our first Vermont winter. By the time we finished the purchase of the property, there wasn't enough time to totally prepare either the cabin or ourselves for the inevitable challenges that were to come. After some negotiation, we eventually secured a place to live on the college campus for the winter—a residence hall nearly destroyed by its previous student inhabitants and slated to be completely demolished by an official wrecking crew soon after our departure.

The building's lackluster appearance worked to our advantage, however. It spurred us on to make sure we had our own place to live as soon as possible. Plus, the excitement of finally having a place of our own meant that we were ready to invest ourselves in our new abode. We also knew that spending some winter days and nights in the cabin would help prepare us for the next year when we did take up permanent residence there. Sometimes, shallow steps are much safer than deeper dives. We had purchased a real dive, to be sure, but one that had potential.

It was clear to both of us that we still had to figure out those Vermont winters that all the locals talked about as soon as they heard of our plans. That is, those locals who chose to verbalize their opinions on the subject. Other Vermonters just looked at our mild physiques and heard my not-quite-muffled southern twang and responded with either utter silence or a half-disguised smirk. Both responses were pretty unsettling for a southerner used to excessive discourse and bewildering smiles as a cover for thoughts like, *You're crazy as a tomato worm in a cotton patch.*

None of the locals bothered to mention mud season to us, the time of year that ultimately proved less predictable and more frustrating than winter. Or maybe they did mention it, but it was simply something that had no parallel in our experiences in North Carolina, Pennsylvania, or the Alps. We certainly didn't realize that roads could become temporary fictions—marks on a map, but with no basis of certainty that modern automobile drivers tend to expect.

Erin and I decided to proceed by getting our faltering cabin in shape for some weekend visits, with as little cost as possible. With the generous help of our new Realtor friend Scott and his tractor's backhoe, we spent the next few weekends jacking up the cabin and putting in new Sonotube concrete footings to fix the failing structure (a North Carolina solution that I later learned was a big mistake in Vermont). The cabin's two rooms were both slipping off their original concrete-block footings, in the process ripping apart the two rooms, with the floor joists on the ground becoming food for ravenous carpenter ants (that species name being an oxymoron if ever there was one).

We spent several weekends raising, leveling, and reinforcing the base of the cabin just before the first snow flew, relieved at that point to be spending the winter in our lonely and decrepit residence hall, no matter how grim its atmosphere. But at that point we coveted warmth more than beauty or comfort, and such unromantic lodging actually helped make the prospects of our next winter in a sparse but cozy cabin seem all the more enticing. The cabin still needed insulation and interior walls—a job for the following summer—while we ourselves also needed a little insulation . . . from the possibility of failing to survive our first Vermont winter.

As the temperatures steadily dropped during each of our late-autumn work weekends, we finally decided to try out a homemade sheet-metal stove I'd discovered one day at a yard sale for $25—a replacement for the woodstove that was stolen from the cabin during its slow demise. I had admired my strength as I carried it into the cabin by myself, not thinking enough about the fact that its light weight should have been a sign of trouble.

Everything was fine when we started the fire with white pine tinder, then added some dry apple branches. It was the addition of a few small hop hornbeam logs that turned the black sheet-metal stove into a throbbing cherry-red box, nearly pulsing with its roaring inhalations of oxygen. The red traveled up the stovepipe and seemed to want to go straight through the roof, with no way to stop the surging influx of air into the stove. A few weeks later, a Pawlet firefighter told me that he loved hop hornbeam simply because its incredible density and resulting BTUs frequently provided the local fire department with some good practice runs.

Once we had gotten the fire under control by plugging the stove's air inlet with a soaking wet towel, I took a quick nap to recuperate from the adrenaline overdose, and we went to the nearby town of East Wallingford to buy a beautiful green-enamel Jotul stove. In exchange for a six-pack of beer, the proprietor threw in a stovepipe oven—a barrel-shaped oven that we installed between two pieces of stovepipe, with the chimney smoke channeling through the outer chamber of the barrel, heating the inside chamber that served as a small oven. We now had our first cabin "utility."

Our "penny-wise pound-foolish" yard sale purchase had nearly cost us much more than a new stove, so we opted for the opposite approach with the new Jotul. The stove's glass door, with its full-spectrum show of dancing colors, was the central focus of our lives in that cabin for many years to come.

Like most things in Vermont, it was a view worth paying for. The stove kept us coming back to the cabin nearly every weekend for the rest of the winter—that is, whenever Carl wasn't dragging me around some place to get educated. Sometimes, I found, it pays to keep your mouth shut and your ears open, and just go along for the ride. Especially if you're a teacher who still needs to learn—and earn—your place in a new environment.

Every homesteader needs a Virgil—a rooted local who can help one navigate the probability of purgatory, avoid a self-inflicted inferno (woodstove-related or not), and find the simple pleasures of the local paradise. These Virgils, guides into the geography and chronology of a place, can be found everywhere—in cities, suburbs, and small country towns, although they may be more anonymous and harder to find in well-populated areas. However, the best Virgils have a hard time remaining anonymous in smaller communities—places like Poultney, Vermont.

Carl was the first person we had met when we pulled up to the college's main entrance, towing a U-Haul trailer behind our pickup in May 1996. With his cigarette, slight speech impediment, and bearish belly, it was easy to wonder if we hadn't run into a backwoods vestige of old New England, poorly disguised in an ill-fitting uniform of a college security officer—the result of questionable casting on the part of a director who had no choice but to work with the locals provided him. But anyone who thought Carl fit into any ready-made role suggesting ignorance or backwoods obliviousness was quickly disabused of that notion.

He would amble into most any social situation and usually interject just the right verbal wedge to work his way into the grain of the conversation. Sometimes he made sure folks felt the force of the wedge, but more often than not they barely noticed how he inserted himself into the dialogue. His wit and charm would soon hang in the air as thick as his ever-present trail of cigarette smoke. The occasional Korean student at the college would be particularly rattled on first encountering him, as he would shift abruptly from an American welcome to a casual greeting in Korean.

An astute observer of human character, Carl had a full repertoire of approaches—and reproaches—that he could use to deal with a spectrum of personalities and situations. Within just a few minutes of meeting him upon our initial arrival at the college, he had us divulging our hopes of homesteading, as well as of establishing a college farm on the campus.

"What do you know about this area?" The question was delivered with what I soon learned was his trademark skeptical glance, replete with a downward tilt of his head and a tightened brow.

"Not much," I replied.

"Would you go to Wall Street and try to start investing with pesos?"

I must have responded with a blank look: It was my first encounter with Carl's pedagogy, full of aphorisms and momentarily perplexing parables.

Carl courteously filled in the blank for me since it was apparently a sample question on my first test—something he would soon refuse to do. "Well, if you don't know much about the people or the place, then how are you going to figure out what to grow in a garden, much less how to survive on your new homestead? You're not in Kansas anymore, Dorothy." His eyes sparkled, and he let out reassuring laugh. But then he looked at me, ready for something resembling an intelligent response on my part.

"Well, I guess I'll have to start asking questions." I'm sure my tone exuded more naive optimism than confidence.

"Yeah, but you'll save yourself a helluva lot of time and maybe even money by asking the right questions to the right people. In my experience, you academic types spend too much time standing in front of the mirror and asking questions of the only person you see."

He looked at me with constricted eyebrows. "There aren't many people around anymore who've got the answers to the questions you don't even know you have yet." His face softened a bit. "I guess I better help you find them before they all die off. Otherwise, you might not survive very long in these parts."

He looked straight at me and took a long draw on his cigarette. "I don't know if you're worth keeping around," and then he smiled and pointed at Erin with the dying red tip of the cigarette. "But I like her already." Erin blushed, but not before grinning.

Uniforms and uniformity. Carl didn't fit into either very well. It was ironic that a man who spent most of his time bending the rules had crammed his unruly persona into the role of an MP in Korea, a bouncer among hard-drinking peers, and now a college public safety officer. By day, he was a well-tanned, shirtless gardener—up by the crack of noon after his late nights of moonlighting—"from college security to food security," he'd quip. Once square and stout, Carl was still a hefty figure, although he was trading his square build for rounded edges.

I asked him once why a cultural rebel kept taking jobs that required him to enforce the rules. "You've got to hire a troublemaker to find a troublemaker . . . And I like working between the rules and the realities." A light chuckle seeped out of his stony expression, and a smile crept up the side of his face that still functioned like it was supposed to, the result of a terrible car accident that had killed his wife and almost him. "Plus, somebody's gotta protect the public good—from people like me!" With that, his chuckle drifted lower into his belly and threatened to pop the lower buttons of his uniform.

Raised partly in the ways of the Iroquois tradition but in the geography of "a white man's world," Carl was definitive about his background: "I'm 110 percent Yankee woodchuck and part Iroquois, whatever that comes out to be. I might not know who I am, but I do know where I belong." Carl had spent his entire life—except for his military stint in Korea—traipsing the terrain between the parallel north–south run of the Adirondack and the Taconic mountain ranges.

From Carl's perspective, Erin and I had a title to our new land, but we weren't yet entitled to it. Since we were living on campus and he had a pass key to our building, Carl had constant access to us during his second-shift rounds of the campus. Carl relished the idea of a farm on campus, though he still wasn't so sure about me. But with a pass key and a job that required him to be both nosey and helpful, he had me cornered.

So I became Carl's student. Somehow Erin got a pass. At times, it was more like assuming the role of a novice Buddhist monk, with Carl asking regional gardening, farming, and ecology questions that he knew I couldn't answer, all to ensure my humility. Any display of unfounded certainty on my part resulted in a firm but well-timed reprimand, ensuring that my confidence didn't get ahead of my experience. At other times, the tutelage was much more pleasurable, with him taking us to have a beer where he knew we'd meet an array of locals much more diverse than the college could ever boast—farmers, slateworkers, trappers, small-business owners, contractors, and retired persons of all backgrounds and ages.

If Carl was a self-made man—an assemblage of parts, pieces, and personalities discovered along the quirky path he'd blazed in the land between two mountain ranges—then his homestead was certainly in keeping with his eclectic lifestyle. The first day I met him, Carl had invited me to his place to see his market garden. "It'll be worth you looking around and watching what's going on for a season before you're on your own gardening up here in the land of ten-week summers." It took me a while, but I finally made time to visit his place.

I'm not sure I would have found his modest smallholding were it not for his ubiquitous blue Dodge pickup truck. Even after finding it, I was ambivalent about venturing to the back door of his house for fear of the chained fury on the far side of his truck, but Carl yanked open the door and yelled, "Dog, shut up! That boy's mostly bones, but I'm not sure yet whether he's worth either of us spending much time workin' on him!"

With that, he had both me and the dog in submissive postures, and he let out a belly-borne laugh.

I walked around the edge of his truck and caught my first glance of his canine compatriot. "What's his name?" I tentatively sticking out a fist for the curly-haired terrorist-turned-terrier. His cool wet nose cautiously sniffed my clenched hand, and then his tail wound up like a prop.

"No sense calling him something he's not," Carl said. "'Dog' works just fine. Anything else is just a waste of imagination."

Dog was chained to his Doghouse between the shop and the house, with a pile of Dogfood cans mounded up on one side of the Doghouse.

"He's an environmentalist," Carl proffered, noting my double take. "He recycles. Better than a lot of humans who'd just scatter all the cans outside somewhere."

Carl motioned for me to walk with him, and as I turned I shook my head. Outwitted and outweighed, it was best for me just to appreciate the age-old role of novice. After all, no one remains a novice forever—you either move up or move elsewhere, and I was determined to stick around, so that left me with only one option.

The house and shop straddled a plateau just below the rural highway that ran above and parallel to his homestead. The rest of Carl's land sloped to the south until leveling off in a flat basin that was once part of Lake Champlain's ancient lakebed. Still a central drainage point, the far southern boundary of his land shifted from prime agricultural soils to some channelized wetlands.

I followed Carl down a path that traversed a steep bank sloping down between the shop and house, both of which Carl had built just a few years prior. Simple in design and basic in materials, both buildings conveyed more pragmatism than elegance. In Carl's view, they were a means to an end—oversight of his fabulous Garden of Weedin'.

The path ran past his greenhouse and down to the garden, an area ranging from 1 to 2 acres, depending on the degree to which the weeds leapt the intended boundary between garden and field. We got to the edge of the garden, where he had rototilled a few weeks earlier. He pulled out a cigarette, lit it, exhaled, and let the smoke drift into the silence of the fields.

"I know what you're thinkin' . . . Yeah, it looks messy. And you can't afford to let things get as messy as I do because people are gonna be watchin' you a lot more closely than they are me." He took another puff.

"But be careful what you call a weed and decide you need to get rid of it. It might end up being one of your best friends, without you even realizing it. Ever heard of the tarnished plant bug?"

"Yeah, they're a problem with strawberries sometimes, right?" I was hesitant, not wanting to risk conveying too much certainty, lest I suffer a verbal whack from the master.

"Okay, good. We might get somewhere after all." He winked at me. "Now, you see those strawberry plants there? Cardinal—a variety released out of North Carolina State, I believe. Something good comes out of that state occasionally, I guess." I opted to ignore the slight slight.

He pointed to some small but vigorous feathery plants in the next row. "Know what that is?"

"Dill?" I suggested, sure to add a questioning intonation.

"Right. And that plant over there in the weeds. What is it?"

"Queen Anne's lace," I responded, a bit more declaratively.

"Good—we're gettin' somewhere. Now, what do Queen Anne's lace and dill have in common?"

"Well, they sure look similar."

"Yup. They're in the same plant family—Umbelliferae. The Latin name comes from the flower shape—an umbel." He paused and looked at me. "Always good to be humble, especially around a crotchety old man like me, eh?"

I didn't bother to say what I was thinking: *Some woodchuck he is . . .*

Carl ignored my silence. "Anyway, an umbel is made up of composite flowers. Know what likes composite flowers?"

"No, not really. Certain pollinators?"

"Right. There's a parasitic wasp that does a number on tarnished plant bugs, and do you know where it lives when it's not takin' care of business?"

"The composite flowers?"

"That's it. So I'm perfectly happy to have this field come right up to my garden, because if I don't have any habitat for those wasps, then the tarnished plant bugs are gonna ruin my strawberry crop. Think about it a little more. You've got your pests, and you've got your beneficial insects. Who's gonna live where?"

He looked at me but saw enough of a befuddled expression that he graciously jumped ahead. "If you had the choice of living with your enemies or with your dinner, where would you live?"

I must have looked a bit more enlightened because he nodded and acknowledged the obvious. "Right. I'd do it, too, except the kitchen starts to get crowded when I put my bed in there!"

I burst out laughing at the image, but Carl wasn't slowing down. "So you gotta remember to make sure there's habitat for your beneficial insects. They tend to like the protection of the fields around the garden. As far as I'm concerned, it's a two-fer. I get to provide habitat for the predators like my wasps, plus I have an organic excuse for not being able to keep up with my mowing."

He let the idea settle in a bit. "There's another lesson here, too. Know how I know about these wasps and their habitat?"

"Well, I doubt you learned it in school," I teased.

"Now don't you go mockin' school. I learned plenty in school. It just so happened that not much of it came by way of teachers!"

He gave me a raised eyebrow. I decided just to take the jab. "Okay, now don't be gettin' me distracted! The point is that you're gonna be out in the college garden you're hoping to start or in your own garden at home, and you're gonna get pissed off that you're spending so much time out there with a hoe and on your hands and knees, trying to get rid of these damn weeds. But if you use that time to look and listen and feel what's going on around you, then you're learning something. And every little thing you learn will make you a better gardener the next year. Eliot Coleman calls them '1 percenters.' Every little thing you improve on combines with a few more little things—until you've improved things 10 percent or more . . . and that's a lot in the gardening world! It can be the difference between breaking even and making a decent profit."[1]

He looked down at his cigarette. "Most of it is about paying attention. You can read all the best books and meet all sorts of people who can teach you a lot, but in the end it's just you in the garden, trying to make sense of it all."

I looked out across the expansive garden, taking in what he was saying and anxiously wondering what the next test question might be. In an effort to forestall another unnerving list of sequential questions, I tried to divert his attention with a distracting comment. "You sure do have a lot planted out here, Carl—and it all looks like it's doing great."

"You trying to point out my character flaws?" he asked, obviously baiting me, the straight man.

"What do you mean?" I felt like I was in the middle of a knock-knock joke.

"My subtle dishonesty." He looked to see if I was still on board with his explanation. "If you plant enough stuff and lay out your garden right, it'll never look like anything is missing even if you do lose something to a bug or a disease or drought. Everybody'll see your successes while you're casually hiding your failures."

He took another puff on his cigarette. "When you get right down to it, it all comes down to common sense. And common sense isn't something you're born with—it's something you're born into. And the way our world is going, not many people are being born into it right now."

I grinned, and he looked up. "Watch it—the verdict's still out on you." He offered half a smile in return.

"But you're right." He looked out at the size and stature of his midseason garden. "There is a lot planted out here. Half the pleasure is growin' it, and the other 60 percent is giving it away."

He glanced over at me with a hint of mischief in his eyes. "*You* might not like my math, but I know a few ladies who do. Sometimes it adds up to a good little bit of fun!"

I tried not to, but I laughed, and Carl let out a giggle unbecoming of a man of his stature. "Hey, speaking of beneficial predators like me, did I mention to you that it always pays to grow flowers?"

For the rest of the growing season, Carl made sure I stopped by every week or two to watch the progress of his garden and take note of any tips he could offer. One day in early June, I pulled up to his house just as he was coming up the path out of the garden, shirt off and cigarette on. He rubbed the sweat off his brow with his forearm and waved me down to the greenhouse.

"Have you paid much attention to this greenhouse?"

"Well, I've been admiring what's been coming out of it." I knew I wasn't impressing him with my observation skills.

"I hope your students pay more attention to things than you do," he muttered. "C'mon in."

The greenhouse was built into the south-facing side of the hill, and it featured a lower level and an upper level, each with a deep floor of crushed slate, bounded by the concrete block walls that stair-stepped up the hill. The wood frame was covered with translucent, corrugated fiberglass panels, and both levels had plants exploding out of their pots and boxes. Most of the transplants had already gone out in the field. The remaining plants in the greenhouse were his backups for any plants that didn't make it in the field, and the rest were destined to be gifts to fellow gardeners.

Not wasting any time in getting with the lesson plans, he tossed out the first question of the day: "You know why I built this greenhouse like this?"

"To maximize the use of the hill?"

"That's part of it, but not the main reason. Now look at what plants you see in the lower section and the upper section. What do you see?"

"Well, up there I see tomatoes, peppers, eggplants, and some sort of squash . . ."

"Pumpkins." His demand for precision seemed to be another way of keeping me in my place. "And how about down here in this level?"

"Broccoli, cabbage, cauliflower . . ." I kept trying to read the labels in front of me, just in case.

"Good. So what's going on with my fancy split-level operation?"

I thought for a moment. "Well, the upper level is warmer."

"Yeah, I can send the heat from this level up to that one and cool it down in here, plus I can keep the air moving just by opening the doors and not using any fans. Now what plant families do you see in each level?"

"I guess I don't know," I replied.

"Oh boy. Well, I guess we started down here in the lower level for a reason. I would've hated to have started up there only to be sending you back down a level."

I blushed, but I was already flush from the building heat coming from the heightening arc of the sun, so I was hoping he didn't notice.

"So I've got my solanaceous crops and my cucurbits up there—they're heat lovin', just like me."

We both laughed at what was clearly the truth. "Down here, I've got my brassicas and my other greens—things that need a warm, tender start but then will bolt and go to seed if they get too much heat. That's why it's best if I can separate my heat-loving and cool-loving plants and give them each the environment they want.

"Notice anything about all these barrels I've got in here?"

"Sure—they're filled with water—probably to capture the heat."

"That's right. Not only that, but if I fill them up and leave them for a few days, the water warms up, and I use it for my plants. That doesn't shock these tender babies with cold well water; plus I'm beginning to think that the algae growing in them might be good fertilizer."

"Wow, I bet you're right." I nodded—increasingly impressed with how much attention Carl was paying to details. "So how much did you spend on this greenhouse?"

"Less than a grand. Even that's a lot for me. But I worked out a great deal for the crushed slate fill, and the fiberglass panels aren't perfect, but they're good enough. You've got to use what you got—not what you think you have to have—or you'll never get started, and you sure won't make any money."

"Makes sense to me."

"It'd better. Plenty of people use money to replace what they lack in common sense. You don't have that luxury. Plus, you won't learn anything that way, and it's not what you want to be teaching your students."

Carl was on a roll now—there was no way I was going to be able to stop him without severing the elder–novice relationship, so I settled in for what looked to be another homegrown homily.

"See, what you're talking about doing here with your homesteading and starting this college garden is something so old that to most people around here it seems like something new—they've forgotten how things used to be done and why they were done that way. If you don't know *why* something was done a certain way, you never get to the point about caring *how* it was done. I'm coming from two worlds that are disappearing fast around here—woodchucks and Native Americans. And you environmentalists don't care enough about either one to keep your mouths shut and your ears open."

"But Carl, don't be calling me an environmentalist. I'm not even sure what one is, but I don't like being pigeonholed."

"Well, whether you like it or not, you're new—at least I didn't call you a 'flatlander.' But I'm holding that title in reserve—just in case you don't pay enough attention to what I'm trying to show you about life around here. And I'd better do it fast, because there ain't many of us left. I'm one of the young old-timers, and the more of them that die off, the lonelier I get. I'm wondering how much longer I even want to be around here."

He looked at me without any of his usual humor or mischief. "I'd probably just go ahead and check out right now except if this college is gonna be full of environmentalists, I need to at least make sure a few of you professor-types know that people around here used to live with the environment and off the land—and we probably know more about it and care more about it than any of you ever will. You guys need to be careful. Somebody says 'environment' and you think of wilderness—then you run back to your houses in a chopped-up landscape, stopping on the way at the grocery store to grab something to eat from God knows where. Then you get home to dinner with all that stuff, and you sit around and talk shit about people like me that hunt for their food—not that we haven't done it for a couple thousand years before the Pilgrims ever even knew what a turkey looked like, mind you."

"C'mon, Carl—you don't need to put me in the same boat as the Pilgrims or the earthy-crunchy crowd . . ."

"All of you just got off the boat, as far as I'm concerned." Before I could catch him, he was on another tear. "And not many of you know how to swim, either. People worry about immigration—Mexicans moving in to help on the dairies. Why not? The people around here who know how to work are all dying off. Hell, I worry about people from New Jersey and the big cities—they're the ones who don't know a thing about taking care of the land because it takes care of you. The migrant workers coming in from Mexico still know how to take care of themselves and the land. But the flatlanders come in, plop their houses right in the middle of the best pastures and hayfields, throw up NO TRESPASSING signs, and then argue with me about how much my vegetables cost on their way to the grocery store. If you want to build a homestead or an environmental college, then you've got to spend some time remembering . . . and the only way you new people can remember is by asking questions and then trying to listen."

This was the beginning of Carl's famous Monday-night tours.

Carl had decided that my education needed to grow beyond his garden. He generally had Monday nights off, so he offered—with utter clarity about the ramifications if I refused—to start taking me on Monday-night tours. We started making our rounds that next week.

On those evenings, he would push the pile of seed catalogs off the bench seat and into the barely existent floorboard of his truck, making room for everything except my feet. Then we would head off onto the back roads of Vermont and New York that eluded even some of the locals. As we crisscrossed the state borders, he would mutter his mantra: "It's about your state of mind, not which state you're in." He was constantly frustrated with the Vermont-fixation that blinded people like me to the rich terrain and traditions of his beloved Washington County—New York, that is.

His idea was to get me literate "in a way you academics tend to forget about." His goal was not just to get me to places I probably never would have seen on my own, but to paint a storied terrain. And he was determined that any newfangled, foreign ideas I might have would be tested and tempered by people who knew a lot more than I did.

Early on in these tours, Carl made it clear how he saw his role as elder in our relationship. "My job is to get you out of your comfort zone. You're the teacher—that's a big part of education, isn't it?"

"Sure it is," I concurred. "I'd just prefer it to be part of the students' experience—not necessarily mine!"

His laugh was just slightly on the demonic side. As usual, he pushed on. "And I'm not interested in just showing you a bunch of organic stuff. You'll find that on your own. I want you to see the full picture of how people have been living around here for centuries. You can call it what you want, but I'm not sure all those labels you environmentalists use are gonna fit all that well—at least not by the time I'm finished with you."

Not so happy to be tagged with his label, I grimaced. "Just keep driving, Carl." He burst out laughing.

The Monday-night tours might have seemed less stressful had it not been for Carl's spontaneous approach. While we were driving around, Carl would point out landmarks of a passing era—overgrown orchards, shuttered farmhouses, and small family cemeteries. But then he would make a sudden turn into a driveway and utter something along the lines of how he hadn't seen this person in nearly a decade, and he hoped he or she was still alive for me to meet and talk with.

If anyone did dare come to the door at Carl's knock, he would re-introduce himself when necessary and explain his goodwill mission— to educate an educator about how people live off the land in these parts.

Sometimes the host was more flustered than I was, but eventually we found our way into conversation, with Carl as an intermediary and backup narrator. I guess Carl had always been slightly eccentric enough that most folks settled into our interviews with relative ease. Oftentimes, Carl would go to the door and hold up a partial six-pack of canned beer like a skinned rabbit, opening up the possibility of a more fluid discussion of the old ways and the new days.

He introduced me to people I probably never would have met through my college work or otherwise. One of the first people we called on was Walt Perry, a local dairyman, potato farmer, and draft horse teamster, who told me, "Everybody told me I was crazy for trying to plant potatoes here. I like when people tell me I'm crazy—it makes me even more determined, and it usually means I'm on to a good idea that nobody else is thinking about enough." Even though Walt died a few years back, Perry's Potatoes remains a staple of our region, supplying grocery stores and even the New York prison system with potatoes.

We wandered over to Bob Anderson's vegetable farm, where he walked me through all the equipment that he had fixed, modified, and even invented for his operation. He was one of the first in the region to experiment seriously with season-extension methods. We also met another pioneer—in preservation and restoration. Floyd Harwood was in his eighties, and Carl drove us unannounced to Floyd's mill and museum. Floyd had been a vocational education teacher in his small town of Hartford, New York, and he and his wife had fully restored the dam, waterwheel, and inner workings of an old mill, to the point that he was grinding grains for visitors and locals and had gathered an enormous collection of antique farm and household equipment. He built a museum out-of-pocket and even put up his own agricultural library for public use.

Carl drove me over to Hicks Orchard to meet Dan Wilson, the young proprietor of the oldest U-pick apple orchard in New York State. A savvy entrepreneur in the midst of a fruit industry laid to waste all around him, Dan clearly had thought strategically how to capitalize on agritourism, and he was eloquent in his description of the difficulties he was facing in trying to raise quality fruit while minimizing the toxicity of the sprays he was using.

Carl even parked the truck along a dusty back road and had me walk down to the riverbottom to meet a dead woman. There was a pile of bulldozed rubble in a small field near the river's edge. Carl started poking through the rubble before telling me where we were. "This is Mary Dodge's old place. The Nature Conservancy just bought it. Now, if anything shady and interesting was going on, this was the place to come find it. This was the Wild West of West Haven. I guess it'll stay wild here with The Nature Conservancy owning it now, but not in the same way it used to be wild."

There was a wistful, mischievous look in his eyes. "I'd probably better not risk offending her ghost by telling you the stories I know that happened right here. Wait till we get back to the truck."

Those Monday-night tours went on throughout much of the summer and fall. It would be a long time before I felt rooted, but it was Carl's determination that helped me feel grounded. I began to feel more optimistic about the prospects for our homesteading venture and for the college garden.

Winter passed quickly, thanks in part to Carl's inherited store of stories, and spring began its slow progression. There wouldn't be time to begin a garden at our homestead that year, but I had all I could handle in establishing the new college garden at that point anyway, and since I only had time to get things planted, not sold, I figured we'd have plenty of produce for ourselves.

Carl helped with the seed order and in cobbling together the various supplies that I needed to get things started. He even offered to share his greenhouse space for the college plants. Despite the tight quarters, this arrangement bought him a little more time to make sure I had my act together.

"You know, a lot of people think I'm wasting my energy spending so much time with you," he told me in early spring. "You have to promise me one thing."

"What's that?"

"That you're paying attention. Because when it's all said and done, if you give up on this garden or bail out of your homestead, you might look a little bit like a fool. But I'll look like an even bigger fool for believing in you."

"Carl, you've got my word."

"That's not enough." He made sure I was looking him dead in the eye. "Show me."

At least once a day, I would run over to Carl's to check on our seedlings in his greenhouse. One morning, I arrived to water plants after he'd had a late-night shift at the college. Carl heard me pull up, and he hung his head out his bedroom window, dressed in just his underwear—and thank God for that.

He waved, cleared his throat and spit out the window, then reached inside for a cigarette. Apparently, he decided to take in a little more of the rising sun to warm up, so he poked out the window until the bottom of his belly rested on the sill. He cupped his thick left hand around his lighter and lit up the cigarette, inhaling the view with the first smoke of the day.

"You know, this is all I ever needed or wanted—great soil, plenty of water, good south sun, and a helluva view. Of course, a good woman to share the fertility with me might round it out good." He let out a belly laugh that I thought would vibrate him right out the window.

"Now while you and your woman are getting settled over there—" He pointed across the valley to the distant ridgeline of the Three Sisters, with Haystack's perpendicular southern edge catching the morning light. "—you remember that I can see what's going on from here. I'll be watching, not interrupting—I've got enough to do and don't have time for it anyway. Better if you make your own mistakes—it'll save me some work always trying to make sure you're listening."

I laughed.

"You think I'm kidding, don't ya? You'll find out that your mistakes are where you're gonna learn the most. That just doesn't work real well with teaching, when you're supposed to be showing everybody the right way, even if you haven't figured it out for yourself yet. Hell, look at me—I'm in my fifties, lived here my whole life, been gardening since I was big enough to poke a stick in the ground, and I still spend half the time scratching my head or my ass, depending on whether I'm in public or in the privacy of my own home . . . hey, you don't mind if I . . ."

"Carl, wipe that grin off your face and get your ass back in the window and in the privacy of your own home!"

Carl got to laughing so hard that he started one of his coughing fits, thanks to a generation of cigarettes. He wrapped it up with a fierce clearing of his throat and a mighty oyster propelled far into the weeds below.

He twisted his hand around, looking hard at his cigarette. "You know, if you white folks hadn't been so damn determined to turn a Native American plant into an agricultural product, people like me might be smart enough just to be smoking it every now and then out of a pipe, not getting to the point where we gotta light up as soon as we wake up."

He hocked another lung cookie down to the weeds. "I'll be right out."

A few minutes later, Carl came out and motioned for me to walk down into the garden with him. He wanted to show me the succession plantings of lettuce that he had going, with a series of rows at various stages of growth.

We got down to the southern edge of the garden and noticed the weeds about 100 feet away rustling. We both straightened up from bending down to look closely at the lettuce plants. A long line of weeds was shaking violently.

"What the hell is that?" Carl grumbled, perplexed. About that time, the weeds in front of us parted and out came Dog without an unidentifiable object in his mouth and something else trailing behind him. I'd seen Dog drag woodchucks up to his Doghouse for a meal several times, but something was different this time.

As Dog came toward us, I realized that he had a deflated volleyball in his mouth, and it looked like he was somehow tangled up in a volleyball net—dragging the net, poles, and anchor ropes all behind him.

Carl shook his head in disbelief, and his security-guard tone came out automatically as Dog walked up to him and dropped the deflated ball at his feet. "You damn Dog—now there are some deprived kids out there somewhere, probably crying and screaming to their mother about some hooligan who stole their fun—and I don't even know who they are, so I can't take it back to 'em!"

He paused, and we both burst out laughing. He looked down at Dog and wagged his finger. "So where the hell are the badminton rackets? If you were gonna take this much, you should've brought *all* the evidence home with you!"

Reverting to his theatrically gruff facade, he picked up one of the stakes still tied to the anchor rope and looked down at Dog, who was now clearly disappointed at the lack of the praise he generally got when he dragged a woodchuck home. "What kind of a retriever are you anyway? I send you out to the neighbors to get me a steak, and you came back with this. Damn Dog can't even spell."

The last time I saw Carl was on a cold April evening in 2004. He was crossing campus, making his rounds to lock up classrooms for the night. His face was puffy and red, and as we were talking, his coughing spells repeatedly stifled both his humor and his constant admonitions and reminders. That didn't bode well.

With a final coughing fit that didn't seem to want to end, he made it clear he didn't feel up to any more counseling or conversation.

"I gotta get the rest of these buildings locked up," he muttered, wiping his nose with a handkerchief. "And I just need to get home and get to bed. No sense me being around here anymore anyway. I'm just a damn dinosaur in these parts anymore, and it's about time for me to go the way of the rest of the dinosaurs."

With that, he turned and started walking into the night. Then he did a tight about-face and looked firmly back at me. "You've been listening to me, right?"

"Yeah, Carl . . . and I've been taking notes, too."

"Good."

I watched him go into a nearby building, turn the light off in the class-room, and lock the door.

Carl didn't show up for his next shift, so a few friends went to check on him. He'd died in the house he'd built overlooking his garden of mixed ancestry—Native American corn, squash, and beans planted amid a host of Old World crops in the deep fertile soils of the valley between the Taconic and Adirondack ranges.

There were more than six hundred people at Carl's memorial service at the college several days later, more than triple the stated capacity of the room where students, faculty, administrators, farmers, and law enforcement officials gathered to honor him. It was his last chance to break more rules and hearts. Some elders die too young.

———

THREE

When Time Was Made of Trees

When I see an old field giving way to forest or the outer walls of an old building giving way to one last exasperated sigh of loneliness and then collapsing, I can't decide whether to call it human neglect or ecological advancement. I have too much empathy for those who dare to cultivate the earth to callously celebrate the surrender of any well-intentioned farmer or homesteader as a victory of nature.

And yet, after putting our money down on a crumbling cabin and an old pasture clearly coveted by the encroaching forest, I couldn't help but wonder whether our forays into this forest ecosystem would be a good thing for the tenantless neighborhood. The solitude of our new home was reassuring, but it also meant that any ecological miscalculations we made would be glaring indictments of our ignorance. Carl's methods of making sure I learned my place before I set out on any misguided trajectories might not have been gentle, but they were effective. It seemed to us that the lighter we lived early on, the less prone we would be to egregious or intractable errors of judgment.

Of course, any time the "green guilt" kicked in, and uncertainties about my own capacity to make good ecological decisions increased, my knee-jerk reaction was always that someone else with less of a green-lean could have purchased any combination of the several empty parcels up Tunket Road and turned them into a development of 25-acre wooded estates strung along the length of the road, complete with power lines and a host of suburban amenities—as was nearly the case a few years prior to our appearance on the scene.

There is, of course, an arrogance in such thinking. None of us likes to think that we're ultimately hurting our piece of the pie—even the least conscientious logger I've ever met thought that nature would eventually heal itself, with near indifference to his minor scarring of the earth's surface. We all find comfort in our individual actions by ignoring the sum totals that actually complete the equation.

Carl had worked hard to try to ensure that I understood the basic elements of the equation in his tromping grounds: the division of land, the addition of newcomers, the multiplication of so-called necessities, and the loss of traditions tied to the land. In his view, it all equaled a society that was losing its grip on its precious shared resources. He also knew that if a culture lost its appreciation for the simple rewards of living close to the land, then protecting that land would have to come more from zoning and environmental regulations than from the intuitive understanding that stems from a sense of rootedness and commitment to a place.

The spring of 1997 finally arrived, and the college semester ended, so Erin and I stored our few belongings, giving away all of our electrical appliances except for our power tools, and set up a modest base camp, consisting of our small tent and an embarrassingly ragged dining fly that we'd found tucked underneath the cabin. In the Northeast, winter's most miserable work is generally done during the hottest months of the year. For us, this included winterizing our shelter with the curse of fiberglass insulation, friendly neither to humans nor to the local landfill. We worked throughout the late spring and summer on the cabin, making it more habitable as a primary residence, adding interior walls and a tiny kitchen area, all the while trying to chase away the constant visits from mice, red squirrels, gray squirrels, flying squirrels, raccoons, and porcupines.

When the weather allowed, we would grab our towels and trek down to the somewhat distant brook to bathe. We brought drinking water up from the Waites' farm and hauled wash water over from a seasonal stream—when it was running—or a reliably filled vernal pool about 200 feet from the cabin. The volume of tadpoles in the bucket often seemed to outweigh the water, but we always scooped them out of the bucket and back into the talent pool of fellow springtime serenaders.

We'd purchased 25 acres, which included about 20 acres of beautiful hardwoods, roughly 3 acres of white pines surrounding the cabin, and less than 2 acres of old field. The big white pines surrounding the cabin served as sentinels for the forest edge. The first tree species to begin filling the open gaps in the landscape, these pines seemed like greedy, hovering family members bearing witness to the dying pasture's last-minute will and testament—uttered in a surrendering tone, fearful of the forest's stealthy advance.

Some would say that there's no clear-cut way to homestead; others consider a clear-cut to be the first act of homesteading. We couldn't decide whether to cut down the white pines and open up the area surrounding the cabin to light and the potential for gardens or to retain the pines and their gifts of shade, wind protection, and open forest floor. The best ecological decisions generally come from waiting and watching, and my penchant for underestimating the time required of most any task, seldom commencing or completing any big project when I think I'm going to, actually served us well in this case.

Instead of initially cutting down any of the beautiful multistemmed trees, we had set to work on preparing the small cabin for year-round habitation. But we continually struggled with the question of whether to cast our lot with the advancing forest or the old pastures. For decades, the dry cows and heifers from the Waites' farm had rummaged through the shrinking pastures up Tunket Road, grubbing for grass and hoping for a windfall of apples with the late-summer and early-autumn thundershowers. To accept the forest's reclaiming of its deed to the constricted clearing meant passively conceding to nature's preference; whereas to rein in the initial advances of the white pines meant that we were real homesteaders, ready to harvest the light, not just hermits squatting in the forested hills.

As it turned out, it was our barter arrangement for two Holstein bull calves that drove the decision to begin taking down some of the pines, along with a yearning for a garden space near the cabin. We had taken a fancy to oxen over the course of the year. Our first 2-ton introduction came in the form of Will and Abe (short for "willing and able"), an oxen team at a festival of rural crafts and skills in Vermont's Northeast Kingdom. I returned from the fall event determined to shed my "oxenmoron" status and reported my newfound interest to Carl.

Within hours of hearing that news, Carl once again pushed his cascading stack of seed catalogs onto the floor to make room for me on the bench seat in his pickup and drove me across the New York State line to meet Herb and Sheri Troumbley. Although Herb had long since moved across the border and into New York, he had coincidentally grown up just down the road from Tunket. He'd raised oxen his entire life, under the tutelage of his father, "Rowdy," a character whose name was apparently somewhat of an understatement.

Besides keeping anywhere between two and six teams of oxen at a time, Herb made yokes and rented them to ox teamsters across the

United States and even a few in other countries. The span of the bows in the yoke, measured in inches, provided a way of setting the expected price per day of the rental—a bigger and more expensive yoke meant a higher rental fee. The proceeds of his cottage industry paid his daughter's way through college, and Herb's reputation as a teamster extraordinaire grew as fast as a castrated Holstein.

As we thought about all of the work that we needed to do, oxen seemed like a reasonable possible source of traction—and, if we changed our minds, we could always eat them . . . but that option appeared about as remote as our homestead at that point.

Only a few weeks after meeting Herb and Sheri Erin worked out a trade for two Holstein bull calves and two rodent-chasing kittens in exchange for her painting a farm logo on a local farmer's horse wagon. Before we knew what had happened, we were carrying up two gallons of milk each day from the Waites' dairy to feed our calves and kittens throughout the summer. Suddenly, clearing some of the land seemed less a question than a necessity. The calves, Pet and Troll (as in "petrol"), certainly liked the shade of the pines, but they clearly preferred grass over pine needles.

In what was to become a trend in housing animals in better quarters than our own, I built a small shed for "the Boiz" before finishing our own cabin renovations. We initially let them roam, searching for food and helping to clear the brush in and around the small existing clearing. That worked well until they one day invaded our dining fly, had dinner, and left a few unwelcome tips outside our tent door, at which point we invested in our first solar device—a solar fence charger. Boundaries began to emerge—but not before Pet had found his way up the porch stairs and into a bag of Erin's homemade soap. He ate forty-nine of the fifty bars, leaving just one for us. I guess he was trying to cleanse his palate.

I don't think we realized just how much those first cattle would change our lives. Nor did we have any real sense of how much the decision to raise livestock would begin to shape our ecological perspective, in much the same way that it had the settlers who had arrived at this place several hundred years before us. In contrast with the early settlers, however, starting to raise cattle didn't put us at odds with our new neighbors, as was the case with the new folks and the Native Americans. Instead, our growing fascination with cattle drew us into the local community and culture, with the Waite family and others from Carl's Monday-night tours warmly welcoming the professor as a student.

Acquiring cattle in the midst of an area transitioning back from field to forest forced me to think more about domestication than I had previously—vegetables and fruits just don't challenge humans or the landscape in quite the same way that livestock do. I was faced with a stark realization: Domestication is seldom benign. And yet we're culturally predisposed to thinking of domesticating plants, animals, and the landscape as our beneficent way of creating order, beauty, and food—not as a rip in an ecological web established long before we came into the picture. We humans constantly run into this web face-first and try to remove ourselves from it, yet we never really extricate ourselves from its tug. We simply rearrange our own entanglement, much like an unwitting insect, struggling to free itself from the nearly invisible gossamer strands for the rest of its life.

Our unwieldy task as modern-day homesteaders is to find a way to rearrange the inevitable strands so that the structural integrity of the web remains intact, while our own lives are reasonably comfortable and gratifying. The American back-to-the-land movement, if it can be packaged into such a rough-hewn term, can be seen as splitting roughly into two groups. There are the Thoreauvians, those who creep quietly into unspoiled terrain and whisper with their pens, and there are the rest who fall untidily into the Nearing camp, bringing shelter, order, and a whir of activity to a place. In both cases, the actual homestead and one's thinking tend to co-evolve, but that constant progression of act and thought is difficult to see at the beginning.

Erin and I weren't quite sure which camp we belonged to, and we didn't consider that one might eventually morph into the other. We simply knew that we had never really felt at home in our suburban upbringings. The level of consumption and a lack of challenge left us feeling empty and unfulfilled there.

I'd lived the transient version of the American dream, moving from place to place across the country and the globe for the better part of ten years, all the while feeling the pang of needing to settle, to try my hand at building and nurturing roots. Erin was still fresh out of college, ready to live artfully, if not artistically, having long been perplexed by the elitist wedge driven between "craft" and "art." In both cases, we shared a deep need to better define the strands of our existence and feel more like inhabitants than migrants. The thrill was the possibility of better identifying the gossamer entanglements with a place called home and then rearranging them into more of a comfortable hammock than a final cocoon.

Going back to the land *should* be daunting because it raises the specter of survival—but not one's own survival. Plenty of people expressed concern for our safety as we retreated a mile into the forested distance and faced our first Vermont winters. After seeing the lives of farmers in the Alps firsthand, trekking up our small hill seemed reasonably tame to us. The most important question of survival seemed to us to be about conserving a relatively intact and stable ecosystem, while building a life for ourselves and raising much of our own food. But we quickly learned that, as soon as reflective homesteaders start talking about growing their own food and thinking about a native ecosystem, things get complicated, if not muddled . . . but more on that later.

I'm convinced that most of us are virtually hardwired, with the light soldering of generations of cultural influence, to prefer clearings to densely wooded landscapes—as homesites anyway—and to try to create them. Like the rest of the settlers who'd come up Tunket Road, we came with an eye for woods and water, but it's also true that our dream was cast more in full light than in mottled shadow. Whether we realized it or not, the landscape history of New England from the colonial era forward was a foreshadowing of our future homesteading questions and endeavors.

New England history is a perplexing retrospective for anyone with a soft spot for sustainable agriculture, forest ecology, animal husbandry, or Native American history. The trees and stones of Tunket Road started telling a long and hushed tale of earlier settlers, many of whom came with intentions much like our own, but whose vestiges were rapidly disappearing under generations of leaves. While Erin and I were both immediately struck by the beauty of the rough and rutted road, flanked on both sides by chipmunk-dominated stone walls, neither of us guessed just how central the road was in telling the history of the Taconic region of Vermont, if not how ecologically blind we pioneers have been.

In many ways, it takes a romantic to begin homesteading in any kind of remote location, although I suspect that most of us over time become steely pragmatists who gladly suffer from occasional romantic flashbacks. But that romanticism risks an ecological amnesia, ignoring the fact that we bring with us an armament of non-native plants, livestock, and ideas. We assume these non-native plants and animals to be our stash of regenerative vittles, the key to self-sufficiency, good nutrition, and agrarian order—and they can be. But with virtually every new species introduction, there is a displacement of some other organism or habitat. Nova Kim, one of our wildcrafting friends who comes from the Osage tradition, reminds me of these choices when she calls her garden vegetables "weeds" and her gathered wild foods "edibles."

This tension is never more evident to me than when I find myself mowing pastures to trade the edible delights of berries, nettles, and milkweed for grass to feed our cattle, who then nourish us. There were, after all, generations of native peoples who fed themselves on what they hunted and harvested, long before people like myself decided that our sustenance utterly depended upon swapping forest and field for pasture and cropland, a feat accomplished only by adding a whole new suite of plants and animals into the ecological picture . . . and a relatively limited number of species at that, at least in comparison with the plants and animals utilized by the original natives of the area.

Tunket Road slowly became a sort of time line for us, with each walk up the hill becoming a revisiting of what was. Carrying several gallons of drinking water and milk up the road once a day helped to slow us down and pay attention to a road that seemed to wend its way back in time. With every walk up and down the mile-long road, it became increasingly clear that "up Tunket," time was made of trees.

Tunket Road may have started out as a Native American path of some sort, probably most used by the Abenakis, the primary original inhabitants of our region. The road is in many ways a walking chronology of New England history, etched into the Taconic landscape.

The Taconic Mountains rise and fall in graceful green undulations across the southwestern flank of Vermont and the southeastern edge of New York, their crumpled topography much like the wrinkles of a half-made bed. Their north–south axis is no coincidence, as glaciers followed the tectonic folds, gouging out swaths of rock and vegetation in their climatic surges and retreats, plucking, scraping, and pushing any geological impediments out of their way. Both Native American and European inhabitants naturally followed the early trajectories of the glaciers; in fact, traveling east to west in Vermont remains a challenge even to this day.

Perhaps we shouldn't have been surprised to discover a map from 1758 that appears to show the main north–south military thoroughfare in this area to include what is now Tunket Road. This route ran northward from Manchester, Vermont, to the strategic crossroads of Castleton. While it might seem odd for anyone—military or civilian—to choose a rugged route over thickly forested hills instead of the flatter alluvial areas along the rivers and streams, it's worth remembering that the lower areas were swampy, mucky, and insect-infested. If your cart didn't get stuck, you yourself were nearly certain to get stuck, repeatedly—by mosquitoes and other winged conspirators that were well equipped to pass on misery and even disease.

While the roads in the hills were not simple to traverse, they were generally less prone to problems related to flooding, heavy vegetation, and disease. The British often upgraded these rugged roads by paving them with logs laid horizontally across the road to provide traction, as these were vital military and trade routes (even then, economic and military interests coincided). Such a road was dubbed a "corduroy road," perhaps stemming from the French term *cours du roi*—"route of the king"—hence, its purported namesake fabric.[1] The British Crown's error that led in part to their own undoing in this region was that they set up a road infrastructure that provided relatively swift movement to the rebelling colonists and their goods and armaments as they worked to dismantle the distant monarch's colonial reign.

Today Tunket Road is once again more a path than a road, serving as the entryway to The Nature Conservancy's North Pawlet Hills Preserve, with a magnificent trail up Haystack Mountain. A hiker beginning the trek up the road is sure to notice the stone walls that flank either side of the road, most of which have tumbled into dirt and duff, thanks to falling trees and the constant heaving and settling of the wet, clay soils underneath. The rocks tend to reveal their sedimentary and metamorphic nature in the horizontal mosaic of stone walls that ride the crests and troughs of the heaving landscape, and there are places along Tunket Road where one gets a glimpse of what Vermont's thousands of miles of stone walls must have looked like in the eyes of each town's "fence viewer," the person appointed and paid to walk the town's fences, looking for breaches—both physical breaches that would allow livestock to pass through and breaches of the public trust when walls did not meet the legal minimum height of 4 feet.

Looking back, we tend to romanticize the bucolic nature of this pastoral landscape, but most folks don't know just how much bucolic activity was really going on as Tunket Road shifted from a Native American path to a colonial road. *Bucolic* comes from the Latin word for "ox keeper," and indeed it was more oxen power than human strength that built these stone walls, if one considers the relative caloric expenditures of man and beast. In the early settlers' desperation to make clearings to provide for their larders and their livestock, they employed the strength and skills of teams of oxen to pull the "stone boats"—wooden sledges built tough and low to haul stumps, stones, logs, and supplies.

The typical oxen of this era did not resemble their black-and-white relatives who now fill much of the Vermont landscape and the state's tourist brochures. In contrast, many of the cattle of that era were a deep brown or a rich ruby-red color, the signature colorations of the first breed of cattle to appear in New England—the American Milking Devon. American Milking Devons were particularly renowned for their low-slung musculature, their fleet-footedness, and their ability to produce meat and dairy products from relatively rough forage. Although few recognize it today, a Milking Devon still adorns the Vermont state flag as a symbol of the early colonial era.[2]

Another reminder of this bucolic era is the tree that grows alongside the stone walls of Tunket, the so-called hop hornbeam. The dense wood of this tree species was used as a "hornbeam," literally a piece of wood lashed to the horns of a team of oxen in lieu of the yoke we tend to think of today, providing roughly the same pulling power of a head yoke, but requiring somewhat less demanding craftsmanship. The flowers of the hop hornbeam appear in June and closely resemble the flowers of the wild hops plant. Their seed is an important source of feed for wildlife, particularly grouse.

Native Americans altered their landscapes, too—just to what degree remains a topic of hot debate. Obviously, Native Americans' impacts varied in degree and scale in different parts of the continent. The European immigrants, in contrast, radically shifted entire ecosystems, primarily due to their "ingredients for sustenance." Just as there is little sense in romanticizing the past, it is probably also misguided to over-correct with a constant negative critique of any culture for its myriad ecological decisions. That said, the Native Americans tended to coexist with the natural environment in this region, in contrast with the settlers, who were determined to manage it, transforming it from its native forest into a landscape of pastures, hayfields, cropland, and villages, with forest filling the gaps in between.

The simultaneous need for open land and wood for building, combined with an enormous annual household consumption of firewood, meant that the colonial homesteaders did not live lightly on the land.[3] Add to that the fact that as the forests were cleared and the excess wood was burned, potash and charcoal both became valuable commodities. Potash was essential for making lye soap, gunpowder, and other products.[4] Made simply by pouring water into an enormous potash kettle filled with wood ashes, potash was one of the first major agricultural exports from Vermont, and it was certainly a by-product of early agriculture in much of New England. Two hundred bushels of wood ash would make approximately 100 pounds of potash.[5]

Potash was smuggled from the Taconic region northward to Canada via Lake Champlain; in fact, it was in the nearby town of Whitehall, New York, on the South Bay of Lake Champlain that the American navy was born, not on a seaside port. Lake Champlain was the primary route of commerce between Quebec and the colonists in Vermont. Benedict Arnold and his compatriots opposed the British Crown's restrictions and high tariffs on potash, charcoal, and other goods that were floated northward to the markets of Quebec, where these items were exchanged for salt and other essential goods. The colonists' fledgling fleet fought throughout the Revolutionary War to keep the route free for trade while daring smugglers continued to sneak their exports to the Canadian border, generally under the cover of fog, darkness, and the early navy's watch.

Forest, field, and fence probably sum up the distinctions and the tensions between the original inhabitants of the region and the influx of settlers in the mid-1700s onward. Native Americans recognized any appearance of the honeybee and several plant species such as common plantain and mullein as harbingers of the coming infiltration of a culture obsessed with domestication and, in many cases, dominion. In fact, Native Americans purportedly referred to the honeybee as the "white man's fly" and both mullein and common plaintain as the "white man's footprint."[6] But it was the livestock that somehow made it across the stormy Atlantic in the putrid holds of ships that were most emblematic of the coming psychology and impacts of domestication.

Livestock tested the veracity and wisdom of their purported domestication, as they were just as eager to explore and taste of the new landscape as were the colonists. The effectiveness of fencing was often more a part of the settlers' optimism than a physical reality for the critters themselves. The problem with livestock being imported to the colonies was that the animals arrived before the fencing did, and probably nothing exacerbated tensions between the new colonists and the resident Native Americans more than the rampages of cattle and pigs through the forests and planted fields of the native populations.

Not only did the livestock have voracious appetites, but the settlers also seemed to have a limitless hunger for more land to increase their livestock numbers. The animals lucky enough to survive the voyage across the ocean were the original breeding stock brought from Europe, and they quickly proliferated. With the European dependence upon livestock and crop agriculture, domestication seemed to demand and even justify dominion.[7] It wasn't long before much of what the early settlers had come for had been disrupted or even displaced by everything they had brought with them (perhaps not so different from today's urban migration to rural New England, in which newcomers bring with them expectations for convenience stores, paved roads, and other "essentials"). With the disappearance of intact forest and certain vegetation came diminished wildlife populations, undermining the promises of the New World's limitless bounty.

Those bound for bounty were bound to set boundaries, and fences made of wood, stumps, and even thickets of briars and bramble eventually gave way to stone walls. Stone walls served several purposes and differ notably from place to place. Initially, fencing was used for exclusion from certain areas such as gardens or grain fields. It wasn't until some point in the 1800s that the role of fences was reversed, and fences became enclosures, a means of confining livestock . . . at least sometimes. These walls also served as a convenient way to deal with the overwhelming supply of stones pulled out of pastures, hayfields, and cropland.

Over time, the stones coming from pastures and cropland started to differ in size and frequency. Stones pulled from pastures and hayfields helped clear the way for the growth of grass, whereas the rocks rooted out from cultivated cropland helped make plowing, harrowing, seeding, and plant growth more efficient. Pastures and hayfields gradually needed fewer stones removed, since the relative stability of a well-managed pasture doesn't promote the freezing, thawing, and thrusting movements of the soil that tend to move rocks toward the surface. Also, smaller stones in areas grazed by livestock or mowed by scythes weren't as problematic as they were in cultivated areas. Therefore, stone walls with large stones were generally bounding pastures, whereas stone walls featuring smaller rocks tended to outline the perimeters of areas plowed for growing crops. The constant disturbance of the soil in plowed areas, however, meant that annual harvests of stone probably at times rivaled the crop yields, at least in weight.

Other hints about previous land use reveal themselves to the trained eye in a place like Tunket Road. The architecture of old trees such as maples and oaks tends to provide clues as to whether these trees were once out in the open, spreading their limbs broadly in open relief, or simply spiring upward, in rapid vertical competition for light and longevity. Heavy branching to one side, especially along a stone wall, is usually a good indication of which area was open, with the best source of light. Big, branching trees in the middle of areas circumscribed by stone walls hint that they were once pasture trees, rugged individualists who were, as the expression goes, outstanding in their field. In recent times, these "pasture trees," or "wolf trees," are usually surrounded by trees a fraction of their girth and in tight, in vertical competition with one another, with neither room nor time for branching until their apexes reach the fast-encroaching canopy.

Along Tunket Road, the historical hints of the occasional "pasture trees" are substantiated by the white pines that tend to congregate in clumps, filling the vertical void in fields that were left to their own devices as farming declined and farmers retired. These white pines are not the shady characters their undersides portray—rather, their top branches openly tell the tale of . . . well, the openings from which they stemmed.

White pines that germinate in open fields have all the advantages of full sunlight and tend to branch rather broadly, but in their early leaps toward the light, their upright ambitions are often squelched in their first few years when the white pine weevil bores into the apical stem, laying its eggs inside. This terminal leader is then killed, with the surrounding uppermost branches taking over its efforts. The result is a top with multiple forks, creating a fine place for a raven's nest but not a tree to gladden a logger's heart. Interestingly, the weevil generally does not like to place its eggs in white pines in shady areas, so an area of weeviled pines typically indicates a former field of some sort.

Scattered among the pines and pasture trees of Tunket Road, "wild" apple trees are yet another reminder of the ebb and flow of the shifting ecosystem. Humans moved apples from their native forests in Kazakhstan to western Europe and beyond, including the colonies in the United States, with the diaspora (literally, "a scattering of seed") of varieties spreading out from the ports of New England and the Chesapeake Bay. The diversity of tastes, textures, and appearances of these apples is hard to fathom, much less catalog, and yet these old apples hold culinary, cultural, and genetic surprises that are a reminder of just how quickly our domesticated world can change. Go anywhere in the world, and you'll find Red Delicious, Granny Smith, and Fuji apples. But go somewhere like Tunket Road on a fall day, and you'll be at a loss for names, descriptions, and recipes for the diverse bounty of apple varieties you'll find. Some of the trees are undoubtedly remnants of the long-gone homesteaders who somehow eked out an existence up Tunket, while others are unique seedling varieties that never had a name beyond the door of the cabin outside of which they were planted.[8]

Like so many places strewn across the hillsides of the Northeast, Tunket harbors the stone remains of long-abandoned havens. When one crests the hill up Tunket Road and is hit head-on with an unexpected open vista of three aligned mountain peaks, it doesn't take long to notice the enormous sugar maples flanking the road, with a not-so-obvious "cellar hole" on the knoll near the maples. The old maps of Pawlet actually call the place "Mapleton," and the collection of cellar holes, some of the maps, and the durable memories of a few old-timers who have died since we started asking questions all indicate that Mapleton boasted several families up until the early 1900s, at which time everyone pulled up stakes and left for an easier life and terrain.

One lingering rumor has it that there was a "halfway house," a place to sleep and to water and rest the draft animals, about halfway over the crest of Tunket Road. Near the purported location of the old guesthouse, there is indeed a stone foundation, not far from where our neighbor Donald Waite remembers the horse loggers of the 1940s camping for the winter. They would drag in their logging tent platforms with the first snows and set up camp for the winter, logging six days a week. On Saturday, they flipped a coin to see who had to stay in camp that night with their horses and equipment while the rest went to consume their wages in the bars of Granville, New York. Sunday was probably a good day to believe in resurrection.

All of the harvesting and clearing of the forest shifted the forest community significantly, along with some changes in the climate. The forests on these slopes were once predominantly spruce, hemlock, and hardwoods.[9] These days, stands of spruce are sporadic at best, and it's less the forest-related activities of local human inhabitants that are shifting the species composition than it is our economic engines. Both national and international trade have introduced new insects and diseases, and our fossil-fuel-driven economy has amplified the impacts of a changing climate and increased pollution.

Insects and diseases have thus far attacked American chestnut, beech, butternut, ash, and hemlock, to the extent that we now have to question each species' survival as an enduring part of the native forest ecosystem. Even the iconic sugar maple faces the documented triple threats of the imported Asian long-horned beetle, acid rain's leaching of calcium from rich forest soils, and a significant warming trend for the Northern Forest. Meanwhile, the versatile and vigorous red maples and the aggressive but short-lived beech saplings (creating thickets called "beech hells") tend to dominate the resulting ecological gaps, creating a new forest regime that makes for difficult choices in whether to utilize intensive forestry management or to leave the forest to its own devices.

Just as we are torn by whether to cast blame or fame on previous generations for their adherence to the tenets of domestication, we must also ask ourselves to what degree our own exaggerated domestication and all of its associated comforts and conveniences is impacting a world we claim to understand better than any previous generation. Perhaps it's not so much the natural world that we don't understand anymore, but rather our own place in it.

All of the hikers who come up Tunket Road to hike Haystack Mountain seem to delight in cresting the hill and reaching a clearing with ancient maples in the foreground, our cattle in the pasture, and Haystack, Middle, and Bald Mountains as the backdrop. What they probably don't consider as they look in satisfaction at the pasture is just how many of the most common pasture species are non-natives: timothy, white clover, red clover, orchard grass, bromegrass, reed canary grass, plantain, and mullein. It is thought that many of these species first appeared on US soil clinging to root-balls of imported plants and as part of the earthen ballast cast from ships' holds for the transatlantic voyages to the colonies and then cleared out for the loading of goods back to Europe, at which point the ballast was shoveled from the ships onto shore. Seed and even some new species of earthworms took hold, and the underground colonization was under way. New England forests had no native earthworms at the time of the European colonization, at least not since they were wiped out in the last Ice Age. The lack of earthworms meant that forest leaf litter piled up and helped to sequester moisture and nutrients. Once the night crawler and red marsh worm moved in, the forest floor became a different habitat, albeit slowly.[10] Other changes aboveground seemed more dramatic, such as the appearance of some reasonably domesticated pollinators—honeybees.

Although it is difficult to say precisely when it happened, at some point in the first half of the nineteenth century, the history of the area along Tunket Road shifted from one primarily of ecological disturbances such as wind, ice, and an occasional fire to a litany of shrinking and swelling "civilized clearings." Undoubtedly, one period in the mid- to late 1800s involved a massive clearing of forest to make way for the international merino sheep craze. It wasn't the sheep that were crazed: It was the farmers and wool entrepreneurs who urged the sheep up the hills of Vermont and into much of the Northeast, with stone walls in slow but methodical pursuit. Several stone walls that we have discovered across the brook from us traipse up the steep sides of Middle Mountain, in an area where the sheep obviously felt more at ease than did the wall builders. It wasn't ecological concerns but rather the popping of this economic bubble in the international wool markets that brought the sheep down from the hills and into the history books, with the forests slowly recuperating on soils now robbed of depth and fertility, thanks to the deforestation and subsequent overgrazing.

Clearings and civilizations, taken too far and too fast, risk supplanting a native order with unbridled optimism—sometimes resulting in irrevocable errors. There are lessons in trying to domesticate the world too much in our own image. Medicinal plants become weeds, non-native invasives pose as ornamentals, and we feign understanding of a world we hardly know.

For Erin and myself, the issue was not about restoring order to the landscape. Rather, we wanted to put the stories back in order so that ultimately our portion of the land's long narrative might, in hindsight, make sense.

FOUR

Oikos: A Household Economy and Ecology

Optimists and realists definitely belong in the same house together, but they sometimes have a hard time sharing the same room. When the room is so small it's hard to change your mind, much less your clothes, things can get pretty complicated at times. Erin and I had committed to downsizing, simplifying, retreating, rejecting, retooling, and reassessing—but we hadn't quite figured out how it was all going to work in our cozy 12' × 28' cabin. I am the eternal optimist, while Erin is the day-at-a-time realist.

Perhaps kittens, pup tents, and people are too much of a species mix, but we had enjoyed three months of intimacy in our tiny tent as we finished insulating the cabin and adding interior walls. After months of planning and a summer of hard work, we were looking forward to upgrading to life in the cabin in the fall when the doubt came out.

Moments of doubt when beginning a homesteading venture are the points of intersection between idealism and pragmatism—a chance to reclaim sanity in the midst of the search for a reasonable (I did not say "simple") lifestyle. I can deal with doubt, but I hate tears when they are someone else's and I don't quite know what to do to fix the situation. Erin, on the other hand, can't stand the fact that I feel like I have to fix whatever is wrong. She would much prefer momentary empathy in lieu of an immediate solution. *Knowing* and *learning* aren't necessarily synonymous—I know what she prefers, but I haven't necessarily changed my approach yet.

All summer long we'd been showering underneath a big white pine, with our solar shower bag hung from a tree branch after it had heated up nearly to a scalding temperature out in the sunlight of the open meadow. On the particularly hot days, we would make a trip to the brook below us to bathe, feeding the mosquito population with the blood-rich tender regions of our striped anatomies. But as the occasional chills of August started to seep into our evenings and early mornings, Erin finally hit a wall of doubt.

I looked up from fixing breakfast one day, and she was in tears. "What's wrong?" I asked, caught completely off-guard after what had thus far been a mellow morning, getting ready to tackle the finishing details on the interior of the cabin.

"What are we going to do about a shower or taking a bath?" she sobbed. "How crazy are we? We don't even know how we're going to stay clean, much less get in and out of here in the winter. We've got cows to take care of through the winter, and you have to get to work. I'll be up here alone . . . and we don't even know how we're going to take a bath!"

I was perplexed. Anyone who knows us realizes right away that of the two of us, Erin is the tougher one. She's neither buff nor aggressive, but she is headstrong, a phrase I'll use to infer both intelligence and stick-to-itiveness. The woman who could easily go a day or two beyond what I could in delaying the need to bathe was worried about how she was going to take a bath in the cabin—after all this time bathing outdoors?

"Erin—I don't get it. We're about to move into the cabin, where you've got four walls—actually seven—that'll give you a lot more privacy than we have now . . . and there'll be the woodstove. I'm sure we'll figure something out."

"So what am I going to do? Put in a shower curtain that comes down from the ceiling and bathe in a washtub? This is nuts . . . this whole idea is nuts! What are we doing? Sure, it all seems ideal and romantic, but what are we really getting into? I'm not so sure this is going to be the fun you think it is. It might be a disaster. And I'm *not* bathing in some makeshift washtub like a cartoon character!"

By late in the fall, we'd figured out how to put a 2-gallon bucket of hot water from the woodstove into a 17-gallon galvanized washtub and take a full bath and shampoo, warmed by the glowing window of the woodstove. Our record temperature inside the cabin during those sauna sessions was 103 degrees, and Erin's biggest complaint once we moved to our new house eight years later was that the shower was too cold and wasteful.

I'll admit the truth from the very beginning: Deciding to scale down, minimize one's possessions, and shirk amenities such as electricity and running water is a luxury. While it may not be a choice of luxury, it is a luxurious choice, borne out of socioeconomic privilege. There's nothing particularly noble about such an experiment, since it is a choice and a privilege to embark on such an experience, with the port of departure being a reasonably comfortable American middle-class lifestyle. What may be an austere choice for an American homesteader is a stark reality for the majority of the world's population.

Erin and I both were dissatisfied and uncomfortable with the plastic cornucopia lifestyle so prevalent in much of middle- and upper-class America, a lifestyle in which there are more expectations regarding consumption than there are lessons about how to minimize it. It's a lifestyle that often breeds ennui and cynicism instead of cultivating engagement and wisdom, and it tends to dilute the notion that a home is where people work together for sustenance and meaning, not just a place where people live together. I've long associated our culture's obsession with fabricated adventure—whether it be out-of-doors, online, or in some other virtual reality—to be the direct result of a lack of challenge and engagement in our everyday lives. Challenges start to appear rather quickly, though, when you decide to forgo electricity, running water, phone, computer, refrigeration, and easy vehicle access.

Both Erin and I had been fortunate enough to hear our professor Sizzo in his classes at Brunnenburg Castle lecture eloquently on Metis. As Sizzo described it, Zeus devoured his first wife Metis, the Greek goddess of wisdom, whose intelligence he feared because she might bear a son to rival him. When he swallowed Metis, he did not realize that she was pregnant. After nine months of misery and a constant headache, Zeus had Hephaestos split his head open with an ax to relieve the pain, and out popped Athena, whom Metis had birthed while inside Zeus's body. Athena, soon to be recognized as the goddess of war, had inherited her mother's intelligence and was given credit for being the inventor of the much-revered bit for controlling horses, a key invention in the taming of the natural world and other civilizations. Over the ages, *Metis* became synonymous with a kind of craftiness, what Sizzo called "manual intelligence."

Metis, this ability to confront the challenges of the world with practical inventions, stems less from genetic inheritance than from nurturing the ability to tackle a problem with intellectual prowess and artisanal skill. A culture that provides us instantaneously with everything we could want and more than we possibly need in ready-made form twenty-four hours a day doesn't foster Metis, the wellspring of innovation. Before we Americans can again rely on necessity as the mother of invention, we first have to reinvent necessity.

Thinking back, I'm not quite sure whether we abandoned most of the standard amenities that we'd grown up with primarily because of our minimal income, the challenges of our homestead's location, or simple philosophical obstinacy. It was probably a combination of the three. We were definitely more concerned with liberating ourselves from debt by doubling and tripling our mortgage payments than we were with being slaves to a host of daily tasks that could have been made much simpler with certain amenities. And in the process, we relished the challenge of figuring out how to make, do, make do, and do without.

Our Realtor Scott went well beyond his expected role by loaning us a generator for our carpentry projects, but we were loath to run it any more than necessary. The noise and smell made our energy consumption palpable, but that type of sensory metering seemed pretty intrusive on the otherwise serene landscape. Photovoltaic panels seemed beyond our means—economically and technically—and the pine trees surrounding the cabin made that option difficult if not impossible anyway. We did need water and light, but beyond that, we felt we could get by with minimal amenities, at least for the time being.

One thing that had impressed me from my first walking of the land was the preponderance of water. Springs seemed to be everywhere. What impressed me then depressed me later, at least during mud season and rainy spells. But finding the right source of water and getting it near the house was still a challenge.

One day I asked Carl what he would suggest doing to find the right water source. He looked up at me and then back down, shaking his head and drawing on his ever-present cigarette. "Hmph, you're definitely not from around here are you?" After a moment of silence that spanned his disgust, he looked at me and responded, "You call a dowser—but don't go looking in the Yellow Pages for one."

The same day that Erin and I had met Will and Abe, the oxen at the rural crafts and skills festival in St. Johnsbury, Vermont, we had run into the dowsers with their array of forked sticks, coat hangers, copper wires, pendants, and eccentric literature. I'd pretty much lumped dowsers and geezers into the same category, out of ignorance more than doubt. But the dowsers drew us over to their table with their smiles and laughter—or maybe it was magnetic attraction.

Before I knew what had happened, I had a couple of dowsing rods in my hand and was pacing the lawn, trying to get a nod from them when I passed over the water main going into the building. I walked and thought hard about water then tried not to think about water. Before I knew it, I needed to pee, so I ran inside and then came back out, as empty a vessel as a thirsty Buddhist.

I tried the forked stick from every fruit tree they had: apple, pear, and cherry. I refused to try the pendant, just because I'm averse to being associated too much with crystals. I was about to give up and dismiss both the science and the art of it all, when an elderly gentleman walked over and asked if he could help.

"Sure," I replied, not sure how he was going to pass on something that seemed neither rational nor tacit. He picked up a forked stick made of cherry.

"Here, hold my hand with your left hand." He extended his right hand to me, and I reluctantly put my hand in his. "You walk beside me, with your right hand holding your side of the stick. Now think about water—not too hard, but don't think about anything else. We'll walk forward at a slow pace. Don't be distracted by me or anybody else around here."

We started walking toward the spot in the big lawn where everybody knew the water line was buried. I pushed about everything out of my mind except how silly this must look, and I couldn't water down that thought no matter how hard I tried. I decided to look straight ahead instead of down so that I couldn't see where they'd marked the line for the water main when we crossed it.

I'm certainly not the strongest guy around, but I'm wiry enough to be tough when I need to be, and I was sure this dowser geezer was in his eighties, if not older. (I was too polite to ask and I didn't have ready access to carbon-dating methods.) Anyway, as we neared the line that I was trying to avoid seeing, the stick began to quake, and I felt an intense tugging on my wrist. I looked down to see if there was any way he could be pushing the stick down. I tightened my grip, and the tip of the cherry branch began bending downward. I heard Erin giggle. As we crossed the line, the tip of the stick bent downward beyond my ability to keep my wrist parallel with the ground. I looked over at him in disbelief. He smiled back knowingly.

"Now you know it's true." His widening grin appeared to be linked to my melting skepticisim. "But you've got to practice on your own to get a feel for it." So he stepped away and let me walk back and forth over the line, feeling the draw of something below the surface of the earth.

I'd only once before felt anything so primordial—while I was searching for a mountaintop Late Stone Age cultic site in the Alps that matched my hunch for where I thought there should be a site. In both cases, it felt like finding something was only going to happen if I peeled away the layers of rationality and simply let the discovery emerge of its own accord. For a while, the end of the forked stick continued to bend despite my wrists' best efforts to hold the entire stick straight out. Then the sensation began to dwindle, and my mentor gave me the dowsing rods. Sure enough, they worked with much less physical effort, to the point that the finesse involved in letting them do their own thing seemed impossibly delicate.

"Part of dowsing is knowing when you're ready to begin, and part of it is knowing when to stop. I think you're done for now." He told me that if he went out and dowsed for hours, even when he was young, he would come home exhausted, ready to collapse. "After all, it takes energy to find energy."

Erin and I definitely needed to establish a reliable source of water at home, so Carl's subsequent affirmation of the reliability of dowsing convinced me that it was our best option. Besides, at that point, it was easier to conjure up faith than dollars.

About the same time, I went over to pick up some lumber from our local sawmill. Phil's Mill had become as much a source of local lore and wisdom for me as it was the best place to buy top-quality lumber for bargain prices.

Phil Hayes had built his sawmill just a year or two prior. If I've ever met a New England example of Metis, it would be Phil. He'd found the metal components of an old sawmill from the late 1800s sinking into the ground as the wood infrastructure rotted under and around it. He'd offered the owner $500 for it, trucked it home, and built a staging area for it. He somehow found another mill just like it, and the owner gave it to him for free so he had any spare parts he might need for the first one. Then he hooked a diesel engine to the mill and didn't even hang out a shingle—he just ordered truckloads of logs from his friends and started milling, building the walls and roof of the mill as he went. The log yard and Phil's local reputation as a jack-of-all-trades were advertisement enough, with people like me coming to buy his beefy, rough-cut lumber from local logs. His jingle was "Come see what I saw," and anyone smart enough to buy lumber from him was guaranteed to get plenty of solid advice on framing, logging, welding, hunting, trapping, beekeeping, and just about any other practical skill. Both the price and the advice were considerably better than anything I could get at any of the commercial lumberyards. Plus, it was closer.

While I was loading up the heavy green hemlock 2×6s, I asked Phil if he knew anyone who might be willing to dowse some springs for me so we could get a reliable source of drinking water established before winter rolled in. "Sure do. When do you want me to come over?"

"Really—you can dowse?"

He looked at me and gave me the traditional Vermont response, without a hint of pride or frustration: "Yup."

Excited already at the prospects of life with our own water supply, I tentatively asked how soon he could come over.

"How about right after work? I'll be over a little after five, and we'll see what we can find."

Phil pulled up in his delivery truck a few hours later and went straight for an apple tree. He grabbed a branch and asked me where I thought I might want to dig a spring. I pointed uphill behind the cabin.

"Anywhere back up there should be protected from any contamination, and maybe we can even get it set up for gravity feed to the cabin."

"Having it run downhill seems like it might be too easy for you guys," he quipped, with a wink. "But let's see what we can find up there."

We headed up into the woods behind the cabin, and we both got quiet. Concentrating so hard on finding water made me have to pee, just like my first dowsing experience. Meanwhile, Phil seemed to combine his dowsing with a reading of the landscape for likely spots to home in on. He started circling one spot, tightening his steps into a spiral. I saw the twig bend—or at least I thought I did. Phil found the center of his signals, and then he walked across what I guessed was a vein and then walked across it again from a perpendicular direction.

"Right here it is," he offered modestly, pointing his boot to the point of intersection. "I think you'll have plenty of water if you dig right here."

I shook my head in mild disbelief and smiled at him. "I'll trust what I don't understand. But do you think we could choose one more spot just in case we don't hit enough water here?"

"Sure." Within ten minutes he had flagged another spot. I tried to pay him, but he shrugged me off. "This isn't the kind of thing anybody should charge for."

A few weeks later, just as our first Tunket winter weather started to spill out of the sky in the form of sleet, hitting the dry October leaves with a hissing sound, Leon Corey came up with his excavator to dig out the two springs. As the growling of the excavator clashed with the clanking of the metal treads banging along on our road, I felt the intensity of our intrusion on the serenity and sanctity of our new home, nestled between the ridgelines of the Three Sisters above us and the Fox Cobble behind us. I felt a pang of guilt as we trimmed out a narrow path for the excavator to access the new spring sites.

Throughout the summer, Erin had discovered pottery and brick shards in the bed of the small seasonal stream flowing down from the ledges of the Fox Cobble when she was filling buckets for wash water, so I knew that we weren't the first to homestead here and harvest the water. However, the rumble of an excavator clumsily wending its way among the white pines and into the deeper hardwoods was a foreboding sound of imminent change. Whatever changes we were about to make to this place wouldn't be erased as easily as those earlier changes made by people well versed in the harmony of wood and stone.

Expecting to hit ledge in 4 or 5 feet, we went down to 8 feet, with water seeping in from the gravelly veins we hit every few feet. We cut a 20-foot plastic culvert in half and put 1-inch holes in the bottom 2 feet of corrugations. Then we sank it vertically in the ground and filled around the outside first with larger stones and then with gravel, leaving an exit for a length of 1-inch black plastic pipe that went through the culvert and down into the bottom of the bubbling spring.

"I guess Phil got the right spot," Leon said as we finished up the first spring. "In a way, I just wish he hadn't been quite so right—I'm getting pretty damn wet and cold!" Within a few hours, we had the second spring dug, too, and we began the process of tying the water lines for the two springs together and running the line aboveground to a spot 30 feet outside our cabin, where we installed a shut-off valve. We covered the exposed line with leaves and pine needles to insulate it, and we hoped that letting it trickle all winter would prevent it from freezing.

At that point, we weren't planning on living in the cabin for very long, and we had no good way of keeping the water line from freezing

if we sent the line from the ground up through the open space between the ground and the recently elevated cabin. We decided to wait until the next year to decide precisely where to run the line and install a frost-free hydrant. We also couldn't afford to pay Leon the extra cost of burying the line in a 4-foot trench the whole length of the pipe from both springs to the cabin.

I couldn't help but think of my dad's story about some of his hard-core Appalachian friends who finally scraped together the finances to put in a well for indoor plumbing. As it turned out, the woman was out when the plumber came to install their first sink. My father was surprised to see the sink installed on the porch, and when he asked what had happened, the husband grumbled, "She's got enough junk in that kitchen already. I didn't see why we needed to add anything else in there!"

We wouldn't have minded an indoor sink at all, and it was a real triumph to get one eight years later that didn't require hauling buckets of water in for washing and out for dumping. However, we did find that we became much more conscious of our water consumption, and, over time, we also saw the results of strategically dumping the nutrient-rich "graywater" around the plants and trees surrounding the cabin.

Having water come gushing out of our outdoor hydrant for the first time was a triumphal moment. Nothing is more of a cause for celebration than prior deprivation, and no convenience seems more essential than easy access to water . . . except perhaps light. As the autumn days shortened and the mood of the forest shifted from bustling preparations to a slow resignation of winter's certainty, we found ourselves torn between rest and restlessness. It's no secret that light is energy, but we Americans have forgotten the degree to which light imparts energy and pushes our human penchant for productivity.

We weren't happy with any of our lighting options. Using disposable batteries in flashlights seemed too wasteful, and we seldom resorted to them except for finding things in the dark corners of the cabin—which, as it turns out, was most of the cabin. Candles seemed too dangerous for the minimal lumens they produced, and we weren't comfortable with the propane lights some folks used in their hunting cabins. We opted to use three oil lamps: one for the cooking area, one for the table, and one beside the bed.

We ended up using that arrangement for five years, until we could no longer stand the smell, or the cost, of the oil. Fortunately, by this time engineers had finally developed white LEDs—not just red and green ones—so Erin was able to make a homemade light from six white LEDs. We hung it above the table and connected it to a car battery outside on the porch. Our visitors thought it was cute. For us, it was a technological highlight, so to speak. The one benefit of the oil lamps, though—like hauling our water in- and out-of-doors—was that we kept close tabs on our consumption and were careful to conserve, as much out of economic necessity as from ecological considerations.

If we learned anything in prioritizing and setting up our cabin amenities, it was that affluence seldom links economic and ecological choices, whereas economic limitations and ecological constraints can be soulmates—and Metis is often the end result of that romance.

Homesteading is an act of defiance and of reliance: *defiance* of cultural norms and habits and *reliance* on self and local community. We homesteaders are cultural curmudgeons who consider our lives to be small steps in re-norming our consumptive, disconnected culture. *Homesteading* seems difficult to define precisely—in the end, it probably tends to define us more than we can define it.

Contrary to the back-to-the-land images most folks have of the quintessential homestead, homesteading is actually much less about location than it is about intent. It means that we want to be accountable for our actions, if only in our own private musings. By embracing the menial and the mundane and searching for the minimum, we homesteaders are trying to envision, create, and assess our individual "household ecologies," which we hope can be woven together into a social fabric that makes more sense.

In the United States, most of us tend to think of our existences in two polarized views: as individuals and as a collective culture. That makes it simple to rationalize our irresponsible economic and ecological behaviors either as individual actions that have no real significance or as cultural behaviors that cannot be swayed. We generally don't think of the household as the place where accountability and accounting begin. However, the Greek word *oikos,* meaning "house," is in fact the root for both *ecology* and *economy*. The boundaries of the house provide us with a means of defining inputs, outputs, and interactions. In other words, the household becomes an ecological unit, essentially a small-scale ecosystem.

We can, from the perspective of our individual households, measure our consumption and our contributions (good and bad) and determine whether these actions jibe with our values or the planet's ecological carrying capacity. Household accounting starts to inform household accountability, and when we stop feeling powerless as individuals or overwhelmed by cultural norms, then we begin to change things as we best can—one household at a time.

It's generally wise to admit the reality of a lifestyle's minority status when making the case for its national relevance. So here's my confession: Homesteading as we tend to think of it is a tiny subculture in our society, and what meager capital we do have is probably not political. Yet there are ample political and economic lessons in the homesteading subculture, and it all begins with the fact that the household unit has some clear boundaries when it comes to its economy and its ecology.

Economy and ecology are inextricably linked in the homestead setting. In contrast, our culture constantly finds ways in our national and international discussions to pit economy against ecology. But when thinking about a household, we simply cannot separate the ideas of economy and ecology. They both exist under the same roof—sometimes in harmony and other times in tension, if not outright conflict. *Oikos* is a good reminder of the inevitable integration of a household's ecology and economy—and of our own place in the world.

A more inclusive and responsible model for homesteading in the near future might be to emphasize the household as an ecological and economic unit. This perspective shifts our sense of individual responsibility for our world to a more accurate portrayal of choices as a household responsibility. Homesteading allows us as household units to account for what we do. Even if we are not absolutely precise in our math, at least we can approximate our impacts on a cultural or even a global scale. The downside of viewing our impacts through the lens of the household is that the conclusions hit home with an unmistakable pointedness. However, finding ways to create a responsible household economy and ecology is immediate and manageable. The accounting and the accountability both seem within reach.

Economic security does not begin on Wall Street or on Main Street. It begins at home. And what transpires in each of our household economies becomes a collective psychology that drives our cultural values and our financial industry. If we don't behave rationally or within our means as households, how could we possibly expect our political representatives, our bankers, our business sector, or even our children to act any more responsibly?

And yet that boundary between home and the rest of the world needs to be permeable. Ideally, it is not about erecting barriers between one's home and the rest of the world. It is more about establishing a gateway that involves making conscious decisions about what comes in and what goes out, not just accepting the status quo.

I hope that we can shift our cultural notion of homesteading from a back-to-the-land search for self-reliance to a quest for a "crafted interdependence" between homesteaders and their communities, no matter the setting—rural, suburban, or urban. Such an approach involves barter, collaborative education, apprenticeships, community service, and shared celebrations. This crafted interdependence between households works on a scale that avoids the perils of numbing anonymity and misguided individualism, neither of which will cultivate much-needed change in the way we make ourselves at home on this shrinking planet.

In a culture flush with a thousand ways to hide or veil anything to do with the ecological messes we create, an outhouse is as good a place as any to unseat our ignorance. The "home of the end result," the toilet can be a place of appreciation, if not subtle enlightenment. In his delightful essay "In Praise of Shadows," Japanese art critic Junichiro Tanizaki espouses the merits of Japanese aesthetics in comparison with those of the Western world. In reference to the Japanese toilet, he notes that "one could with some justice claim that of all the elements of Japanese architecture, the toilet is the most aesthetic. Our forebears, making poetry of everything in their lives, transformed what by rights should be the most unsanitary room in the house into a place of unsurpassed elegance, replete with fond associations with the beauties of nature."[1]

About the time that we'd finished most of the interior of our cabin, our tree-sheltered bucket-toilet started to become increasingly uncomfortable in the chilly fall rains, so we assembled the leftover wood from our rehab operation and set about building an outhouse/toolshed with all recycled materials. Erin found old metal roofing and a fine old door at her new job running the town landfill and recycling station. The door had perfect windows for framing Haystack's peak—we just had to position the outhouse correctly to gain the ideal contemplative view, in homage to Tanizaki. The mail slot still intact in the door provided the opportunity for passing notes back and forth. The most difficult part of the construction was designing a toilet paper holder that would prevent the mice from destroying the bulk of a roll in just one evening. Surely it doesn't take that much paper to wipe a tiny rodent bunghole!

It seems ironic that one of the twentieth century's hallmarks of a civilization coming of age was the toilet-test: If a culture decided to use perfectly clean water as a vehicle for moving feces and urine to a facility where these undesirable elements were removed and the water could then be resanitized, it was a sign that the culture had progressed. I am not suggesting that we go back to an era of human waste running in open ditches or sewers through cities, overwhelming the olfactory senses and resulting in a host of diseases. However, we seem today to be locked in a technological stalemate in which we don't even want to think about our daily "end result," much less reconsider our ways of dealing with this natural and daily effluvium.

Drying the organic wastes left from sewage treatment plants and then shipping them via truck and rail to out-of-state incinerators, as we do in parts of Vermont, seems a bit ludicrous. Even if we can't bring ourselves to reconsider using perfectly clean drinking water to transport poop and pee (and everything else we subsequently dump into the system—anti-biotics, household cleaning chemicals, paint residues, hygiene and birth control products, et cetera), why can't we at least adopt some "ecological education stations" that could double as both water treatment plants and biological research stations, like John Todd's Living Machines?

John Todd, an ecological designer based at the University of Vermont, has worked to create simulated wetlands and water ecosystems that treat wastewater "biologically." Granted, most sewage treatment plants also treat wastewater primarily with biological methods, since bacteria do 80 to 90 percent of the work. However, John Todd's Living Machines incor-porate various versions of organisms—from bacteria to snails to fish to plants—into a progression of sequential "living" tanks inside a green-house. As the wastewater moves through the tanks, beginning with anaerobic and aerobic bacteria, the water becomes visibly and quantifi-ably cleaner. The end result is that the water comes out of the system in compliance with EPA standards, and, in the process, the solid wastes are broken down and consumed by the living organisms in this ecological train of events.

In the past I'd had some pretty disgusting encounters with hole-in-the-ground outhouses that seemed like Venus flytraps designed for humans—first you're enticed in, then the ammonia knocks you out, and you subsequently fall into the pit, never to be heard from again. If that possibility weren't bad enough, the even worse possibility was being splashed from a poop-plop. We had no desire to replicate those bad experiences or to risk contaminating our groundwater with the resulting seepage around the outhouse. So many of our negative experiences with outhouses and even high-tech composting toilets stem from the fact that the nitrogen has virtually no carbon complement to minimize smell and maximize composting action.

We decided early on that we wanted our toilet facilities to be outside, since our cabin was too small to dedicate many square feet to a toilet—and the potential for odoriferous reminders of such a mistake was too high. Besides, we'd discovered that our trips to the privy (is that short for "private" or "privilege"?) treated us to nighttime serenades and celestial shows that we would have missed entirely were it not for the beckoning of bladders and bowels.

Plenty of folks encouraged us to get a chemical toilet, but that made no sense to us. Without heat and a power source to run a fan or a propane burner, a composting toilet wasn't an option we could consider—nor could we afford one. So we settled on the option with lowest cost and technological infrastructure: a 5-gallon bucket with a toilet seat from the town landfill and sawdust from Phil's Mill.

Soon thereafter, we found a copy of Joe Jenkins's hilarious and informative guide on converting crap into a crop—*The Humanure Handbook*.[2] As Jenkins confirmed for us, the sawdust and toilet paper provided just the right 25:1 ratio of carbon to nitrogen, and our toilet residues, food scraps, and household waste paper never filled our homemade 4' × 4' compost bins in less than a year. The sawdust captured most of the urine and mellowed the smell of the feces, and whatever liquid did remain at the time of emptying the bucket every four or five days was readily absorbed by the carbonaceous materials already in the compost pile.

That's not to say that dealing with one's own waste is all that elegant. There are usually discussions about whose bowels are more productive and whose turn it is to dump the bucket. And then there were the times that the contents of the bucket would freeze . . . solid. The resulting "poopsicle," as I called it, wasn't nearly as messy to dump, but it did require some thawing out before it could be removed from the bucket. A little time near the woodstove—when no guests were expected—usually solved that problem.

Of course, I once set our fancy new $19.99 bucket toilet with sealing lid too close to the woodstove, only to find that the lid had melted and readily sealed itself to the seat. A razor blade soon fixed the dilemma, but the lid bore a constant reminder of my outhouse misadventures, only one of which nearly scarred me.

We used the outhouse also as a toolshed, and when we got a cell phone, about four years after moving into our cabin, it turned out that the outhouse was the only place that we could get reception at the time. I have no idea why. At any rate, to make a call, I would go to the outhouse, face south, hold the phone in my right hand, and get reception most days. Facing east, in the direction of the toilet, would not get reception, so unfortunately I never had the opportunity to "multitask." Obviously, we did not generally tell people where we were calling from. "Oh, I'm at home . . . Yeah, we do get reception here sometimes, if we're standing in the right location! (chuckle, chuckle)"

It was on one such occasion that I went out on a surprisingly warm spring afternoon to call our excavator friend Leon about an upcoming job. The sun was shining intensely on the front of the outhouse, and sounds of spring were everywhere—frogs bellowing, robins singing, and water gurgling from the porous ground. I was just finishing the conversation when I felt the outhouse shift slightly, then sharply, and as I leapt out with a cry appropriate for an outhouse's calling, the entire structure fell forward, stopping only when the front edge caught on the large, flat stepping-stone at the doorway.

"What's wrong?" our contractor queried, clearly concerned.

"Uh, nothing." I tried not to stammer. "I guess I just lost my balance out here." No amount of explanation would have sufficed. Nor was I eager to be the butt of the jokes at the local general store for the next decade. Once again, mud season had gotten the best of me, with the thawing of the mud on the front side of the outhouse allowing it to sink with my weight and pitch forward. It took me four hours in the mud the following day to build a base firm enough to jack the outhouse back up and stabilize it until mud season was over and terra firma was once again something I could trust to be there when I needed it.

The joy and the challenge of homesteading is that it puts us face-to-face with our ecological choices. We are forced to confront our cultural upbringing that gives us disappearing poop, anonymous food, and ravenous landfills. I'm reminded often of the cultural admonitions delivered to me by Mary de Rachewiltz, who was raised in a peasant family in the tiny village of Gais in the Pustertal region of the Italian Alps. As she watched me sort the castle's garbage and recycling and cope with the unmethodical composting efforts of the American college students living there, she would shake her head and say, "Where I grew up, we never had garbage. We didn't even have a word for garbage. We had only what came from the earth, and then it went right back to the earth when we were finished with it."

We Americans can't conceive of a world without garbage, and we don't want to imagine a world in which dirt, death, decay, and defecation are a visible part of our lives. However, we simply can't be good ecologists or household economists if we demand that the finalities of our ecological loops are hidden from view and consciousness. We have to be conscious to be conscientious—and nothing helps deconstruct our daily assumptions better than stepping into another culture.

FIVE

Looking Forward to Yesterday:
Weaving Chronologies for the Future

I've always found that it's hard to know where I am without looking elsewhere—geographically or historically. Elsewhere is pretty important for understanding one's own place in time or on the map, and home-steading relies heavily upon cultural and historical knowledge, both of which seem to be at risk in a society hell-bent on cultural homogeniza-tion and an electronic future.

Stepping into another culture is particularly helpful when one wants to better understand how to live a less consumptive life. There simply aren't many role models in the United States for ecological balance. And the models that we do find are generally living on the fringes of culture, often in sequestered environments and sometimes in polarized opposi-tion to the rest of their community. It helps to find an entire culture that understands and lives the sustainability ideals that we so readily preach from our comfortable sanctuaries in a land of plentiful excesses.

Homesteading is like a rich winter stew, concocted with a mixture of mentors, places, ideas, and passions—all simmered on the woodstove over the course of a snowy day, with the occasional thick bubbles erupt-ing from below and jangling the cast-iron lid. It is a weaving of head, hands, and heart with the warp and weft of people and place.

It also involves a steep learning curve. I suppose that's why I've always found homesteading and mountain cultures to be siblings. Cleverness and stubbornness are staples in places where the terrain traditionally leaves people to their own devices. From the hollows of the Southern Appalachians to the pastures and peaks of the Alps to the hills of Vermont, I've been fortunate to find an enduring history and a history of endur-ance nestled in the crumpled topographies of mountain landscapes.

In a world that increasingly embraces transience and disposability, we find ourselves returning to a search for meaning that endures. The

Latin root for the word *endure* originally meant "to harden, to make lasting." Perhaps it should be no surprise that mountains are often the final refuges of lasting wisdom that can guide us in how to find a reasonable egress from irrational progress—essentially how to craft a life in a manufactured world.

I woke up on September 4, 1983, to the unfamiliar smells of a past not my own. I'd never inhaled the accumulated scents of so many generations as I did my first morning in that farmhouse from the 1600s— hints of multiple species of wood, smoke from fires burned for heat and light, wooden fruit bowls brimming over with pungent pears, apples, and grapes, and the descending wood smoke from the kitchen ovens in the farmhouses that clung to the slopes above and below us. And as I stepped out of the old farmhouse and into the courtyard of Brunnenburg Castle, I caught the slightly dank scent of firewood drying in preparation for the winter, combined with the rich smell of moss and gentle molds emanating from the larch-shingled roofs and the cool, shady corners of the castle's stone walls.

Brunnenburg sits on a peninsula of glacial till on the edge of the village of Dorf Tirol—or, as the Italians renamed it after seizing the territory following World War I, Tirolo di Merano. At an elevation of 600 meters above sea level, Brunnenburg's strategic promontory straddles the southern flank of the mountains separating Italy from Austria, high above the Vinschgau Valley. The castle's fanciful turrets and swallowtail crenellations convey a Bavarian count's early-twentieth-century imagination and belie the castle's original strategic simplicity. Brunnenburg was less a castle built to house and hoard its own riches than one designed to protect its nearby neighbor, Schloss Tirol. Schloss Tirol rides another outcropping of ever-dwindling glacial till just a few hundred meters above Brunnenburg. It was there in Schloss Tirol that the wealth and fame of the entire region resided—so much so that the region conceded to its power and became known as the land of Tirol.

Nearly crumbling myself just from the power of the vista, I took in the Old World tapestry spread out below Brunnenburg. It was a geometry of inheritance, with farm boundaries crumpled across the steep landscape but clearly evident—walls, fences, and hedgerows stitching the farms and homes together with the overlapping threads of time and topography. Orchards and vineyards seeped out of the village centers in the valley and climbed their way up the sides of precipitous mountains, stopping only when slope and aspect slowed them down. Altitude appeared to be no barrier here, and the Alpine imagination transgressed the boundaries of pragmatism that the American mind would have erected far sooner.

Here was a place to learn—a place where the past was somehow receding a bit more slowly than the future seemed to be approaching. The South Tirol—now an autonomous and predominantly German-speaking province in the Alps of northeastern Italy—carefully tended to its deep-rooted history to ensure its identity before moving forward. Without its past, its future was uncertain. The South Tirol's long struggle for autonomy within the Italian state depended upon declaring its unambiguous cultural heritage—a heritage challenged by the infiltration of the Italian regime in the early twentieth century and the region's subsequent annexation by Italy after World War I.

Although I didn't realize it at the time, my first view from the castle was an introduction to this cultural schism, with the farms riding up the steep slopes on all sides being largely of traditional Tirolean heritage and the more modern architecture on the valley floor stemming primarily from an Italian influence. The Italian regime had first moved into the valleys, taking over the basic civic infrastructure such as rail transport, hydroelectric systems, and the postal service, while the Tiroleans clung to the slopes and their cultural roots. I could see and smell a culture that I had tried in vain to imagine from home, but it would be a long time before I could understand or articulate what I was encountering. All I could guess at this point was that the past was going to be a big part of my future.

As I came around the farmhouse corner early that first morning, nervously exploring the many-nooked terrain of my home for the semester, I nearly ran into a slightly hunched figure coming from the lower side of the farmhouse. He lifted his head, and I almost winced at the suspicious glance that he shot my way from a nearly wooden face. I greeted him with a nervous nod and scurried past, not quite sure of his role or my place at the castle.

As it turned out, I'd had my first encounter with Lois, the castle's *K'necht*—essentially the primary worker on the farm. A true Bergbauer, or mountain farmer, Lois was brought to the castle by his stepsister Mary to help maintain the farm attached to the castle. Lois was from the

Pustertal, a rugged Alpine valley near Austria where he and Mary were raised by the same stepparents on an isolated mountain farm.

Mary was the daughter of the American poet Ezra Pound, and she and her husband, Boris de Rachewiltz, had begun to inhabit Brunnenburg Castle just after World War II. Although they soon came to own the farmhouse and the farm the laws in the region carefully protected tenant farmers, to the point at which it was difficult for the Rachewiltzes to begin using their farmhouse and the land surrounding the castle, even though these adjacent properties were part of the legal title to the castle. The Rachewiltzes finally were able to take control of the castle farm just prior to my arrival with a group of fellow students from St. Andrews College in North Carolina.

We were the first group to spend the semester at Brunnenburg Castle as guests and students of the Rachewiltz family. Mary was immersed in maintaining her father's literary archives and in setting the historical record straight on what he wrote, said, and intended, while Boris ducked in and out from his various archaeological and anthropological studies throughout the Mediterranean and Africa. Upon each return, he seemed to add to the castle's artifacts, bringing mementos from his excavations in Egypt and his forays into the various tribal cultures of other parts of Africa. Meanwhile, their son Siegfried—Sizzo—was fresh from finishing his dissertation in comparative literature at Harvard and was beginning to assemble a museum devoted to the disappearing tools and waning traditions of the Alpine agriculture in the politically complex land of South Tirol.

The Rachewiltz family inhabited the upper and more distant reaches of the castle, while Lois lived below us in the students' farmhouse, serving as a cultural sentinel of sorts. He wasn't certain what to make of us, and we certainly didn't understand his perplexing, timid curiosity. He averted any direct eye contact for the first few weeks, although it became increasingly common for us to discover him quietly watching us intently from above, partially hidden in a window or behind the thick cover of grape leaves in the vineyard.

As part of our studies and our compensation for the family's hospitality in hosting us, we worked a day and a half on the farm—clearing rocks, cleaning up old dumps from the previous tenant farmers, building terraces, picking apples and pears, opening up new exhibit space for the museum, and finally bringing in the much-awaited grape harvest.

On those workdays, Lois preferred to work alone, but inevitably needed our many hands to complete the tedious jobs that called more for energy than for know-how.

Nonetheless, he seemed to be in a constant state of tension during those workdays—at one moment displaying with absolute, unspoken clarity his unfettered disgust over our ignorance of how to do any manual labor efficiently, but later taking great delight in ridiculing us for that same lack of common sense. Lois saved most of his bombastic words and his less frequent humorous quips for chiding anyone—American or otherwise—who did not understand his basic tenets of mountain farming: Keep it simple, think about winter year-round, and do it as it had been done forever in the Pustertal or else don't do it at all.

Little did I suspect that I would be Lois's working companion several years later, much less that I would end up trying to don his mantle as the castle farmhand when he unexpectedly died of a heart attack. Ironically, for such an outwardly crusty character, he died while thoughtfully picking wilted blossoms off a flowering shrub. He had indeed softened over the years, and he'd grown a bit more accustomed to the ignorance and odd ways of American college students—to the point at which I began to watch with bemusement as he took a shine to various females who passed through. A student would know that she was the target of his affection when Lois started tossing pebbles at her from various strategic vantage points in the castle or from his post at the entrance to the agricultural museum. In a few cases, he even decided to betray a bit more of his affection by throwing tiny pebbles at her window. None of us could ever quite imagine the potential personal transformation that might sweep over Lois were any of the women to respond to his rocky advances.

The cultural barrier between Lois and myself was perhaps stronger than the language barrier. It wasn't until I had spent another semester at Brunnenburg as an instructor in 1988, and then returned to work on the farm and oversee the college programs from 1990 to 1993, that I slowly began to transcend both barriers and started to understand Lois's difficult lot in life. It was his generation that had to span the gulf between a traditional way of life that had changed very little over several centuries and the sudden onslaught of modernization. His worldview was in direct conflict with a new era of technologies and consumer expectations. His scythe was transformed into a weedeater; his *Korb* (woven basket carried on one's back) became a tractor; his quiet nights of stillness in a farmhouse shifted to evenings of television programming; his pastures and hayfields became orchards, vineyards, lawns, and sometimes resorts.

Life as Lois had known it in the Pustertal became a relic, partially enshrined by the agricultural museum that wended its way through the labyrinthine grounds of Brunnenburg Castle. He must have felt some bitterness at watching the tourists walk through the museum, mesmerized by the tools and traditions that were slowly migrating from barns and daily chores to museum walls and videos—seemingly unaware that their vacationing lifestyles were directly contributing to the demise of the culture they had come to admire.

Throughout most of the world, the last half of the twentieth century represents a time when one generation was leapfrogged by technological and economic developments. Lois's generation—whenever it occurred in various cultures—was the generation in the South Tirol that was perhaps the last to understand the details of how a human's seasonal tasks over the course of a year both created and maintained an agricultural ecosystem that had persisted for hundreds, if not thousands of years in one particular place. And the fact that the Alpine cultures had survived for nearly a millennium on such extreme slopes—with the challenges of soil erosion, avalanches, and brutal weather—meant that they had indeed accumulated a wealth of ecological knowledge that was sequestered in the minds and memories of the mountain farmers.

In our collective rush to embrace unprecedented economic and technological growth, we inadvertently leapt beyond culturally encased ecological wisdom, wisdom that we now find ourselves trying to understand and, in part, to reclaim. Whether it is a conscious act or not, we homesteaders constantly find ourselves struggling to rediscover and conserve this knowledge for future generations. When our lifestyles— if not our very lives—depend upon this knowledge, we tend to take it seriously and hopefully pass it on to the next generation. If we simply entrust libraries and universities to store this knowledge, we are missing the point. Ways of doing belong to the landscape, and ways of understanding should be nearly inadvertent lessons, taught and learned in the fields, forests, and homes of modern homesteaders.

It's easier to romanticize the past than it is to really understand it. And there is a difference between going back and looking back. I am passionate about looking back for clues to constructing a future that makes ecological sense. As someone who would now be dead from Rocky

Mountain spotted fever and permanently crippled from a perfectly placed cow's kick to my knee were it not for modern medicine, I am not interested in calling for a nonsensical retreat to the past. However, I am convinced that our generational leapfrog into the future nearly robbed us of the vast stores of traditional wisdom that allowed societies to subsist and even thrive in their cultural closed loops. In contrast with the traditional farming cultures of the Alps, much of American agriculture has yet to prove itself to be what we would call—for lack of a better word— "sustainable." We are all too often trying to substitute chemicals, fossil fuels, bioengineering, unethical livestock production, and unjust labor practices for thoughtful, hard work and sophisticated ecological knowledge passed down from generation to generation.

Technology may be leading the way, but the ultimate destination is seldom clear. As a result, we find ourselves in uncharted and often treacherous terrain. In contrast, homesteads are at the very least living repositories for an inherited understanding that can be wedded with appropriate scientific and cultural advancements. Homesteads can also be safe harbors for endangered crop varieties and livestock breeds. Perhaps our greatest and most fragile inheritance from our history of domestication is less the land than the genetic caretaking of our agricultural plant and animal species. Yet inheriting the stewardship of these species makes no sense if we do not understand how to manage the carefully crafted agricultural ecosystems of which they are integral pieces.

Our culture talks a lot about sustainability. But we seldom live it, and the notion is often intellectually amorphous and detached from the rhythm of our daily lives. However, slopes give me hope.

The slopes of the South Tirol—like those of the Andes and the Himalayas and other mountainous regions that have been farmed for centuries—are far steeper than many of us would dare inhabit, much less farm. Yet the demographic pressures from approximately AD 800 onward forced many of the Tiroleans to build their farms on slopes steep enough so that the farmers often have to wear boots fitted with spikes or even crampons to work in their fields. The USDA would shriek in justified horror at the plowing of slopes as steep as those farmed by the Bergbauern. And, true enough, the use of standard American cultivation techniques would definitely lead to unfathomable soil erosion. Even in an area as flat as Iowa, poor farming practices have led to the loss of more than half of the state's topsoil in less than one hundred years.[1]

However, the Bergbauern have plowed slopes of incredibly steep mountainsides for at least a thousand years, and many of the individual farms have remained in the same location and in the same families for a good portion of that time. In fact, some of these farmers on the steepest slopes did precisely what we would assume to be ecological and economic suicide: They plowed with the slope, vertically—not perpendicular to it, as we typically recommend with contour plowing. As it turns out, plowing across these particularly steep slopes would create terraces that would only wash away with a rainstorm of any severity. So the Tirolean farmers have traditionally used an ard in lieu of a plow with a moldboard. The ard has a hardened, triangular point that cuts open a furrow but does not turn and flip the soil like a moldboard plow. These steep slopes would be plowed with the help of power from draft animals, humans, and eventually motorized winches.

In order to plow such steep slopes, farmers would often anchor a rope or a cable horizontally across the top of the field. They would then attach a double pulley that would travel the length of the upper horizontal cable while also allowing another rope to be threaded through the second lower pulley, such that the other rope would move up and down the slope. A draft animal, a winch, or another person would be attached to one end of the rope going up and down, with the ard attached to the other end. The source of power—animal, human, or motor—could then pull the farmer and the ard up in one direction and restrain them as they went back downhill. The resulting furrows were undoubtedly fragile, but farmers took great care in maintaining these fields.

These mountain farmers literally felt the weight of the future generations that would be dependent upon the health of the fields. Not only did they haul composted manure from the barn to the field, often in baskets on their backs or with hand-pulled sledges, but they also would dedicate a vast amount of energy in the spring to loading up the soil that had accumulated at the bottom of the field after the growing season and carrying it back up the steep slope to the top of the field where it could be distributed evenly. As one farmer noted to my photographer friend Erika Hubatschek, each farmer bore the literal and metaphorical burden of "this field on my back." Any ecological missteps meant that the chances for the next generation's survival had slipped. Each step of every season mattered, and it was only through such careful management of these relatively small farmsteads that so many of the farms remained productive and in one family from the early Middle Ages until now.

The fragility of this life, however, meant that personalities were often tempered and hardened to be as resilient as the tools. And keeping the farms intact for one generation after another meant that strict inheritance laws developed, with winners, losers, and mere survivors. The farms in the Tirol region developed the tradition of the *geschlossener Hof*, or "closed farm," meaning that the farm always went to the eldest son. The son's siblings were allowed to stay on the farm as laborers when possible, allowing the siblings food and shelter but usually minimal autonomy. Lois did not inherit his farm, and Mary's sense of compassion and responsibility for him brought him to Brunnenburg.

Early on, I seldom understood the cultural context of Lois's often gruff exterior or the language of his occasional explosive outbursts. Just as they were delivered in thick Tirolean dialect, they were tightly tied to his upbringing in what we would consider to be a relatively poor "peasant" family.[2] I usually knew when the words were about to fly, as Lois would let out a tight-lipped *"Putana . . . ,"* with a few cleaner religious declarations soon following in a less-controlled escalation of colorful dialect. With just a little physical distance, these verbal escapades could be pretty amusing and easily interpreted if they involved Lois at odds with any of the castle livestock.

Although their reign was relatively short-lived at Brunnenburg, the breeding pair of peacocks that strutted about the castle for several years were Lois's cultural nemesis. I can't help but think that the peacocks' association with monarchs somehow enflamed Lois's ingrained sense of Bergbauern pride—he was not about to be subservient to any person or animal feigning royalty. Yet it was his job to feed and house the peacocks, and the trouble began each evening, when he thought it was time for them to go to their stall in the barn, whereas they considered it time to roost . . . in the highest perch possible.

There was a giant cedar tree growing right beside the castle that seemed to be the perfect strategic post for the peacocks to settle in come dusk. As Lois started shutting up the museum each evening, he would commence his initial efforts at getting the peacocks down to his level and into the barn. Seldom did his first attempts to shoo them down work. By the time he got the museum locked up, he would begin to get serious, with his coaxing calls evolving into perturbed strings of insults. If these efforts weren't successful—and they seldom were—he would add injury to his insults by introducing a barrage of pebbles into the conversation. Once a pebble found its mark, the peacocks would give their godforsaken screech that always sounded like Herod's murder of the innocents and flap noisily down to ground level, where Lois was again fully in charge. The high entertainment on those evenings was when the battle of wills sent Lois high up into the cedar, even above part of the castle, where he asserted his dominance with a few well-targeted pebbles. He took the dominion aspects of domestication quite seriously.

His work in maintaining that dominion was never complete, however. The castle sheep were constantly using their wits to find new holes in the fence surrounding the vineyard—and then playing really dumb about finding their way back out again. One man against about a dozen sheep on a steep slope with terraced rows of grapes that resembled more a labyrinth than a well-conceived horticultural operation could provide an hour's worth of comic relief for someone standing above, while Lois hurled curses and stones down upon the woolly lot. If the sheep were indignant about the assault raining upon them, they feigned ignorance instead, making Lois all the madder. My amusement turned to empathy and self-pity once Lois died and I was left to fend off the fleeced invaders on my own. I hope I did Lois justice with my accumulated barrage of dialect curses, not about to let those damn sheep pretend they didn't feel the prick of a good Tirolean verbal dressing-down, even if it was with an accent and questionable grammar.

Few things tended to frustrate Lois or Mary more than seeing me or anyone else mow grass . . . and just leave it. Coming from suburban America, land of the lawn, I was utterly perplexed as to why it was such a problem either to mow the areas around the castle for aesthetic purposes or to leave the downed grass in the orchards or around the edges of the vineyard. It really wasn't until years later, once I had cows of my own, that I understand that mowing grass was, in the eyes of the mountain farmer, a harvest. Mown grass was a crop. It didn't matter how small the area or how distant it was from the barn—hay was meant to be harvested and stored. It was the key to winter survival for the animals, and the animals were the key to winter survival for the humans. Tiroleans have traditionally gone to incredible extremes to harvest hay. They would leave their farms to hike above tree line, often above 6,000 feet in elevation, with their scythes and whetstones and cut hay—even in spots where they had to use footwear with metal spikes and, in the most extreme scenarios, ropes to mow and rake. Once they gathered the hay, they would get it back to their barns with draft animals, cable-and-pulley systems, hand-pulled sledges, or ingenious "backpack" devices.

Mowing grass and not harvesting it was, then, a travesty for Lois and Mary—a pronounced disregard for the bounty upon which any good farm was utterly dependent. To waste it was to call into question the covenant of domestication, an unspoken agreement in which humans and the land nurtured each other. And life in the Alps is simply too fragile to risk treating any gift of nature as irrelevant.

Over the years, I have come to realize the stark contrast between homesteading in the United States and in most other parts of the world—a sense of space. In the United States, we are both cursed and blessed with a sense of spaciousness that stems from having such an abundance of land. The result is that we tend to lose a sense of preciousness for each acre, if not each square foot. Even homesteaders with seemingly "small" parcels of 10 or 15 acres would be land-rich in most of Europe. The difference manifests itself in how we view and treat the land. By the time I left the South Tirol to farm in the US, I'd decided that the best way to be a good farmer is probably to become an excellent gardener before graduating in scale.

In the South Tirol, every swath of grass was traditionally coveted as a key to sustenance. In harder times, even grass and brush along roadsides were used for livestock and fire tinder, particularly by the poor members of the community. Grass is the medium between sunlight and healthy meats and milk. It is probably also the greatest gift of our "civilized" clearings, but it requires herbivores that are capable of transforming the cellulose born of contemporary sunlight into stored food energy that we can savor—and perhaps even be thankful for. The value of every green bank and swale was driven home again when I was leading a study tour of the region in 2006, and we saw farmers mowing with scythes and raking the hay right up to the edges of three sides of a small village bank, with the patrons driving up in their high-end cars hardly taking notice.

From my first visit to the South Tirol, I was fascinated with the Austrian-style scythe, with its straight snath and thin, razor-sharp blade standing in marked contrast with the heavy, curved snath and thick blade of its American counterparts. The Austrian scythe was a refined tool suitable for fields freed of rocks and brush over the course of twenty or more generations, whereas the rugged American scythe was sculpted to handle the coarse terrain of a newly settled land. The nearly silent efficiency of the Austrian scythe caught my ear, and the sweeping arm-length arcs of its path on the steep slopes turned the hayfields into brushstrokes. But it was the fast rhythm of tapered stone on the thin metal blade that wandered around the contours of the farms that really captured my curiosity. As I watched the whipping motions of adept farmers sharpening their scythes and tried to detect the best method of sharpening, I noticed just how many variances existed. Somehow, it seemed like learning to mow with a scythe would exorcise my long-lasting disdain for mowing lawns, and it might also open the door into the Bergbauern culture a bit wider.

As it turned out, my first step was a misstep. I asked Lois if I could borrow his scythe. He looked at me with a crumpled brow, bowed his head slightly, and shook his head back and forth: *"Nein."* I always loved it when I understood every word uttered to me. Whenever Lois's dialect was too much for me, he would compensate with terse clarity.

Had I paid closer attention to the intricately decorated scythes, scabbards, and whetstone holders in the museum—as well as to a long mythological understanding of sharpness—I might have realized my error. The ornate attention given to these implements and their covers was a reflection of the pride of their owners, not only in the tools themselves, but also in their sharpness. Sharpness was critical in the life of a Tirolean mountain farmer, and having a keen edge over other men gave one a certain power and prowess. All metallurgy has historically had an element of mystery and power to it. Metals made the tools and weapons that built the cultures that created empires—and a guarded secrecy about how to create, shape, and sharpen metal objects was quite common at least since the time of Hephaestos, the crafty blacksmith god of Greek mythology. To make a long myth short, I was inadvertently asking Lois to share his edge—not a cool thing to do to a Tirolean farmer. The rebuff was short, but my understanding of its cultural significance was long in coming. I did realize, however, that I needed my own scythe, and I needed to learn to sharpen it myself.

I'd seen Lois in the haymow of the barn, using some contraption to do something to his scythe, with the end of the handle hanging in the crook of a stiff wire hanging from the ceiling. He straddled a bench that had the blue metal contraption bolted to its front, slowly pressing down on a handle with a red rubber grip on the end. When I finally got up the courage to ask Lois what he was doing, he said—without looking up, still intent on his work—"Dengel'n." Okay, I thought, just what I needed— a terse one-word answer that I didn't understand. "Dengel'n" sounded like a description of what happened when I ran out of underwear. At any rate, not a good way to build one's cultural confidence.

But I did begin to see what he was doing. As he started from one end of the scythe blade, he inserted about a 3-inch section of the sharp edge of the blade into the device (a *Dengelmaschine,* as I later learned it) and pressed down on the lever with his right hand. When he pressed down, he would "dengel" each section of the blade's edge, until the new crescent edge of gleaming metal went from end to end. "Dengeling" gave the blade an incredibly thin and sharp edge, taking out any minor nicks and burrs that were the result of hitting stones and other hard objects. Such accidents were inevitable, since the skill and efficiency of the mower were measured not just in how much ground he could cover in a given time, but also in how close to the ground he could mow. High stubble behind a mower was considered an inefficient use of time and vegetation. Getting a clean cut at the base of the plants was ensured by a careful but rapid sharpening of the newly shaped edge with a whetstone, a task that had to be repeated with great frequency.

I soon learned that the Dengelmaschine was a modern form of "peening," or hammering the edge of the scythe with a peening hammer. The farmer peened the edge of the scythe blade by moving it across a small anvil as he hammered it, creating an edge similar to the Dengelmaschine, albeit perhaps not quite as uniform. These small anvils were often the end portion of a metal stake that was sharpened and could be driven into the ground for stability. The farmer could do the peening right in the field, minimizing interruptions and maximizing mowing efficiency.

Determined to step a bit farther through that Tirolean cultural door, I went to the toolshed and looked for a scythe that wasn't attached to anyone's manhood. Back in a dark corner hung several dusty scythes in a neat line, their snaths aligned in order, with each blade carefully draped across a beam, as was the custom. I pulled them down one by one, examining the worn blades. I knew that a novice needed a shorter blade, so I avoided the one with a blade that was nearly 3 feet long and opted instead for a blade of about 2 feet. Despite the rehabilitated scars on its fine edge and a loose bond between blade and snath, it looked like a potential willing partner that I might coax into cooperation.

I went to find Sepp, the vineyard worker and respected pruner who had come to Brunnenburg to oversee the renaissance of the somewhat neglected castle vineyards. Sepp could make *gregarious* seem like an anemic adjective, and nothing gave him greater pride than sharing the history and culture of his homeland with anyone who risked showing even the remotest interest.

Sure enough, all I had to do was bring the scythe out into the light of day and Sepp came my way. "Ah, yes," he uttered in a thick dialect imbued with a light but curious speech impediment. "So now you've found a good Tirolean dance partner! And she doesn't look too bad!"

I asked Sepp how he sharpened the blade. "Quite well—see!" He pulled up his pant leg and showed me a scar that went across the lower part of his calf muscle. "That's where a friend caught me with his scythe when we were mowing together. We Tiroleans know how to keep a scythe sharp!" he proclaimed with a chuckling wink.

Sepp helped me figure out the subtleties of the Dengelmaschine, inserting the edge of the blade a few inches at a time and then squeezing the metal edge into a cusp of thinness. Once I worked my way along the entire blade's edge with the Dengelmaschine, he had me hold the scythe upright in front of me, with the blade arcing threateningly to the left and my right foot lightly on the handle parallel to and sitting on the ground. He showed me how to hold the top of the tip with my left hand and pull the long, elliptical whetstone from the water-filled plastic sheath attached to my belt, the water running down my hand as I held it upright and perpendicular to the lower edge of the scythe blade. He gently grabbed my wrist and helped me find the correct angle for holding the stone against the newly dengeled blade.

"Always start on the right, at the big end of the blade," he said, "and draw the stone to the left and down across the blade's edge. Don't just whip the stone back and forth—move it across and down, across and down—horizontally. First on the front side of the blade and then on the back side. Keep the same angle with the stone and the blade on both sides of the blade. Across and down on both sides. And always go the same direction. Overlap your last stroke with the new stroke just a bit. Before you know it, it will sound like music! But don't try to go too fast until it feels natural—otherwise, you're going to slice a finger to the bone."

He paused. "And you don't need to have as many scars as I do!"

I looked up, and Sepp was pointing to his heart, smiling. He was known as quite a romancer, so I wasn't so sure his pain really exceeded his pleasures, despite his marital woes.

I worked on feeling the slightly gritty grain of the dripping stone pull down and across the molecular smoothness of the metal, stripping the edge of any metal not aligned with the angle of intent. The dark, sweeping crescent of the scythe now boasted a thin, gleaming edge of freshly minted sharpness. Sepp then picked up the scythe and stood it upright against the barn wall. He scratched a mark on the wall where the metal edge ended near the handle. "This is how you adjust the blade's angle," he noted, loosening the two screws on the snath's metal ring that held the blade in place and at the proper angle. He pointed to the scratch on the wall again, aligned with the corner of the scythe's blade, and he kept the handle firmly in place on the ground as he swept the blade across the barn wall like an upside-down pendulum. Each time, he would move the tip of the blade down just a bit, until the tip was finally lined up with the mark as the blade went back and forth across the wall. He then tightened the adjustment screws with the special wrench for their inset heads, and he handed me the scythe.

"Jetzt bist du ein echt Tiroler," he said with a twinkle in his eye, as if he were passing on the command of the mowing militia.[3] "Once you reach my age, Philip, you're ready to start using the *Motorsense*"[4]—pointing to the weedeater hanging from the rafters.

I filled the plastic sheath for the whetstone with water, clipped it to my belt, and perched the surprisingly light scythe over my right shoulder, headed for the vineyard to try my hand at mowing. I felt like I was headed out with the peasant's militia, although I think I probably looked more like the Slim Reaper than a soldier ready to mow down anything in his path.

The tendency of a new mower is to follow the shape of the scythe and try to make huge crescent-shaped lunges, mowing an enormous semicircular path that surrounds him. The trick, however, is a controlled, gentle sweep, using the finesse of the blade to mow just parallel to the ground, but without "losing one's edge" to a hidden rock or root. Mowing contests were once a spontaneous part of the work itself, but when they do occur these days, they are generally ways of keeping a cultural tradition alive and in the public eye. Traditionally, speed was important, but so was the

cut's evenness and its proximity to the ground. Stems left standing signi-
fied a deficit of skill and care.

As I was learning German, I quickly realized that the stock, everyday phrase *"Alles ist in Ordnung,"* or "All is in order," meant more than
"Everything is okay." It meant what it said—all is in order, as it should
be, and details matter. Attentiveness to detail indicates control, and
having some element of control was an important anchor for farmers
in the Alps, who lived in a very unpredictable world. When things went
downhill in that environment, they went downhill fast. This sense of
order easily translated into an aesthetic appreciation, so order, beauty,
and control became soulmates.

Over time, these values became part of the ecological fabric of the
region. Mowing and grazing specific areas over a period of generations
encouraged certain plant species while discouraging others. Mowing was
a critical part of life in three of the four levels that made up the mountain farmers' lives: the valley floor, the mountainside farms, and the
high pastures and hayfields above tree line—the only exception was the
rugged mountaintops that had no agricultural utility. For several millen-
nia, inhabitants of the Alps have taken their livestock from their farms
to the grassy areas above tree line to graze the nutritious alpine grasses
and to use the open areas immediately surrounding each farm for hay
production instead of grazing. Sending the village's cattle up to communal alpine pastures has allowed farmers to bring in the hay closest to their
barns, although they also have worked hard to transport some portion
of the much-coveted hay from the upper elevations back to their barns.

As it turns out, the grazing and mowing of the steep slopes above
treeline evolved into a delicate ecological pattern that helped alleviate
some of the ecological havoc wreaked by avalanches. Careful grazing
and mowing of the steep slopes helped keep the grasses short, so that
when an avalanche did occur, the plummeting ice and snow did not take
the turf along, simply because the snow and ice were not able to lock
on to the long vegetative stems of untended grassy areas. In fact, the
mowing of some of these steep areas by hand and machine is now subsi-
dized by some governments, not just to help the farmers economically
but also to help minimize the erosive effects that stem from avalanches
ripping away precious turf on this precarious terrain.

My own sense of ecological harmony in learning to mow with the
scythe was perhaps more naive and romanticized. When I compared

the difference between slipping a whetstone and sheath onto my belt and hanging a scythe over my shoulder with harnessing the heavy-duty weedeater to my back and donning a full-face shield, I had the choice of enjoying a full day of the scythe's whisper, birdsong, and tourists' trailside laughter or enduring the high-pitched whir and slap of the weedeater and its acrid exhaust.

Some days I would mow alone in the terraced vineyard, carefully working around the vines and posts of the trellised grapes. As with so many jobs on a farm, I found the rhythm soothing but the monotony challenging. It generally took me about five full days of mowing to make my way through the entire vineyard. Sometimes Sepp would join me with his *Motorsense,* sweat pouring profusely from his beet-red face as he whirred and whipped his way between rows of vines. Between tanks of gas, he would wipe not just his brow but his entire balding head with his handkerchief, cursing the fact that his vices had deprived him of his chances to retire. He would mutter, sputter, and putter with the ever-finicky weedeater, dealing with jammed trimming string and a misanthropic carburetor while I whipped the scythe's delicate edge with the whetstone, happy to be liberated of the sounds and frustrations of modern technology.

I was tempted to dismiss the weedeater for its inefficiencies and aggravations—it demanded constant tinkering and visits to the shop, and we inevitably had to mow around the younger vines with the scythe, lest they be damaged by the indiscriminate slap of the trimmer. However, I did discover that the weedeater had its role, particularly in mowing tightly against the wooden trellis posts. When I returned to the States years later and began mowing around our homestead in Vermont, I discovered that the scythe had its niches, too, but the weedeater was particularly useful in mowing under electric fence lines and right up to the fence posts, eliminating all of the weeds that would otherwise divert the electrical pulses from their intended four-legged targets.

When we don't have the opportunity to learn how to use the tools of the past and discover their efficiencies and subtleties, we can't compare the advantages and disadvantages of older and more modern tools, much less determine which ones are more appropriate for certain jobs. A homestead probably allows for more experimentation and romanticism than a farm in thinking about and utilizing certain technologies. However, a farmer's pragmatism also risks calcification, resulting in an unwillingness to try different ideas, be they old or new. Finding a comfort in dwelling in the nebulous world between yesterday and tomorrow is a skill that a young and seemingly progressive culture like our own tends to ignore.

I'm not sure Lois ever found that comfort, but he was a constant reminder that the past was a relic to be reckoned with—not to be disregarded or discarded.

Sizzo had promised to come to pick me up at the train station in Bozen following a quick trip home to visit my family after eight months in my role as an ill-informed Alpine farmer. I stepped through the station's main entrance, laughing quietly as usual at the guardians of the doorway—fascist icons of hyper-muscular men and women hunkered down to work with the new tools of the Industrial Age. They were all holding the tools of hope and prosperity—jackhammers and gears and other industrial symbols, all a reminder to me of how mistaken any of us can be in romanticizing the past or the present.

Sizzo pulled up to the curb just as I was stepping out. His greeting was warm but troubled. I wasn't sure whether I was quite ready to ask what was wrong, thinking that it maybe had been my poor choice of a vacation time, right in the middle of the August harvest preparations. As charitable as always, Sizzo asked about my time home. I eagerly caught him up with what had been a fun and much-needed visit with my family and friends.

He seemed slightly distracted throughout my reasonably succinct overview, and not due to the traffic—which he only partly paid attention to anytime he was driving—at least from my skittish perspective.

"So how have things been here?" I asked, ready for him to reciprocate and catch me up on the activities and everything that needed to happen last week but didn't, thanks to my untimely vacation.

"Well, I'm afraid we lost Lois last week . . ."

"What? Wait—do you mean he died?" I felt myself plummeting into deep disbelief, realizing only in part what it meant for me or for life at Brunnenburg. "Why didn't you call me?"

"I know, I know . . . we thought about it, but we didn't want to upset your time with your family, and we knew you would only worry about what had to be done when you returned. And you can go visit his grave in the village tomorrow—it's really a nice testament to him."

"I—I can't believe it. What happened to him?"

"Well, there's an irony to it all, given Lois's gruff nature. He was out by the entrance to the museum, picking off all of the dead flowers near the gate to keep himself occupied. Next thing we knew, he was on the ground, having some sort of seizure or heart attack. So he went in relative peace, with flowers. Sort of ironic for a tough guy like Lois, I guess."

I nodded, and we fell into a brief silence. I was reeling inside, wondering if the jet lag had spawned a tailspin of a dream.

"So I'm afraid it's not just that we lost Lois." Sizzo's words jolted me back to the certainty of what was happening. "We've lost an era . . . we've lost a perspective, really. It means that Brunnenburg isn't quite such a living museum or a working Alpine farm anymore."

He looked over to see how I was absorbing it all, knowing that I was going to feel the burden of responsibility as much as anyone at the castle.

"We're going to have to do things a bit differently," he continued, "without all of Lois's reminders—politely delivered or not—of how it's all supposed to be done. The traditions are part of the work, part of the tools—and we both know that it's the few remaining mountain farmers like Lois who keep it all alive."

He glanced my way again. I wished he would just watch the road, but this time it was because the tears had started.

"So I hope you're ready to step into his boots . . ."

Not sure what else to do, I nodded affirmatively.

He looked back at the road, but it was obvious that he was still focused elsewhere.

"It's a big role to fill, and things will change, I know that. We're already working on getting rid of the sheep—they were his tie to the Pustertal and his life there."

I winced. The sheep bells had become one of my favorite parts of the landscape, especially when they would suddenly start ringing in rapid unison—a sign that Lois was chasing the animals out of forbidden terrain.

"You just need to keep concentrating on the vineyards," Sizzo said. His voice seemed to soften as his thoughts teetered between the past and the future. He was clearly thinking more about negotiating the challenges back at Brunnenburg than he was about navigating our way through the labyrinth of narrow streets, swarming with pedestrians, bicycles, mopeds, and vehicles of all sizes. Nonetheless, he somehow continued his rapid shifting and swerving through the tight traffic and twisting terrain.

"You'll just have to try to remember how Lois saw the world. You were lucky to see part of it."

I nodded, not having anything to add in any language. We both fell into a respectful and uncertain silence that lasted until we pulled up to the castle gate. We pulled my bags out of the car, and I felt a weight much heavier than my bags as we slowly walked past the spot where Lois had fallen.

I remained at Brunnenburg for several more years, working hard to find my way closer to Lois's world, despite his distance. In the meantime, I'd fallen in love with Erin, an art student who'd come to Brunnenburg and was as entranced by the world of the Bergbauern as I was. I was also beginning to resent the number of summer days that I had to spend in a rubber suit with a respirator, spraying the castle vineyards against a constant barrage of diseases. Despite the fact that most of our sprays were relatively low-impact in comparison with the much more aggressive pesticides used elsewhere, I just couldn't reconcile the use of most pesticides with my emerging understanding of agriculture and ecological systems. Also, in the universal spirit of farmers and homesteaders, I was longing for independence, regardless of whether it was a mystique or a mistake. I just wanted the opportunity to make my own decisions.

And then came a letter from my grandparents, asking if I would consider coming back to their farm in the Sandhills of North Carolina to help out. Their age and declining health meant that staying on the farm was becoming quite difficult for them. Although Grandmom didn't write it in her letter, we all knew that staying on the farm was the only thing that was going to keep Grandad mobile and alive in his battle against Parkinson's disease. He'd beaten the prediction of being wheelchair-bound by more than two decades, but the accumulating impacts of the disease were taking their toll on him, and certainly on Grandmom.

I was still teetering between what I thought was the simplicity of homesteading and the complexity of farming. I didn't feel like I knew enough to do either very well, but I did know that mentors mattered. Although I couldn't have named it, most of my adult life was essentially a search for what the Japanese call *nusumigeiko*[5]—stolen lessons—the subtle "tricks of the trade" that come from one's observations during what we used to call an apprenticeship, a word derived from the Latin meaning "to grasp" or "to seize."

But we have relegated the idea of an apprenticeship to times gone by, to the point that the word has now drifted into rather archaic usage. Perhaps it is our cultural penchant for equality that has trivialized the depth of learning that comes from consciously choosing to live in someone else's shadow.

Stolen lessons emerge from patient trust that learning in the light of someone else's shadow comes primarily from glimpses into the ordinary. Stolen lessons are perhaps less about claiming huge chunks of knowledge all at once and more about noting and accumulating the subtle illuminations that come from walking daily in the lengthening shadow of someone bigger than oneself.

This kind of learning involves groping in the mundane tasks and rhythms of a chosen life until one is ready to claim the shadow as one's own and slowly fill it with color and life. Books, forests, fields, food, and the playful seriousness of farming had all conspired to send me searching for a practiced life, but I knew that I still needed more stolen lessons from people who could teach me how to live on the land, off the land, and with the land.

I decided that I needed to walk in my grandfather's shadow while he was still mobile and lucid—before true darkness set in. I left the South Tirol with a heavy heart, but with a sense of responsibility to family who had nurtured me for so many years. My time abroad had often reminded me that there was still much more to learn at home, as the lens of distance tends to magnify the familiar.

Round bushel baskets with wire handles on two sides. Rectangular half-bushel baskets with wooden hoop handles. Decorative round red and green peck baskets with comfortable folding wire handles. Baskets of peaches, grapes, apples, nectarines, string beans, lima beans, pecans, okra, sweet corn, collards, broccoli, and of course strawberries in quart containers and watermelons and cantaloupes rolling around on countertops and in cool kitchen corners.

From as far back as I can remember, wooden baskets of all sizes and descriptions appeared whenever Grandad showed up for a visit or at most any social function, his car or truck filled to the brim with the bounty of the current harvest, the sweet scents coming through the door behind him and the omnipresent fruit flies in hot pursuit. Growing up with Grandad meant measuring my own physiological advances by how far I could lean into his trunk or truck and what size basket of peaches I could pull out and take into the house. It was a long time before I could extract a 40- or 50-pound bushel basket of peaches from deep inside a car trunk, but the timing was about right. Once I began to grow into my own and could finally handle a full bushel, he was beginning to feel the advances of Parkinson's disease.

Nothing brought greater delight or family celebration than the peaches. Our family could gauge the waxing and waning of the summer by which peach variety was in season. They came in the same order each year, although the timing sometimes shifted a week earlier or later than the usual ripening date, or an entire variety got wiped out by a freeze: Whynot, Hamlet, Derby, Candor, Norman, Troy, Winblo, Ellerbe, Biscoe, and Emery.[6] Grandad and his plant pathologist colleagues had named nearly all of their new varieties after the tiny little towns surrounding the agricultural research station that they established deep in the Sandhills of eastern North Carolina, although his colleagues did deviate with one modestly sized but succulent peach that my family still awaits every year—the Clayton, named after Grandad. And there were the grapes they brought into the area, hoping to catch the imagination of a few curious connoisseurs and entrepreneurial vintners: Carlos, Noble, Fry, Jumbo, Higgins, Magnolia, Doreen, and Nesbitt. Other than the magnificent longleaf pine, spicy pork barbeque, and all the elements of beachfront property except the waterfront, the Sandhills didn't have a lot to brag about prior to the beginnings of the peach industry after the Depression.

I always wondered why Grandad ended up in such a hot and sandy landscape instead of in the mountains of western North Carolina, where he had initially done most of his fruit research and agricultural extension service with apples. Of course, he did it because he loved peaches, grapes, strawberries, and melons, and the Sandhills were a good place to grow them all. But knowing Grandad, he probably also did it because he felt like the people and the Sandhills region needed an economic boost and a source of pride. He was always finding ways to get money into the hands of the people who needed it and trying to keep it out of places where he didn't think it needed to be—like banks. "Money's meant to be in circulation," he would say to me. "It's not helping anybody except the bankers just sitting in a bank."

But he also liked people to earn their money and to understand the worth of a dollar. I worked for him a few summers and on winter breaks and finally for the last year that he was able to stay on the farm, and he never paid me an hourly wage above that of his other general laborers. He made it clear, without ever having to say it, that formal education didn't trump practical skills on a farm. It was a good lesson, and one that I never resented. Of course, he would always find a way to slip me an extra grandfatherly twenty-dollar bill "for gas" or some other porous excuse that didn't quite hold water. I knew the values he was trying to impart—they jibed with my leftist leanings and his Depression-era economic values. Besides, I wasn't there for the money.

Despite my sense that the relatively flat Sandhills landscape and its brutally hot and muggy climate didn't really fit my vision of where I wanted to farm, I kept returning, drawn back to learn more about food and farming from him and Grandmom. Every meal was a feast, and hot afternoons and cool evenings were spent on the porch, prepping every kind of fruit and vegetable raised on the farm into some sort of canned or frozen goodness. Those times at the table and on the porch were also opportunities to prepare for the upcoming tasks on the farm and to preserve family stories. Shared laughter kept the isolation of the farm's big sky world from turning into melancholy.

It had taken me a while to grow into the place, and Erin never quite did, despite her love for my grandparents. Located about a mile from the Sandhills research station that Grandad and his colleagues had established for North Carolina State University, the farm didn't quite fit my ideal, with a farmhouse, barn and outbuildings, shade trees, maybe a few animals, and an idyllic fishing pond. My first visit to the newly purchased farm when I was twelve dismembered that pastoral image rather quickly. I arrived to find myself plodding through sand as thick as at the beach, with a stuffy camper and a few sheds serving as the living quarters and farm infrastructure. The tallest trees near the house and sheds were the peach trees, and you've got to be about the height of a yardstick to revel in the shade of a peach tree, with its minute stature and small canopy.

The farm that they had purchased might have been a tabula rasa, but it was also nearly a "tabula erased," with enormous gullies that seemed improbable if not impossible in a land so flat, at least to my view. The first thing Grandad did was to plant thousands of yellow pines to hold the soil and to provide a future marketable crop. He also built and stocked a pond, both to challenge the beavers to a duel and to consolidate the water moccasin population. Then came the peach orchard and the grape vineyard, with other fruits and vegetables interspersed in the vast open stretches in between. He'd been a researcher and professor for more than three decades when he bought the farm, and some might have thought that he was seeking to practice what he preached . . . except that he never preached, not about anything. There were enough ministers in the family working on that skill set.

Rather, Grandad knew enough to know that he certainly didn't know it all and that he wasn't done learning. Despite having helped develop more than a dozen varieties of peaches and having written or contributed to more than 130 scientific publications—ultimately earning him the nickname "Dr. Peach"—Grandad's humility and piety came out time and again in the orchard when I asked a question about why something was happening: "I guess only the Good Lord has that one figured out so far, Philip."

I always admired his ability never to feign knowledge or enlightenment, despite the fact that his middle name, Newton, was an homage to a certain distant ancestor whose primary scientific interest in apples was at what speed they fell, regardless of variety. Despite the reams of research on diseases, pests, cultivar immunities and susceptibilities, and control methods that he had accumulated over the years, Grandad was never eager to be the center of attention or the final authority in the various peach growers' meetings, "You know me, Philip," he said once, with a deadly twinkle in his eye and one side of his mouth lifting into a half smile, "I'm just a social hound."

I didn't realize just how methodical he had been in his research or his own record keeping until I got to the farm his last year there and starting working through his notes and his publications, trying to be a better farmer myself and eager to garner more of his knowledge while I could. I could visibly see Parkinson's gradually robbing his yearly records of their legibility, but the despicable disease never diminished his passionate curiosity for what realities and observations each new season would bring. The process of discovery simply never ended for him. In fact, I'm sure the thrill of discovery not only kept him alive but also kept him out of the inevitable wheelchair the doctors continued predicting for him. He lived for each successive fruit and vegetable crop—just to see what it brought—and he pruned, hoed, picked, and drove far beyond what was probable or prudent.

Driving was the real problem. It wasn't that he couldn't stop the truck when we were driving around the farm—it was just that his rapid braking accelerated all of us sitting in the back of the truck. In an instant, all of us gabbing and teasing in the truck bed would be transformed from our sprawling, carefree postures into a human accordion as Grandad hit the brakes and then gunned it to compensate for the sudden stop. After watching the tumbling and the subsequent untangling of human limbs in the rearview mirror a few too many times, he gradually accepted the role of being a gracious passenger. It was well worth the several minutes of helping him into and out of the truck both to see his delight at sampling the farm's fruits and to hear his observations in the orchard, vineyard, and fields. There was always something to be savored and noted, even if it was only a spectacular sunset or the reassuring *chat-chat-chat-chat-chat* of the irrigation system watering the melon fields.

One might think that his interests were tightly tied to taste, but I nearly choked on the peach I was eating when I asked him once if he ever tired of the taste of peaches, since we would eat a dozen or more a day many times: "Ever since I got the flu in the 1970s, I haven't been able to taste much of anything . . . I can't even smell a good fart anymore."

Nonetheless, he never forgot how to relish a good homegrown meal, and he had a voracious appetite for a man in his eighties. He could still pick out the perfect peach, somehow detecting the right balance of sweetness, acidity, and smooth, moist texture.

I won't go so far as to claim that it was the final few months of nursing home food that killed him, but I do think it helped him decide it was time to move on. He and Grandmom both made it clear that the worst thing about having to leave the farm for their assisted living quarters was the shift from a farmer's table to a dietitian's gustatory gulag.

They both persisted on the farm longer than any of us thought was prudent, but in hindsight I have to admire their tenacity. I think they both knew that moving full-time into their assisted living quarters meant that their meals would shift from being their greatest joys to their greatest disappointments. Their marriage was the evolution of the perfect lifelong team as grower and cook, and leaving behind the tastes and seasonal wonders of the farm probably felt like giving up the essence of whom they had become over the course of more than fifty years of marriage.

Grandad's way of leaving this world was to stop eating once the medical staff decided to puree his meals, since they feared that his difficulty swallowing due to the Parkinson's would cause him to choke. I'm glad my mom smuggled in one last fried chicken dinner to him in an emergency room visit before some doctor determined taste, texture, and visual recognition to be irrelevant to the ingestion of a meal. Science has yet to learn that there's an art to knowing when nourishment is no longer food and mere existence is no longer living.

Grandad and I saw eye-to-eye on most things. I think my wanderlust perplexed him a bit, though he understood my inherited love for land, labor, and good food. Our biggest disagreement, but one that we never let separate us, was over the use of chemical fertilizers and pesticides. I'd seen and felt the ill effects of the spraying of pesticides and defoliants on the cotton fields surrounding my college campus each year, and I was utterly miserable dressing in a rubber suit and respirator to spray pesticides every few weeks in the vineyard in Italy for three summers.

I also felt torn while working on the Sandhills farm. I was uncomfortable with the use of so many chemicals, but I was just as uncomfortable with having the farm foreman, Phillip Williams, be the person spraying them all of the time, even though he had the pesticide license and much of his own equipment that he used on several farms. I didn't want to be the one mixing and spraying the chemicals, but I also didn't want to simply leave it to someone else. I believed that those who were reliant on the application of chemicals for the success of their crops should at least share the burden of risk. I have long had a real disdain for fruit barons who sit in air-conditioned offices while their workers—generally migrant laborers or impoverished locals—do the risky dirty work.

Farming with Grandad—someone whom I deeply loved and respected—meant that the labels and aspersions that divide so much of the agricultural world in the United States haven't ever worked for me. Organic versus conventional, sustainable versus industrial—all of the black-and-white categories deny not just the spectrum of approaches to producing food but also the history of how we got to where we are. Farming with Grandad essentially provided me with a view of five generations of farming, from his parents to my own rapidly growing children.

The whole issue of synthetic sprays and fertilizers could have been the cause of a family schism, but over time I've decided that our family differences in opinion over the use of synthetic chemicals in agriculture are rooted in the historic progression of scientific understanding.

Grandad grew up in an extremely poor sharecropping family in South Carolina, with the family's "fortune" tied up in cotton and their subsequent misfortune linked to what he called the "damned ole boll weevil." The boll weevil wreaked havoc on farming families across the South, and picking cotton with the foliage still intact was an added layer of misery. Thus, the development of pesticides, defoliants, and fertilizers appeared, at least to many people, to be a way to help farm families out of poverty and to fuel the nation's farm economy. The last letter his mother wrote to him on September 8, 1949, one week before she died, was not one of despair, but it did describe the challenges their family faced:

> Father is better, too, tho' busy trying to take care of the peanuts during these rainy <u>days</u> & <u>nights</u> too. He has all of them pulled up & hauled into the yard. We have picked off 'bout 2½ bu. Sold one-half bu. at .50 per gal. Sure is a muddy bad job while it's so rainy. We've had lots of rain but no storms. Had some wind one day, which blew down corn right much. Think most everyone's cotton is a flop this year . . . All we know is dust when its dry, mud when it rains, & <u>peanuts</u>.[7]

Grandad and his peers weren't the ag-chem conspirators that are conjured up in our contemporary organic tirades against "industrial agriculture." Rather, they were often the inheritors of enormous crop failures, farm foreclosures, and work that teetered between boring and brutal. They loved what farms could produce—in terms of family, individual character, community values, financial return, and wholesome food. They tended to choose what they thought were the most promising and immediate options of their time—mechanization and chemical inputs.

Nonetheless, Grandad and some of the scientists of his era saw plant breeding as the best ultimate tool for fighting pests and diseases, even though plant breeding was in his era a slow and arduous process that required painstaking research, large tracts of land, and people with time and resources to test the results. The development of a single peach cultivar often required hundreds if not thousands of crosses over a span of several decades. Such breeding can be done much more expeditiously today, and with considerably fewer resources, albeit high-tech resources.

Grandad didn't particularly care for the use of a lot of the chemical treatments that were common in the fruit industry, and yet he saw these chemicals as a stopgap measure until advancements in plant breeding and other scientific advances could eliminate the need for so many sprays and fertilizers. Furthermore, the high humidity, poor soils, and insect pests in places throughout the Southeast made market farming with the cultivars of Grandad's era difficult, particularly in fruit operations.

The collective optimism common among Grandad and his colleagues with regard to the emerging tools for pest and disease control meant that it was difficult to foresee the tremendous costs that we would eventually pay for all of the unanticipated accumulations of toxins and nutrients that stemmed from synthetic pesticides and fertilizers. A high diversity of plants and the possibility of annual rotations make organic gardening relatively simple, but as soon as a farmer creates a monoculture of fruiting perennials—particularly at the scale required in market farming—the farmer has created an enticing, long-term habitat for a host of pests and diseases, with no annual shift in crops or planting locations to break the problematic cycles. When cultivar resistance can't meet the challenges of an onslaught of pests and diseases in a fruit-growing operation, sprays and other inputs tend to be the grower's next tool of choice. (Many consumers don't realize that many organic fruit operations actually spray their crops with more frequency than so-called conventional operations, albeit with organic chemicals that seem to have fewer detrimental effects than more potent and persistent chemicals.)

While I was never as comfortable with synthetic chemical use as Grandad was, I did understand his story and how he got to his perspective. Early in my musings on the possibilities of organic agriculture—anathema to the agricultural world I grew up in down South—I asked him one day what he thought of organic agriculture. I was so amused and slightly disturbed that I immediately wrote down his reply in my journal: "It's got a little truth in it. But people who are into organic gardening are like religious fundamentalists. It's like religion, sex, and anything else—you can go nuts over it."

Grandad was first and foremost a pragmatist. His first graduate student, Robert Aycock, put Grandad's research and teaching career into context for me:

He felt very strongly that students were being denied access to and familiarity with problems in the field. At that time (as is the case now) with the burgeoning availability of government funds to ostensibly encourage so-called basic research, many students, often influenced by young faculty members, did not look with favor upon the challenge of solving disease problems for the immediate relief of North Carolina growers. Dr. Clayton argued successfully that in the words of an early pioneer plant pathologist the science of plant pathology began in the fields and granaries of this country and that basic laboratory work, although important, should be directly in support of plant disease control.[8]

My generation inherited the conglomerated and confusing results of those investigations and the vast array of associated solutions—some that worked, some that didn't, and some that were effective but with unforeseen long-term consequences. In Grandad's era, the shift to what we too readily lump together and call "industrial agriculture" was not necessarily born out of malevolence, ignorance, or profit motives. He and many of his contemporaries wanted to advance agriculture for the benefit of farmers and consumers. They actually lived the hard work, misfortune, and occasional misery that we now tend to relegate to migrant workers in the United States and to peasant farmers elsewhere. Unfortunately, the costs of some of their solutions took a generation or more to emerge or to be understood. The tragic irony for Grandad—as was the case for some of his colleagues—was that the Parkinson's disease that ultimately killed him may well have stemmed from his contact with pesticides. Current, ongoing studies seem to be revealing a strong link between pesticide exposure and Parkinson's, with the likely culprits being organophosphates and organochlorides—key armaments in the fruit industry.[9]

On the flip side, however, the irony that is seldom articulated by my peers in the sustainable agriculture world is that Grandad and his colleagues also laid the foundations for much of the current success of organic agriculture. Grandad and his contemporaries studied cultivar resistance; the life cycles of insects; the pathology of fungal, bacterial, and viral diseases; soil chemistry; and various cultural methods. They developed fruit varieties and rootstocks that resisted devastating diseases such as peach tree short life and bacterial leaf spot. They used the scientific method to reduce many of the pest and disease issues facing farmers to carefully refined understandings of the natural course of events with suggestions of how best to intervene. They embarked on rigorous investigations into the specific elements of big problems. And they were working in a particularly difficult arena, since most fruits are perennials—not easy crops to manage organically when grown on any substantive scale, particularly in hot and humid regions with mild winters.

Organic or sustainable agriculture is dependent upon the kind of research that Grandad and others like him have provided us, but we can't stop there. Our current challenge is to reassemble those detailed understandings of particular pests and diseases into a complex ecological equation that represents a full-scale ecological system. It is clearer now than ever before that we can't afford to think just about the peach tree, or the orchard, or even the farm. It all belongs within a larger ecological context that extends far beyond the individual farm and that requires a variety of lenses if we are going to develop an agriculture that makes sense for humans and our environment.

Thinking about "agro-ecological" systems means thinking out loud and with others, people from various disciplines who each carry a piece of the ecological puzzle in their disciplined understandings of the world. Grandad was probably right in his gentle warning that those of us from the "organic" world can become myopic evangelists for a fundamentalism nearly as problematic as that of the prophets for profits in the ag-chem world. We are all too eager to jump on a left-wing bandwagon (it looks a lot like a *Vanagan*) and embrace concepts like "systems thinking" that feel intellectually invigorating and all-encompassing—but that can also allow us trade the mega for the micro, the grandiose for the details.

Looking through Grandad's field notebooks from the 1940s and '50s reminds me of how we transform an accumulation of details into scientific understanding. He traveled to farms throughout the region for decades, noting weather conditions, bloom times, disease conditions, fruit quality, cultivar differences, and varied responses to fertilizer and pesticide applications. The idea that a researcher like Grandad and an advocate of organic agriculture like myself shouldn't share the table and exchange ideas is a travesty to the pursuit of a better agriculture.

One of Grandad's favorite quips to his students and to me, as he noted differences between trees that had pesticides applied to them and those that did not, was, "An unsprayed tree? How can you unspray a tree?"

Whether Grandad or I initially knew it or not, it was a question that helped to define my complementary interests in homesteading and sustainable agriculture. When Erin and I heard that there was a small college in the hills of Vermont that was putting the environment at the core of its curriculum and had the need for an organic garden, we decided that we just couldn't live without mountains. And we couldn't imagine a better place than Vermont to learn more about homesteading . . . or how to unspray a tree.

SIX

The Simple Life:
An Ecological Misnomer

The simple life should not involve getting locked in a chicken house by an ox. Such a predicament may, however, involve simplemindedness on the part of the homesteader and a rather complex strategy on the part of the ox.

I'd stepped up into our henhouse, mounted on an old hay wagon chassis, and reached into the battered military-green Civil Defense metal barrel to scoop out several buckets of chicken feed to put into the hanging feeder. I'd finished chores and had put our oxen, Pet and Troll, into the lush pasture surrounding the henhouse. More eager to scratch than eat at that point, Pet had followed me over as I fed and watered the layers and promptly cocked his flank up against the wooden sides of the structure, working out the itches with his rhythmic rubbing. The fifty chickens and I seemed to share the sensation of mild seasickness as the mobile coop swayed and squeaked with his hip undulations. "Pet—cut it *out*!" I yelled through the hexagonal chicken wire, punctuating my irritation with the exclamation point of a sharp bang on the plywood wall right beside his head.

Nonplussed, he looked up with half a glance and slowly meandered to the end of the coop with the door. Deciding to shift to a few other itches, he rubbed the right side of his face and his horn up against the door. As the swaying of his thick neck increased in velocity, the scraping of his horn against the door increased in volume until the Dominique chickens all bolted to the farthest corner in one black-and-white blur, with the exhaust cloud of fecal dust seemingly aimed right at me. I sharply pounded my fist at the wall just opposite the scraping sounds: "Pet, go find a tree to scratch on!" Determined to remind me who was boss—or at least *Bos*—Pet gave a final scrape and meandered over into the early-morning shade, leaving me on my own.

I finished filling the feeder and pushed on the door to get out. It didn't budge. *Huh?* I pushed again with my shoulder. The door gave just a bit at my shoulder but not at all near my hip, where the rotating wooden latch was located. *Nooooo,* I thought, *he couldn't have . . .*

Turns out that he did. I was locked inside the chicken house by a cloven-hooved prankster. In the middle of the pasture in front of the cabin. I somehow doubted the likelihood of Pet returning to end the joke—it seemed that he had already delivered the punch line and was in the shade ruminating on the genius of its delivery. It was the first time I'd ever envisioned cattle snickering—they're just not that prone to being self-congratulatory, in my experience.

How am I going to get out of this one with both my dignity and the henhouse intact? I wondered. I knew that I could definitely push hard and break the latch, but I hated to tear up the new exterior siding on the coop. On the other hand, it beat telling anyone what had happened, much less calling for help from inside a chicken coop. Besides, there was only one person available to call, and she already had enough dirt on me without adding this story to the collection.

About that time, Erin stepped out of the cabin to visit the outhouse. I let her go in and take care of business while I decided whether I really wanted her help. By the time she slammed the outhouse door shut, I'd decided that I would rather bear the brief humiliation to follow than spend time fixing the latch. Plus, I knew I'd still have to tell her what had happened at some point. It was just one more unexpected incident in our growing litany of homesteading adventures.

"Erin," I shouted, "could you please come over here?"

"Come over where? Where are you?" she asked, looking down toward the vacant pasture, seeing Pet but not me.

"Here—in the chicken house."

"What do you need me in the chicken house for?" She was mildly irritated, since it meant changing from her clogs to her boots.

"Ummm, to let me out," I replied, somewhat cowed.

"What do you mean, let you out?"

"Pet locked me in." I was wishing that I could mumble it instead of saying it loudly enough for any stray hikers to hear.

Erin doesn't burst out laughing that often, but this time her laughter bolted out and echoed back—any pride I had disappearing with its brief reverberation.

She put on her boots and walked bemusedly down the path and into the pasture. "You need something?" I could hear from her tone that her smirk was fully intact.

"Yes. Out. I could've broken the latch, but I didn't want to have to fix it." I needed to make it clear that I had some authority in the whole situation.

"Yeah, and it wouldn't have been as much fun for me if you had. So, how soon do you want out?" she teased.

"How about right now? My feathers are getting a little ruffled."

I'm not sure who coined the phrase *the simple life,* but I wish it were one that we could buck. Homesteading is quite the opposite. It's far from simple. It may mean minimizing luxuries, but the counterpoint is that it also means maximizing necessities—all in stark contrast to global trends in the opposite directions.

Perhaps the notion of the simple life came from the idea that the elements involved are relatively simple, either in function or in number. While that may be true, it is the relationships and the interactions among those things that are far from simple, not to mention the choices of which ones to utilize and which ones to reject.

For years, I've struggled with whether I can define homesteading or even whether it's a good idea to try, at the risk of creating a definition that is, by nature, exclusive. However, I think I can begin to distinguish between *homesteading* and *not homesteading.* Homesteading is about purpose, intent, action, observation, and reflection, and then determining the best subsequent course of action. It is *not* about accepting things as they are and simply riding the cultural wave. It *is* about determining one's place in the world and then constantly crafting and recrafting a life that seems more appropriate—ecologically, ethically, emotionally, aesthetically, economically. It is simultaneously a juxtaposed act of ascetic detachment and of spirited engagement. It is about taking control of decisions while also accepting the unanticipated, whether it comes by way of social circumstance, economic shift, Mother Nature, a culmination of personal choices, or even a cow.

Homesteading is a selection of nouns and an anticipation of verbs. In sum, it's a way of thinking about the world and one's place in it as a series of interlocking systems. It's a study of the *logic* of ecological, while also savoring unlocked mysteries. Whereas I once wondered why I bothered to study philosophy when my deepest longings were to homestead and farm, I gradually began to see ecology as the philosopher's science. That realization led me to enroll in a graduate program in conservation biology at Antioch New England soon after moving into our cabin. I needed help in putting our lives into an ecological context.

So much of ecology is about divining, defining, interpreting, and predicting systems. A homesteader's ecology is about putting oneself directly into that context, not allowing the science to be peripheral to one's own existence and simply living as if the ecological relevance of our own actions should be considered only when we have the compunction and the leisure to do so. It is also about living on the edge—in the company of curiosity, compassion, and companions of all persuasions.

Erin and I had assembled a relatively small collection of things to begin our homesteading up Tunket. The few belongings we did have became fewer as we moved into our renovated cabin in the fall of 1997. We had given away all our electrical items, except for our small array of power tools, moved our clothes and kitchen wares into the house, and put our tools in the outhouse, dubbed the "Toolet Shed." We had our ever-reliable Nissan truck, Erin's old Plymouth Acclaim, and our bikes. That seemed to be about enough, and there wasn't room for much else in the intimacy of the 12' × 28' cabin—except for intimacy, but it was even hard to make room for that at times, given the demands of the days. We'd built a small 10' × 12' calf shed for Pet and Troll, which I expected to leave standing for a year or two at the most. As it turned out, we didn't dismantle it until an apple tree helped bring it down ten years later.

The cabin consisted of two rooms, with the main living area measuring 12' × 16', while the 12' × 12' room was reserved primarily for sleeping and storing our clothes. Our days revolved around the woodstove, the tiny kitchen, and our modest corner table—originally a recycled countertop placed on stacked milk crates, with 5-gallon buckets for seats. That setup worked for a while, until we finally tired of guests getting up off their buckets and tipping the tabletop into the laps of the people on the opposite side. Fortunately, we somehow never lost a well-balanced meal to anyone's inadvertent mishaps, but the kerosene lamp and candles were more of a concern and much more difficult to catch without getting burned. Erin always compared life in the cabin to living in the tight confines of a boat, and the table's occasional dips and swells were a good reminder of that analogy.

We laughed that our lives were essentially made of buckets—buckets as seats, toilet, springwater containers, dishwater basins, bathwater vessels, stepstools, tool containers, icemakers, compost storage, vegetable totes, livestock feed and water carriers, water hydrant covers, and even varmint protection. We used them for just about everything except clothing. Several weeks prior to moving into the cabin in late August of 1997, Erin and Maggie, her mom, worked out a basic kitchen layout in a 6' × 6' area and built it from the scrap rough-cut lumber left over from our cabin renovations. Complete with a table for our three-burner propane stove, utensil storage, spice rack, dry goods shelving, and our $25 plastic utility sink, that tiny kitchen somehow served us—and all of our curious guests—for eight years.

There was one conspicuous gap in our kitchen accoutrements: a refrigerator. We didn't have electricity to power one, and we couldn't afford to buy a new propane refrigerator at that point, as they cost well over $1,000. It would be five years before we had a source of refrigeration other than springwater and winter weather. In the cold months, we would use the outdoor temperatures and containers of ice to keep foods cold, and in the warmer months, we would use coolers with springwater and a bucket lowered into the springs to maintain storage temperatures of 45 to 50 degrees.

Over that time, we shifted from a Yukon-hermit tin-can pantry approach to a diet increasingly made up of vegetables, meat, fruit, dairy products, and herbs from our land and our neighbors, with significant tutelage from the Waites, Carl, and organic gardening guru Shep Ogden. However, the lack of temperature-controlled storage constrained our choices in all seasons, since we had neither a refrigerator for the warm months nor a root cellar for the colder months. Our search for seasonal foods, preservation ideas, and low-tech storage methods became cultural, historical, and geographical, with visits to living museums such as Sturbridge Village, Hancock Shaker Village, Billings Farm & Museum, Landis Valley Museum, Plimoth Plantation, and—perhaps our favorite—the Museum of American Frontier Culture in Staunton, Virginia.

Living museums are repositories of knowledge, tools, crafts, buildings, books, and staff that warehouse waning traditional knowledge that can sustain contemporary culture in ways that we too often neglect.

Sometimes we need our cultural paradigm shaken, and other times it's best to challenge our chronological paradigm. The interpreters in these museums tend to be people who have thought long and hard about the contrasts between life in previous eras and our modern world, and they often eloquently reveal the dialectical tensions that they have discovered from essentially "living" in two worlds. A day spent at a living history museum can provide months of reflection and surprise moments of illumination for homesteaders.

Lighting was another perennial challenge that we constantly explored at living history museums. Adequate lighting became a growing concern once I began my conservation biology graduate studies at Antioch New England in Keene, New Hampshire, during the winter of 1998. I traveled there every Thursday and Friday for two and a half years, returning home with loads of homework to complete by kerosene lamp and candlelight. I was lucky that my professors understood that my lifestyle was congruent with my studies, so they conceded to taking handwritten papers when I wasn't able to type the final drafts on the computer in my college office.

In a flock of environmentalists, it's an easy thing to demonize electricity, but buying lamp oil by the case—all for a handful of lumens—does not create a very bright eco-luminary. And reading textbooks by lamplight or turning on a battery-powered flashlight to get a solar-powered calculator to function will probably not generate a lot of first-rate conservation biologists.

Yet the romantic warmth of that soft lamplight and the radiance of the woodstove, all in the confines of a small cabin, were real. Never was the solace more evident than when one of us would return from work and snowshoe the mile up from the road to the cabin after a heavy snow, seeing the amber windows glow in flickering silence. For the person inside, the clomp of snow-clad boots against the stairs and the clink of removing and storing snowshoes meant the return of a welcome companion. The door would whip open and shut, and the wisp of loosening layers would commence, with the conversation always beginning with the weather, until the newcomer settled into a slow melt in the tattered armchair by the woodstove.

The one who had stayed home to tend the fire was almost always considered the lucky one, with Oshie and Solstice—our matching sister cats—reminding us how the wisest creatures pass the winter. If we all could magnify our ideas about eating locally to include living seasonally, we would do much less wandering in winter. Most creatures' home ranges diminish significantly during the winter, with caloric expenditures and the risks of travel minimized. Rest and reserves are the tenets of winter survival for most species, but we humans try to carry on as if every season were the same. We do little to tailor our jobs or our social lives to fit the realities of the winter season.

Yet there's no sense in pretending that the short days and long nights of winter are all that quiet and restful on the homestead, particularly if wood heat, livestock, and heavy snowfall are included in the equation. Winter may make one want to stay indoors, but it seldom affords us that opportunity. The chores and duties seem all the more urgent and timely, and they are probably a good excuse to stay healthy—if the occasional stress doesn't kill you first.

In New England, the entire calendar year seems to swirl around winter. Either it's here or it's coming. In either case, there's plenty to do to ensure that it's greeted with confidence and comfort . . . and a hearty dose of humor. Stoics may be better suited than grumps to survive a harsh homesteading winter, but the folks who weather winter the best are those who match winter's shenanigans with an equal dose of playfulness. The aesthete may fare nearly as well, but sometimes it's easier to find ways to laugh than it is to find beauty. Besides, too many aesthetes are inclined to pursue their passion through a window, taking great panes (of glass) to buffer themselves from the cold.

As we worked our way into winter routines that made sense over the eight years in our modest cabin, the biggest challenge seemed to be laundry. We did some handwashing in a washtub and our ever-reliable buckets, purchased a small hand-cranked washer that relied upon hot water and vacuum pressure, and occasionally used an old-fashioned wringer, but the loads inevitably seemed too frequent and too large to handle if we wanted to spend our time doing much else. Erin did most of the laundry, often while I was at work. She would put everything into our laundry bags, load them into the sled, and nestle herself into the load for the steep downhill portion of the trip to the vehicles parked at the base of Tunket Road. She doesn't tend to be a daredevil, but she has no fear on a sled, and the laundry seemed to bolster her courage, to the point that she would rip down the icy hill with a velocity that terrified me. At the base of the hill, she would stick out her left foot, snow flying up and over her, and take the 90-degree turn at the bottom with a slight fishtail that a good NASCAR fan would reward with a ring of the brass spittoon and a two-syllabled southern "Daaaa—mnnn!"

Our ability to pay off our mortgage in three years' time was a tribute to Erin's thriftiness, and her laundry routine was but one example of her creativity and determination. She would throw in the loads of laundry at the Laundromat, make a quick trip to the grocery store while it was washing, and then would pack it back into the laundry bags wet. Once she got to the base of the hill, she would park the vehicle and off-load the heavy-laden bags of wet laundry back into the sled, pulling them uphill with the groceries. She was never cold by the time she made it back to the cabin, although the laundry was sometimes partially frozen if the temperature was anywhere near zero. She always claimed that she was saving money and also helping to increase the humidity in the cabin by drying the clothes at home, as the woodstove more or less eliminated most of the moisture in the air inside.

However, there were times when the loads seemed too big, the temperatures too cold, and the night too late to opt for the simplicity of pulling the laundry up with snowshoes—especially with an infant on our backs, as was the case once our first son, Asa, was born in 2002. After one particularly long day of work and errands, we arrived at our usual winter parking spot at the base of Tunket Road. It was a frigid January night with groceries, three weeks' worth of wet laundry, a six-month old Asa, and an ample supply of fresh snow that would make the pull uphill all the more difficult. We agreed that we should put the chains on the truck and try to make it uphill, although we opted to put on just two chains instead of the usual four. The three of us crammed our bulky winter selves into the cab of the truck, and we started heading up, the depth of snow taking us by surprise.

"Okay, Erin, hold on to Asa, here goes . . ." I gunned it to get uphill, the chained front tires of the truck repeatedly pulling us toward the deep snowbanks on either side of the road. The engine howled, and we fishtailed in and out of the main tracks. We whooped with glee as we made it to the top of the hill, and the rest of the road was a cinch. We got to our parking area below the cabin, unstrapped little Asa, and reached back in the dark to get the laundry, sled, and groceries. The bed of the truck was empty. In darkened disbelief, I got out my flashlight to look— we'd forgotten to close the tailgate. Erin took Asa into the cabin, and I spent the next hour pulling the recovered sled to collect the laundry and groceries strewn along the pitch-dark length of the road and throughout the snowbanks, eventually finding everything except a can of refried beans, which showed up that spring in relatively good condition. I ate them and christened them authentic Vermont Brrrrritos.

Sleds have been nearly as prolific and important to our lives as buckets. I remember being perplexed by the vocabulary used by my boss at Brunnenburg, Sizzo—the curator of the agricultural museum there—whenever he referred to implements used to pull things, primarily in snow but also across treacherous steep slopes. He would inevitably use the word *sledge,* whereas I was accustomed only to the term *sled.* For me, a "sled" was something used almost exclusively for recreation, with a verbal vestige being the implement pulled behind a draft animal, mostly in days gone by. For Sizzo and his Tirolean farmer counterparts, however, there were a host of devices used for transporting people and things through the snow.

A *Schlitten*—or sledge, as it was in fact called in earlier times here in the United States—was for pulling hay, manure, wood, livestock bedding—anything that needed to be moved in winter, either by humans or with the help of draft animals. In fact, winter was often the preferred time to move such heavy, bulky items—a prime example of what the Tiroleans would call *Vörtl,* a dialect derivation of the German word *Vorteil,* meaning "advantage." The Tiroleans use the word Vörtl to express the possibility of turning a disadvantage into an advantage. In this case, one is using what some would consider to be the curse of snow and ice as an advantageous means of moving things with less friction than would be the case in other seasons. Human power was often used in lieu of draft animals, simply because of the difficulty of traversing much of the terrain, and many of the tasks were oriented so that the annual movement of materials tended to be in a predominantly downhill direction. *Rodelschlitten* is the equivalent of tobogganing for recreation, but with the rider seated upright on a slightly elevated platform, allowing for more control with one's feet—critical on such steep terrain as one typically finds in the Alps.

We started to see the logic in the use of snow and even ice to help us move objects and materials around the homestead. If one's tasks are generally oriented to occur in a downhill direction, a sledge starts to become much more appealing and practical than a wheelbarrow, particularly in rough terrain that transforms a wheelbarrow into a groin-destroyer. We soon learned to dread the immediate loss of snow and frozen ground, since mud quickly displaces snow and ice in Vermont, and any mode of wheeled transport—from a one-wheeled wheelbarrow to a four-wheel-drive truck—often has to be abandoned as a viable means of moving materials for weeks at a time up Tunket. If need be, we can always pull in several hundred pounds of livestock feed by sled across the snow, but we are at a virtual loss once the snow turns to mud. Even now, with a slightly improved road and a four-wheel-drive tractor, we have to assume that we will have several weeks each year when anything that comes in must come in on our backs. Our neighbor Donald Waite succinctly put it into proper Vermont perspective for me when I expressed my satisfaction at how smooth our road was one winter: "Yup. A snow road is a good road." And then he wisely added a caveat, "Until it's not."

I've never been very excited at the prospect of plowing our road, whether it's by tractor, truck, or draft animals. I've tried all three, with my success correlating closely with the increased amount of horsepower used, but I've been reliant on force and not finesse. Finesse is usually a good indicator of a reasonably sound ecological practice, whereas force should probably have one thinking about the relationship between ecology and thermodynamics. Spending hours to clear away what nature will eventually take care of generally seems like an exercise in frustration and ecological inefficiency to me, particularly when I could be using that time to walk, snowshoe, sled, or ski on that same road, all the while also keeping healthy and warm and paying close attention to the subtle joys of winter. We tend to savor the winter walks up and down Tunket Road—the walks are a retracing of observations and thoughts over the past twelve years. However, there are times when being able to drive to one's doorstep and get supplies—much less small children—in and out quickly and with minimal effort can be pretty nice. The insurance company seems to prefer knowing that emergency vehicles can get in and out, too, but that's another story, for later . . .

And yet the theme of that story is vulnerability and risk. We live in an odd culture that goes to extraordinary lengths to minimize vulnerability and risk in daily life, then pulls a blink-of-the-eye, Janus-inspired about-face. Having eliminated most of the hazards associated with daily subsistence, that same culture then invents and generates costly forms of recreation and entertainment that are fundamentally based on risk and vulnerability.

One can't help but wonder whether we might not have a lopsided view of reality—and perhaps misaligned priorities—by eschewing life-style choices that at times involve discomfort, deprivation, or difficulty for the sake of living a bit more in sync with nature while aggrandizing energy-intensive (from both human and fossil-fuel perspectives) recre-ation that produces primarily adrenaline and vicarious entertainment value. The option that seeks to minimize long-term risk by trying to live lighter and healthier is culturally suspect, while the pursuit of high-risk sports is magnified and praised.

It is true that risk and vulnerability almost always teach us impor-tant lessons about our inner fortitude, our physical condition, even our personal priorities. Putting oneself on the edge can be transformative. In that regard, risk and vulnerability, whether in the homesteader's rooftop construction or in the skydiver's ether (between plane and terrain) are much the same. Both have an objective; neither one can ignore the risks; both strategize for safety. And yet, the difference comes in whether the end product of the activity results in fulfilling the basic human needs for food, water, shelter, and warmth.

Whether we recognize it or not, we all live in a constant state of vulner-ability. In a sense, homesteading is at once a declaration of vulnerability as well as a response to that vulnerability. The risks are acknowledged, accepted, and engaged. Life is lived with no pretenses to the contrary. It is lived intensely for the moment and strategically for the future. It puts us back in the ecological web, where we belong—not just footloose and fancy-free, having to invent moments of intense risk for momentary fulfillment. The things that we create in the process of confronting risk and vulnerability on the homestead—nourishment, habitat, and crafted comforts—are meaningful, enduring, and sometimes even ecologically appropriate.

In New England, winter is often the primary fulcrum point of vulner-ability, or at least occasional discomfort and difficulty. Feeding the fire two or three times each night because it was -20 degrees 4 inches from the edge of my bed, or going to the outhouse when it was 10 below, or carry-ing 40 gallons of water 100 yards twice each day for cattle because the barn hydrants froze—any one of those times would have been inoppor-tune moments for someone to come and ask me about "the simple life"—

especially in the outhouse, I suppose. Teeth gritted and eyes narrowed, my response in any one of those scenarios might have been something like, *"Drop the 'simple' part. And don't try replacing it with 'complex.' It's just life. Bare bones. And sometimes bare buns when they shouldn't be. But don't forget that it's about living, too. Don't lose sight of the verb."*

Homesteading in North America seems to have a traceable vein of thought with a strong literary component, and several authors have tried to unravel the question of why so many of us—okay, maybe "a few" is closer to the truth—have opted out of a relatively comfortable lifestyle in pursuit of a life with both less and more. Rebecca Kneale Gould actually created a chronology of the American "homesteading movement" in her book *At Home in Nature: Modern Homesteading and Spiritual Practice in America,* theorizing that Thoreau's retreat to Walden was, in many ways, the point of departure for the rest of us, even if we didn't quite realize it.[1] One theme of her fascinating book is the pursuit of a critical question: Why do homesteaders, usually people who could be comfortably floating in the relatively placid currents of the American mainstream, place themselves in the seemingly intentional dilemma of having to navigate the turbulent and often poorly charted waters that too many have inappropriately dubbed "the simple life"?

Gould strikes gold, in my view, when she carefully lays out a well-constructed argument—built around her literary and cultural chronology—that the common element in American homesteading is probably not religion or spirituality, but rather what we might consider "spiritual practice." For Gould, it is the act of homesteading—the daily and seasonal rituals—that provides its allure and rewards. Gould proposes that it is the spiritual practice of homesteading, not so much a common belief system, that seems to pervade the disparate and diverse homesteading population.

Jeffrey Jacob takes a sociological perspective to investigate what fuels the North American homesteader and how differing visions and versions manifest themselves on different homesteads. In his book *New Pioneers: The Back-to-the-Land Movement and the Search for a Sustainable Future,* Jacob also explores spiritual motivations, as well as technological, ethical, economic, social, and ecological drivers.[2] In his conclusion, he weighs the successes and failures of homesteaders as "new pioneers" in re-creating social, economic, and ecological realities on their own terms and turf. He neither romanticizes nor denigrates their efforts, and he sees the diffuse homesteading movement, if it can be called that, as a quest for change. Thus far, he thinks, the results are not strikingly definitive, but nonetheless he sees homesteading ventures as important experiments that might shift our culture's excesses and exigencies one homestead at a time.

Understanding and predicting the social and cultural impacts of homesteading is just as difficult as understanding and predicting how an ecosystem will respond to change. In both cases, what once seemed relatively simple is now looking much more complex. That complexity can be overwhelming or even demoralizing to someone who wants to trust that her homesteading experiments or his ecological observations and understanding might provide at least a small contribution toward improving the human condition and its link to the natural world. However, confronting complexity—not running from it as so many back-to-the-landers tried to do in the 1960s and '70s—is the only way we can expect to make our way through the quagmire of ecological and social issues we face, if we look honestly into the mirror.

These days, as I look out the bedroom windows of our new house that we finally began inhabiting in 2005 and reflect on the gardens, the pastures, the hedgerows, and the complex of outbuildings we've constructed over the years, the ecological complexities bounce back off the shimmering water of the new pond, once an unusable wet spot that constantly mired our agricultural intentions. What would have happened if we had not purchased this land and began reclaiming these old summer pastures that were rapidly working their way back into the surrounding forest ecosystem? Is it better to let old fields like these become forest instead of producing food and capturing sunlight for our solar hot-water and electrical systems? What is the correct approach in a world in which we are fragmenting ecological habitats with development while we are simultaneously centralizing agricultural production in distant places? Is it better to let others elsewhere produce our food and energy or to have a fragmented, diverse working landscape that ensures we are accountable for meeting many of our own needs? Would these old fields, left to their own devices, have reverted to a native ecosystem? Do we even know for sure what that native ecosystem looks like? Do we now have so many non-native plant species and modern disease pressures that a native ecosystem is even possible? And assuming we do know what that native ecosystem would looks like, what if the natural succession takes it in another direction with different species and plant communities? Should we then redirect the process through a careful restoration project?

All of these questions seem particularly pertinent to us, since we live adjacent to The Nature Conservancy's North Pawlet Hills Preserve and part of our land is now under a conservation easement with The Nature Conservancy. We are literally straddling the worlds of ecosystem conservation and preservation. A conservation worldview typically involves maintaining some aspects of a working landscape, whereas a preservation approach generally opts for minimal human impact or resource use. Both have their merits and their place.

The science of ecology has its literal roots in the abandoned fields of the temperate climes of the Northern Hemisphere—"clearings" like the one we decided to habit "up Tunket."[3] Ecology was certainly not born at a given moment, or even from perfectly clear parentage. But the people whom we consider to be the progenitors of ecology through their amorous flings with Mother Nature seem to have spent a fair amount of time pioneering a new field of science by studying the old fields around them.[4] The propensity and ability of those old fields to transition back into forest, prairie, or some other surrounding ecosystem have long been a point of fascination for ecologists and have been the basis for a lot of important ecological theory and principles.

The concept of succession—ecological changes in vegetative composition and structure—stems in large part from scientists' observations on how old fields transform into different ecosystems. Concepts such as "pioneer species," "secondary succession," and "climax species" began to emerge from these observations. Scientists began investigating how different biotic (living organisms) and abiotic (the physical environment) elements could interact to yield certain plant communities, wondering aloud whether the newly forming plant communities should be considered native, new, or some hybrid thereof. In many ways, the emphasis was on determining, defining, and describing the likely interactions among different species, as well as the interplay between these species and their environment.

Initially, scientists studying ecological succession seemed largely inclined to create a formulaic, linear world in which $a + b$ resulted in c, albeit with many more variables included in the equation. In other words, an old field in a particular ecosystem could be expected to go through the established stages of succession, with the normal cast of regional characters, and ultimately would result in a predicted "climax" ecosystem. Predicting change, even by means of that fairly mechanistic approach, seemed difficult enough.

As the science of ecology has progressed, however, ecologists have increasingly acknowledged that their work is more complex than perhaps first imagined. Not only has the stage become crowded with an enormous and continually growing cast of characters—ranging from soil microorganisms to imported plants, pests, and diseases—but the knowledge about the multiple layers and levels of interactions has also expanded exponentially. The reverberations of any ecological pebble thrown into our ever-expanding pool of knowledge go deeper and farther than we ever anticipated, often with unanticipated results.

Ecologists still have to have a solid grasp of the scientific method, which generally helps lead them to a distilled answer to a very specific question, but they also have to think more broadly about populations, processes, patterns, and predictability. As a result, ecologists are moving toward an increasingly sophisticated and integrated approach, with a vanguard of researchers and theorists pushing their peers toward an interdisciplinary harvesting of understanding, often called "ecological complexity." In essence, ecological complexity involves moving from a mechanistic, one-dimensional view of the pebble in the pond to a highly dynamic, three-dimensional view that employs every vantage point, from a microscope to a satellite. Ecology is shifting away from an approach that could be characterized as unidirectional and deterministic to a study of complex, nonlinear systems.

That shift is not necessarily simple for us to swallow. After all, we are finite human beings in search of predictability. That predictability helps us understand not only the natural world, but also our role and responsibility within it. It's not that that predictability is more elusive than ever—it's actually a bit closer in many regards—but the potential for ambiguity is perhaps in clearer focus. Our hunch is that predictability is now more likely to be accurate if we think of systems and not just species.

No one was more important in pioneering systems theory than Vermont's own Donella Meadows, coauthor of the international bestseller *The Limits to Growth,* who—perhaps not coincidentally—began stepping out of her more formal teaching and research roles to homestead and farm before her tragic death in 2001. She described a system as "a set of things—people, cells, molecules, or whatever—interconnected in such a way that they produce their own pattern of behavior over time. The system may be buffeted, constricted, triggered, or driven by outside forces. But the system's response to these forces is characteristic of itself, and that response is seldom simple in the real world."[5]

However, no matter how we name, describe, or categorize our world—be it by way of species or systems or any other label—our descriptors are limited because they are human constructs. Nonetheless, these constructs are our language of self-discovery as we make ourselves at home on a planet still new to us.

Ecologists gravitate toward universal concepts and generalities, but there is a danger that the concepts that work in one ecosystem may not work in another. In fact, most of the theories regarding the succession of old fields were developed in the Northern Hemisphere, and they begin to fall apart in tropical and Mediterranean-type systems—climates in which slow or arrested succession thwarts the theoretical vegetative progression toward some climax plant community.[6]

I made the mistake of bringing my southern ecological understanding of soils and their relative stability to New England. A basic homesteading principle should probably be that what works in one environment does not always work in another. I was proud of all of our work in salvaging and winterizing our cabin, and the new Sonotube footings that we'd poured looked great to my southern construction eye. The cabin was perched tidily upon the eight new footings, each of them 3 to 4 feet deep and based on what I thought was stable earth and stone.

Frost sounds rather innocuous to anything that's not green and leafy, so I didn't take the term too seriously when I heard Vermonters use it in reference to winter's gradual penetration of the soil. Little did I know the degree to which water, soil, and wildly vacillating temperatures can conspire to topple fleeting human grandeur aboveground, in ways that are subtle but cumulative.

Our cabin rode out the first winter with little noted change in its demeanor. However, after the first few winters, we started to have more respect for what New England "frost" can do. That respect soon turned to frustration and fear. The length of our cabin runs north to south, with the eastern back side built slightly into the darker, forested hill and the western facade facing the mountains and the afternoon sun. Water seems to run down our hill in most every form possible—rivulets, seeps, springs, and occasional torrents. Unfortunately, the modestly leveled area where the cabin sits became a resting spot for water in its downhill journey, despite all of our ditches and other diversions.

Water gathering on the shaded back side of our cabin apparently colluded with our clay-rich soil to heave our cabin up and over. The footings on the front of the cabin might have resisted the onslaught, but, as it turned out, they only cowered deeper in the protective shelter of their mud-rich haven. The warm western sun thawed out the ground in the front of the cabin weeks before the ice even disappeared in the back of the cabin, so as the back-side footings heaved, the front-side footings dipped and tipped. By our eighth and last winter in the cabin, there was an astonishing—and terrifying—9-inch elevation difference in the front and back sides of the cabin, over a span of only 12 feet.

Our son Asa couldn't play with balls—they simply rolled to the west side of the cabin as soon as he set them down. It did make fine entertainment for the cats, however. Since we had neither a TV nor a computer, our best adult entertainment came from having guests sit in the wheeled desk chair that we had in the living area. They would sit down and immediately begin a nearly undetectable advance toward the wall, often not quite realizing what was happening.

I did not sleep well our last spring in the cabin, trying to envision ways to extricate ourselves from a capsized cabin in the middle of a dark night if a warm spring rain finally allowed the front, downhill footings to pitch forward and let the cabin tumble toward its obvious inclination. We needed to put most of our financial resources into our dream of building a new house, so we had neither the time nor the money to put in a new foundation for the cabin. With my limited time to work on the new house during the academic year, I just wasn't sure we were going to be able to move out of the cabin and into the new house before my ecological misjudgments had created a self-constructed downfall. I hadn't foreseen the conspiracy of ecological forces working against the simplicity of my original assumptions and construction.

But building a homestead or a farm is never a simple matter.

SEVEN

Framing a Life

Originally, I had thought that we would use our cabin as a base from which to build a bigger, better, and more efficient house, within a year or two of moving in. However, we allowed our forays into livestock to begin dominating the plans (as they have done ever since, it seems), so I began building a pole barn for Pet and Troll a year after having moved into our cabin. In a trend that was to continue, I began construction in the fall and faced the threat of the first snows while racing to get the roof on.

We wanted to build a barn that we could grow into, so I had laid out a plan for a 24' × 24' structure with a red metal roof, divided into four interior quadrants for various uses. Despite some financial help from my grandmother—who somehow never seemed to resent our decision to farm somewhere besides the North Carolina Sandhills and continued to support us in our dreams—we were tight on money, so we couldn't afford to hire an excavator to level the site. We just built into the slope, doing what excavation I could do by hand, just as we'd seen done time and again in the Alps. We again went to Phil's Mill for our lumber, all hemlock and white pine harvested from nearby forests. Fortunately, Phil's truck could deliver just about as much lumber as I could afford with each biweekly paycheck and generally as much as I could utilize in my narrow windows of free time on weekends and in the evenings.

With the exception of exploiting students, colleagues, and Donald's tractor to help me raise the nine 20-foot telephone poles for the barn infrastructure in early October, I was doing the construction myself until I reached the point where I was simply unable to raise the ridge beam and rafters alone, thanks to the weight of the stout green hemlock boards that Phil had cut one or two days prior to the delivery—if not that very morning.

An old Tirolean farmer once told me an adage his father had passed on to him: "If you don't have a good roof, you don't have a good house, no matter what's under the roof." If I had learned anything from Tirolean architecture, it was that big overhangs are the key to the longevity of a house, and the Tiroleans should know. A tour around any village there will have one remarking how many houses and barns were originally built in the medieval and Gothic eras—and they are still intact. In talking with a lot of locals about the best choice for the barn roof, I became convinced that metal roofs make a lot of sense in the Northeast—they're reliable, economical, long lasting, and relatively simple to install. We opted for a red metal roof, a choice that turned out to be the beginning of another trend that was to continue with the rest of our buildings.

Other than having an impervious roof, nothing is more important than getting water, snow, and ice away from the house when it comes off the roof. Overhangs can also be crucial elements in providing proper shading in the summer, while allowing the full burst of the low winter sun to enter into the house. I'm still perplexed by the minimal overhangs on houses in the Northeast and wonder if this standard style should be attributed to the early architectural influences from Britain—a region less concerned with the buildup of ice and snow around the edges of a house or the penetration of hot summer sun than is the case in New England.

Early one brilliant December morning, I managed to set the ridge beam of the new barn atop 10-foot 6×6s alone, using ladders, a pulley, and a tripod. I felt the sense of isolation and independence that I thought I'd always wanted, climbing atop the upper deck of the new barn in full view of the surrounding mountains. But as I struggled to keep my balance while setting the ridge beam, with its 3-foot overhang 24 feet above the ground, I started to question my sense of obstinate independence. Thinking that I had gotten through the most difficult part of the process, I collapsed into a contented heap on the wooden deck after getting the last and most dangerous section of the heavy hemlock beam in place on its posts.

After relaxing in the low-hanging winter sun, I got up and cut the angles for the first two hemlock rafters. I decided to start on the high western side of the barn to stabilize that section of the ridge beam in case a storm came—most likely from the west. I reconfigured my tripod made of 12-foot 2×4s, with a pulley hanging from the middle, so that I could hoist each rafter roughly into position and nail it into place on the ridge beam. Once I got the first rafter up, however, I simply could not keep the rafter or the still-wobbly ridge beam in place well enough to hold the beam and the rafter tightly together, while holding a nail in one hand and my hammer in the other.

Sweating, thirsty, and utterly frustrated at myself for being too proud and stubborn to ask anyone for help, I lowered the rafter with the pulley rope as I descended the ladder, holding on to the end as I gently lowered the still wet 2×8. *What am I going to do now?* I thought. *Eat lunch, I guess,* my stomach responded.

I sat down to eat the peanut butter and jelly sandwich I'd brought over from the cabin earlier. No sooner had I sat down than I heard the low rumble of a vehicle coming up the road. Donald was coming up. I wondered if Pet and Troll had gotten loose down the hill again. He stopped to put his truck in four-wheel drive and bounced up my rutted path to the barn. He cut off the engine, and, before getting out of the truck, he pulled out his little box of matches, lit his pipe, whipped the match flame into a tiny wisp of smoke, and put the match in the ashtray.

He stepped out of the truck and grinned at me, his pipe between his teeth on the right side of his mouth.

"I thought you might be needing some help." He leaned into the truck and pulled out his hammer. "I just finished chores and was getting bored, so I thought I'd come check on you." He spent that afternoon and the next day helping me place all of the rafters, graciously donating all of his precious time between the day's chores. I learned an important lesson about homesteading that day: Interdependence trumps independence.

I eventually finished that first barn. It worked well enough that winter just with a roof, walls on the second floor, and tarps for walls on the lower floor. We were ecstatic to have a place to put the tools that didn't fit in the outhouse and to store our growing accumulation of recycled windows, doors, wood, and other construction materials.

If I were ever to build a homestead from scratch again (and I'm not sure I have the energy to do it another time—not while holding down a job), I would first build a tool shed or barn before I did anything else. Not having a place to store tools and materials is inefficient at best. Sleeping with tools stashed under one's bed doesn't necessarily make a lot of sense, either. We reveled in the versatility and utility of our new barn, and each year it took on new uses, with the upper level eventually becoming a studio for our guests and apprentices, but that wasn't until we later built a second barn, as our homestead began to morph into a small, diversified farm.

However, I could not have built anything on our homestead had I not been wise enough to leave college with a philosophy degree in immediate search of some practical skills, preferably involving tools, wood, and mountains.

It's not that I left college with no tools. Philosophy is a tool. Sharp-edged, precision-oriented, form-giving, it puts edges on the world and mortises the intersection of *would* and *should* with pegs of reasonable certainty and seasoned stability. And if homesteading depends upon rethinking and reshaping the existing constructs with which we have framed our culture, then some training in how to think about a disciplined reconstruction of our current paradigm of ecological excesses can be pretty useful.

"No ideas but in things." That's how William Carlos Williams described the poet's task. Avoid the ambiguity of the esoteric; link ideas to physical realities. Philosophy degree in hand, I left college in 1985 feeling the need to see ideas become things. In my mind, getting a handle on tools was the first step . . . it was only years later that I discovered one of the most challenging aspects in the evolution of toolmaking was just that—figuring out how to attach a handle that would last.

Once again, I was looking for stolen lessons for building a practical life. I just wasn't sure who was willing to be the victim of such a painful larceny. Unfortunately for that person—whoever it was—I was starting pretty much from scratch.

I could hear the throaty roar of the old Jeep truck pushing its way up the hill, its tires catching on the gravelly road. A few of the summer staff had arrived at church camp early to help set up for the coming flood of staff and campers. We had all unloaded our gear in our cabins and were chatting with Bart, the preacher partially disguised as camp director, in the shade of the pavilion. We were already feeling the intensifying humidity that seemed to wedge its way tightly into every cove and valley of the Southern Appalachians.

The familiar blue Jeep from my days as a camper rumbled its way to the edge of the pavilion and stopped, and an enormous arm leaning on the open window raised up slowly to give us a gentle wave. The door opened with a metallic screech, and out stepped a figure that made the cab of the truck seem undersized.

"C'mon over and introduce yourself to the crowd, Dennis," the camp director shouted. "Folks, this is Dennis, the camp's Ranger. If it needs to be fixed or built, he does it."

Dennis was wearing what I later learned was more or less his uniform—a white tank-top T-shirt and blue jeans and a timid if not mischievous smile. I couldn't believe just how solid he was—he reminded me of the pictures I'd seen of the enormous chestnut trees that had dominated these mountains decades earlier. His forearms were as thick as my thighs, and I ambivalently went to shake his enormous hand, not sure whether it would crush mine. Instead, Dennis shyly offered his huge hand and gave me a firm but gentle squeeze, complemented with a warm "Good to meetcha." His size wasn't just my fanciful first impression—I later learned that he'd once been chaining down a load of logs when one rolled off the top of the log truck and hit him on the head and shoulder. It didn't even put him all the way to the ground, and he continued to work the rest of the day, albeit with a terrible headache.

If Dennis even bothered to size me up during our brief handshake, he didn't betray it—and it wouldn't have taken him long anyway. He headed straight for Bart, the director, to see what tasks he needed to put us on in order to prepare for the opening of camp later that week. Dennis had enough experience with college kids to know that there was energy to harness, but not a lot of know-how, so the tasks had to be geared to getting the grunt work done. We were most skilled at moving stuff around and perhaps elementary cleaning. Otherwise, our college educations hadn't advanced us to the degree of being overly helpful, even though we were all hoping the week would be filled with hammers, nails, and power tools—not tarps, tables, push-brooms, mops, and toilet brushes.

The next few days were a flurry of activity, with our reckless energy channeled by Dennis's methodical checklist approach to getting buildings, bathrooms, and campsites ready for the coming flood of campers. None of us made it to breakfast with more than ten or fifteen minutes to spare, but we all ran to the dining hall at the clanging of the noon bell. It was there that I first met Dennis's wife, Bobbie, the cook. Bobbie was a hands-on-hips disciplinarian—she expected order and she gave orders, and once I met her father, Bob, a navy man, it was clear where she was coming from. Even Dennis jumped to it when she distinguished between how things were and how they needed to be, and she didn't take crap from anyone. But Bobbie had a soft spot that wasn't hard to find. She was out to set things right in the world, but she also didn't mind when things got a bit out of kilter, particularly for people she found troublesome. The glimmer in her eye would grow until it seeped into a smile and then into peals of laughter—and then it was back to setting things straight.

Dennis would tip the cart on purpose whenever he had a chance, usually by yelling "Snake!" at opportune moments, sending Bobbie into an utter fluster. There were simply too many copperheads and rattlers around for Dennis's warnings not to be a distinct possibility. Once it became clear that Dennis was the real snake in the grass, he would get a volley of well-aimed punches from Bobbie, who could clearly hold her own. It looked like the Appalachian version of a Swedish massage, with Dennis's face feigning intimidation under the cover of his massive arms and his bare shoulders and arms showing the red points of impact. Sometimes, he would make up some story that he knew would get Bobbie riled to the point of loosing a colorful stream of mumbled curse words that echoed through the church camp kitchen—with Dennis revealing the truth only after she'd had a cathartic release that no one appreciated more than him or her father Bob. It was just too much fun watching the person clearly in charge and in control lose her composure, even for a few seconds.

Although I had come back to the camp to be a counselor, as I had dreamed of doing ever since my first summer as a young camper, I realized after only a few days that I was jealous of Jim, the college student hired to work with Dennis as an assistant for the summer. Dennis was the teacher I'd never had in my formal education, and he could do all the things that I was beginning to see as so important to becoming the self-reliant homesteader I wanted to be. Dennis could fix or make anything he wanted, it seemed. He was the perfect camp "Ranger," as he called himself. He was a carpenter, plumber, mechanic, electrician, mason, excavator, logger—if it needed to be done, he did it. If he didn't know how, he knew who to ask. And then he would try it on his own.

By the end of the summer, I'd seen just how much Dennis knew and how much I didn't know, and I'd found out how much I enjoyed Bobbie's cooking and the way she served up the truth for anybody that needed a good helping of it. With trepidation, mostly at the possibility of being refused, I asked Dennis if he thought the Ranger could maybe use an assistant for the next year. Normally, the camp shut down in late fall and only the director and the Ranger stuck around, but the camp was in growth mode, and there were a lot of construction projects that needed to happen. I figured if there was ever a chance to learn the basics of what I needed to know, it was with Dennis.

Despite what was probably his better judgment, Dennis not only backed up my request but also somehow got Bobbie to agree to give me their extra bedroom, with the agreement that I would contribute toward groceries. After years of working with students as farm and homestead interns, I realize now more than ever just how patient Bobbie and Dennis were, taking in a total greenhorn and sharing their lives and their table with me for nearly a year—one of the best years of my life. I couldn't run a circular saw, chainsaw, or tractor, and I wasn't much more experienced with a hammer or a level. Most of my education had been someone telling me something. Not much of it had been someone showing me how to do it, much less doing it with me to ensure that I understood the subtleties of doing it the right way—and then expecting me to do it on my own, with decent results and without breaking anything.

Dennis was always overly conscious about what he considered to be his lack of education, but as far as I was concerned he knew everything I needed to know, plus some—and a lot more than I could learn in a year. He got the basics from his school days, but his real education happened in the woods—logging and building and living off the land with his dad, a man who went from logging the precarious slopes and ravines of western North Carolina with horses to the modern era of skidders and dozers. Dennis had logged with his dad and his two brothers until the woods just got too small to hold them all and Dennis wanted a change of pace with a variety of challenges. The camp Ranger job fit the bill perfectly.

We would start each day with Bobbie's hearty breakfast, working through the priorities and Dennis's off-the-cuff problem-solving, ranging from engine repair to building design. I was amazed at what coffee, bacon, biscuits, redeye gravy, and country music could do for bringing clarity to the day. By the time we were done with breakfast, I could hardly wait to get started.

I'd done well in school and always enjoyed "book-learnin'," but working with Dennis meant that each day had a real conclusion, with the possibility that something was better than it had been when the day started. Success was measured in just how tangible those results were, so it took me a while to understand and appreciate that a few hours of head-scratching before diving headlong into a project meant that we did things right the first time and we only had to run to the lumberyard once.

Bobbie's coffee and my young hormones made it tough for me to sit still while I tried to follow Dennis's step-by-step logic as to how best to deal with the situation at hand, but I soon learned the costs of not conceptualizing a project all the way through to its end, with a detailed understanding of the feasibility and practicality of each necessary step. He combined his knowledge of tools, machinery, materials, physics, aesthetics, and local experts to figure out any given project or problem. Dennis always felt that the end product was a direct representation of his skills, so while his style was gentle, his standards were always high.

Bart, the camp director, was forever throwing some dilemma or fanciful construction project at Dennis—usually at the risk of having Bobbie hurl a frying pan at Bart's head for his poor timing or prioritization. I would watch Dennis work for days or even weeks trying to figure out how to tackle the project at hand, often waking up in the middle of the night with the answer. He hated coming to the end of the day without a solution for whatever he was working on, and while he was in his monster La-Z-Boy chair with his big feet up watching TV with his three-year-old daughter Lindsay in his lap, he would be problem-solving in his head while we were all distracted with the blue-blare coming from the tube. "Philip, I think I finally got it figured out!" he would say, just before going to bed or as we dove into breakfast the next morning. He would sketch out the solution and then put everyone to work getting together the needed supplies and equipment. Dennis's whole way of tackling a project was an enduring lesson in how to do whatever needed to be done, even if it seemed impossible.

Bart came by at breakfast one morning—inappropriate and intrusive timing in Bobbie's mind. I could tell by the way she bit the right side of her lower lip and tightened her grip on the cast-iron frying pan holding the redeye gravy. Maybe she thought the piping-hot gravy was more than Bart deserved, but she didn't seem to be too reticent about threatening with a frying pan when need be. Bart sort of knocked, but while on his way through the door—a real pet peeve of Bobbie's—and his overly enthusiastic "Good morning, boys—oh, and hi, Bobbie!" was a sign of another overnight revelation that the good Lord must have bestowed upon him. We looked at him like the Israelites must have done when

Moses came down from the mountain, but with more suspicion and a bit less respect. "So Dennis, I've got a project for you!"

"Oh no, now what, Bart?" Bobbie rumbled from the stove. "He's already rebuilt the whole camp for you. Now what do you want?"

Choosing to pretend he didn't hear, Bart continued. "Dennis, I had a great idea last night at 2 AM: I want you to build a fire tower on the top of the mountain back of camp. I think it should have two decks big enough so that we can have a whole group sleep out on it!"

Bart must have assumed that the pall of disbelief that immediately settled over the room came from our concern for the kids' safety, not the status of his own mental health. "Well, of course you'll need to build railings so that they can't roll off in their sleep—not even the kids we'd just as soon lose."

Dennis put his hand around pretty much the whole coffee mug, looking into its untapped reserve. "When you thinkin' we oughta do this by, Bart?"

"Oh, I thought we could have it ready for this next summer," Bart replied. I heard Bobbie's frying pan drop to the burner. I was quickly learning that part of being in the construction trade is that one person's whimsy fast becomes another person's burden.

"Well, building a fire tower ain't no real problem, Bart. But how do you want to get all of the building materials up there? Helicopter?"

"That's why you're the Ranger and I'm just the camp director. I just get to deliver the midnight revelations as they come to me." Bart started making his way back to the door. "I know you'll figure something out. You always do. Well, sorry to interrupt—I got to get up the hill to meet somebody." The spring on the screen door squeaked as Bart edged out and disappeared with a cursory wave, the screen door slapping shut as if to fill the void of our disbelief at how little prophets have to do with what actually happens.

"The nerve!" Bobbie exclaimed. "Coming in here, interrupting my breakfast, and putting this crazy-ass project on your plate before eight o'clock! Why, that son-of-a- . . ."

". . . -biscuit eater," Dennis interjected, putting his enormous hands over Lindsay's tender ears, winking at me. "Awww, c'mon, Bobbie, he just came in before work because he smelled your redeye gravy cookin' from down the road, and he was hopin' for some biscuits. And you didn't even give him none! You should be ashamed!"

"I just about gave him some—right up the side of his head," said Bobbie, shaking her frying pan. "It'd be the first time anything good went through his brain! And if you're not careful, you'll get what he deserves, just 'cause I'm ready to serve it up to somebody!"

Dennis's eyes twinkled. He picked up another biscuit and split it open, dampening the steam coming out with some butter that melted right away. "Philip, pass me the 'lasses, please."

"You want mo'lasses or less 'lasses, Dennis?" Just as molasses was a staple on Bobbie's table, that joke was a staple in our morning breakfast routine.

"I need mo'lasses today—none of that diet stuff. We got some figurin' to do."

It wasn't long before Dennis had hatched a plan. He ordered telephone poles, lumber, and all of the necessary hardware and began packaging it all in bundles. He scouted out a path for his brother Gary to pull all of the materials up the mountain with his skidder, and we began clearing the path and finally the site for tower itself. We cursed Bart's crazy ideas as we parked the truck at the farthest point we could get it up the mountain every day, dragging the chainsaws and other equipment up the hill. But whenever we reached the top, we took in the view with a reverence deeper than any I found in the Bible studies down the hill. The waves and troughs of the Appalachians stretched as far as we could see, and the idea of getting a vista from above the treetops fired our enthusiasm for the job. "There's times I dream of driving an eighteen-wheeler all over this country with Bobbie just to see more of it," Dennis said one day. "But I sure know why I love callin' these mountains home."

For days, we cut our way through the thickets of rhododendron and mountain laurel, following the flagging from our initial mapping of the road, until we were finally ready to have Gary come with the skidder and pull up the supplies. Dennis set me and Dale, Bart's son, to digging the four holes for the telephone poles. We dug and pried rocks until the handles of the shovels and posthole diggers were too short to get out any more dirt and rock. Gary came the next day, and we bundled up the telephone poles behind the skidder. I'd never been that close to a skidder in action, and the roar of the diesel engine and its ability to negotiate its way through the steep terrain thrilled me. I was seeing human ingenuity in action, with Dennis leading the way.

Dennis and Gary devised a brilliant method of using chains, pulleys, and the skidder cable for raising the telephone poles into a near-vertical position in order to get them positioned and into their respective holes. Then the chainsaw carpentry began, and I watched Dennis use his ornery yellow-and-black McCulloch chainsaw to do things that its engineers had probably not imagined it could. The way he used it, its whine reminded me of a nest of angry yellow jackets.

We built mini platforms on each pole for cutting notches for the frame of the first-floor deck and then proceeded to build that deck. Once we had a full deck and a hole for the stairway, we heightened the risk by building the notch-cutting platforms as high as we could go. Dale and I squelched our fears by challenging each other to a notch-cutting contest— two poles each. We took turns creeping up the aluminum ladder to the cutting platforms, lashing ourselves to the poles, and nervously yanking the cord on the chainsaw while balanced on a tiny plank. The sensation of cutting those notches above the treetops was about as terrified as I ever want to be. But Dennis had thought through every stage and step of the process. Within a few weeks, his ingenuity had reached new heights, and I was convinced that anything could be built with enough experience, cleverness, and determination.

Dennis was proud of his work, but he was also humble, and one thing he conveyed to me over and over again was that you earn your way into any job. He wouldn't let me or Dale use a tool until he was sure that we understood its nuances and approached it with respect. His shop was his kingdom, and no one used it or his equipment without his permission. He was passing on what he had learned in growing up—jobs in the trades are to be earned, not given. Education was incremental and based on repetition and humility.

Dennis mixed humility and humor in equal doses, convinced I think that a good laugh was a healthy reminder of one's limitations and place in the experiential pecking order. One day he was showing me how to install a toilet in one of the camp buildings. We got the toilet properly seated in the floor and hooked up the water line. He sent me under the building to check on the exit drain and told me to look up the pipe where he was holding a flashlight to make sure there were no obstructions. "Nope, it looks good, Dennis!"

"Check again, son . . . I think there's something blocking it."

I peeked into the pipe again, only to hear the flush come too fast for me to move out of the way. He'd sent me another reminder.

Reminders can, however, come with retributions, and I did devise a way to remind him who the real boss was. I found a *Playboy* magazine hidden in one of the cabins when I was cleaning, so I took it back to the house. I asked Bobbie if she was game to stick the magazine under Dennis's side of the bed and then "find it" that night when she was adjusting the covers before she and Dennis went to bed. Bobbie heartily agreed.

That evening, I watched Dennis come barreling out of the bedroom, covering his head with his hands, with Bobbie in fast pursuit, pummeling his back with the base of her fists, magazine in hand. "You filthy son of a gun, I never expected my Ranger to bring this kind of trash into my house!"

"But, Bobbie, honey, I never . . ."

"You don't 'Bobbie-honey' me when I'm finding stuff like this in my house!" She whacked him over the head good and chased him into his chair in the living room.

I don't think I ever did 'fess up.

Any good building that I've done on our homestead is built on the foundation that Dennis so generously provided, combined with the constant artistic perspective provided by Erin. Like me, Erin found her college art experience more about ideas than things, with the homestead allowing both of us to convert abstract into concrete, wood into did, and see into saw.

Fortunately for me, Erin sees things in pictures and has an amazing aptitude for turning any of my one-dimensional concepts into three-dimensional realities. She also sees humans as organisms of habits, and when a building doesn't match with those habits to maximize practicality and efficiency, she gets frustrated. As we observed the seasonal cycles of the land around us—water, ice, mud, sun, shade, vegetation, wildlife behaviors, and livestock preferences—we began to configure an evolving plan of where and what to build.

Following my time with Dennis, I had plied my skills as a carpenter throughout the years, learning how to build at the expense of others—highly recommended for the apprentice but perhaps less desirable for the homeowner, except for the low labor costs. In much the same vein, Erin had shifted her college art studies from her strong background in drawing to a newfound interest in sculpture, giving her several years to concentrate on form and function.

We began to find ways to integrate our skills without too much conflict. When conflict did arise, it was generally because I was thinking of a structure from a macro level, and she was deep into the nitty-gritty of how the buildings were going to serve their purpose. That meant that I needed to slow down and refine the plans . . . plans that were more often than not in my head and not on paper—a source of frustration for an artist who also happened to be the daughter of a civil engineer.

I'd known one friend whose marriage ended in divorce due to the stress of designing and building a house together. Neither of us wanted that to happen. As it turned out, we had a lot more building to do together.

EIGHT

Of Scale and Skill:
Homestead or Farm?

"What's all of this broken glass around the coop?" I asked, reaching inside the coop to grab one of the beautifully patterned Barred Rock chickens.

"Oh, that's to keep out the coons," he said. I don't remember the fellow's name, but it's probably just as well, given the number of times I've passed on the stories of his peculiar misadventures. "I just broke up all of the bottles and jars we had in a big trash can and scattered all of the glass around the coop, hoping the coons would cut their feet if they tried to get any more chickens."

The five hens and two roosters sat on their perch, preening their perfectly patterned black-and-white feathers—the barred appearance from which they got their name. One of the roosters cocked his head slightly to the side and gave us a hard look, signaling what I took to be a certain skepticism on his part. Maybe it was the fact that it was early afternoon and he was watching the New Jersey transplant—still in his pajamas and slippers—trying not to step in the multicolored Maginot line of his own creation.

I wasn't completely sure whether the rooster was more skeptical of the method of protection or the originator of the idea. I was still trying to decide myself, although I suspected that the coons had already made up their minds. I laughed to myself, imagining the coons' chattering transformed into a dialogue in which the humans assume the role of hapless wayfarers, finding their way into the woods but not out. I suspected that the coons had a distinct home-field advantage in this case.

I was unsure whether I was seeing an isolated case of poor judgment or a mismatch of mentality and geography, but I probably would have made up my mind more quickly had I been more a part of the local gossip circle. I hadn't yet heard the story of the time when this man's wife had graciously cleaned out the ashes of the woodstove—into a card-board box—and set the box out on the wraparound deck of the house. The smell of smoke alerted the handyman who happened to be there that day, but not until there was a perfectly rectangular hole in the deck, outlined by a charred perimeter, with smoke drifting up from the ashes and embers now scattered safely on the ground.

Nor had I heard about how the husband had somehow leapt from the bank of their pond onto a partially submerged rock a few feet away in order to see the fish—only to slip on the rock and break his leg. Flatlander errors in judgment have long been of significant entertainment value in a land with poor television reception and minimal cable connections.

Despite their penchant for comical mishaps, these flatlanders were generous, and they'd invited Erin and me to take their chickens since the adult version of the fowl didn't take to their grandchildren as well as the juvenile form of cute and cuddly chicks. As we finished loading the chickens into the capped rear of our truck and slammed the door tight before any of them escaped, the wife asked if we might want to take a pig the next year if they bought a piglet for the grandkids to play with during the summer, before it got too big.

I took off my baseball cap and scratched my head. "Well, let's see how this goes first. We're getting a bit of a menagerie up at our place—steers, cats, chickens." I slapped my cap back on. "But being a southerner, I sure do like bacon and barbeque!"

They both shot me a disapproving glance, and I didn't have to look at Erin to know that she was giving me a similar look. She wasn't eager for us to start deviating from a vegetarian diet. She'd found herself eating too much meat in college, and it didn't jibe with her concerns about the factory farming of animals—or mine, for that matter. I'd seen the transformation of the eastern North Carolina landscape from farms to production units for poultry and swine. Farmers had traded independence for contracts and barns for animal warehouses. The animals obviously hadn't been consulted in the negotiations, and they were usually the ones that ultimately suffered the most.

If I had any doubts about how real the consequences were, they were shoved aside by two bulldozers near Rose Hill, North Carolina, several years prior. I rode shotgun for the delivery of a not-so-valuable tractor-trailer load of wine grapes to Duplin Winery, an operation that my grandfather had supported in its start-up phase some years earlier. With no real threat of being held up by anything other than traffic, I let down my guard and savored the steady course of tales that the truck driver, Shufford, told for the entire distance.

When we arrived at the winery, I ran in to ask where we should take the grapes. The owner of the winery pointed out the scales that they used just down the road, so Shufford drove us to the scales, where we pulled in behind another tractor-trailer. I looked at the trailer and couldn't figure out what it was carrying. "What's he got in there, Shufford, stumps?"

Shufford peered through the windshield. "I don't know—is that what those things sticking out of the top of the trailer are?"

I looked again. The stump roots had hooves.

"Shufford, those aren't stumps—those are hogs! Oh man—they're bloated!"

"Well, that explains all the damn flies comin' in here! Roll up your window, and I'll get the AC goin' again."

We watched as the tractor trailer in front of us puffed a quick cloud of exhaust and rumbled forward. We pulled up farther and onto the scales, while the other truck slowly made its way to the huge factory in front of us. As we waited for our weight ticket, we followed the progress of the truck, which had backed onto a ramp of sorts. The driver stepped out of the truck and checked to ensure that the rear of the truck was properly secured. As the driver stepped away, the front of the truck began to lift, pushed smoothly and steadily with the force of an enormous hydraulic cylinder underneath, its steel piston slowly unsheathing at an increasingly vertical angle.

No one was behind us, so we idled. We watched in disbelief as bloated hog carcasses tumbled out the back of the truck and down an enormous concrete ramp. As the velocity of cascading hog carcasses increased, two bulldozers appeared from either side of the ramp and began pushing them into what we assumed was the equivalent of an industrial cauldron. It was then that we saw the sign for the factory that owned the scales we were using. These far-from-little piggies were headed for market—as pet food. The issue for me was not the pet food—it was the scale of production.

Several months later, the dam on a hog lagoon in eastern North Carolina burst, releasing 25 million gallons of hog waste into the New River, killing an estimated 10 million fish and closing 364,000 acres of coastal wetlands to shellfishing.[1] Then, in 1999, Hurricane Floyd hit eastern North Carolina, and the torrential rains that inundated the region contaminated the Neuse River basin with manure and carcasses from hog and poultry farms, wreaking havoc on the river's ecosystem all the way to its outflow into the Atlantic Ocean. Ecologists are still researching the long-term impacts of the pollution resulting from these weather-related events.

Not only did Erin and I struggle with the environmental impacts and animal welfare conditions created by industrial animal agriculture across eastern North Carolina, but my grandparents' farm was just one town down the road from the tragic fire in a poultry processing plant in Hamlet, North Carolina, where the emergency fire exit door had been chained shut, purportedly to prevent workers from smuggling out chickens. When the conflagration broke out on September 3, 1991, twenty-five workers were burned to death and fifty-six were severely injured because there was no way out.[2] Despite our preference for a diet that included meat, we simply couldn't justify the costs we were seeing for animals, humans, or the environment with the usual methods involved in large-scale animal agriculture. I'm not sure we realized just how long and complex our food journey would be, as we tried to reconcile our tastes with an unsavory menu of ethical choices. But having eggs from our own free-range chickens seemed like a source of animal protein that we could justify without any real qualms.

With promises to take good care of their chickens, Erin and I took our free flock home. I certainly overdid it on the coop construction, building an insulated, coon-proof structure that virtually guaranteed that any demise of our chickens would stem from either negligence or hunger on our part, not hunger on the part of the wild residents of our neighborhood. I was more concerned about making the coop weatherproof and critter-proof than I was about providing adequate ventilation, but the chickens seemed rather forgiving. Once we'd habituated them to the coop for three days and let them out to forage with no glass-lined chicken wire barriers, they felt right at home—too much so, as it turned out. They showed up on the mudroom steps, begging for food, and they pecked away at the silver coating of the TekFoil barrier that we'd installed on the bottom of the cabin floor joists to help keep out drafts and rodents.

The fresh eggs made it worth all the trouble, however, and we began surprising our guests with the stunningly orange yolks and viscous egg whites of our free-ranging feathered friends. We began to wonder

whether there might not be a market for eggs that were so visibly superior to the ones we'd both grown up with.

We'd started to think increasingly about markets and what we were aiming for with our homesteading. Self-sufficiency, independence, market gardening, diversified livestock production, cottage industries, craft and art—all of our accumulated notions of what it meant to homestead and to farm swirled around in our heads and our conversations. Sometimes the various possibilities interlocked, and at other times it was clear that they were in direct competition with one another.

While there is certainly a homesteading tradition in the United States, it tends to have a long history on the outer edges of our culture. And in our current era, it is seldom a tradition passed directly from parent to child. Most of us enter the homesteading world not as a continuation of the lifestyle that we grew up with, but through a rejection of the tenets of a culture of excess that surrounds us. We frame our homestead musings with expectations of creating an oasis of homegrown food, self-made shelter, independent power, the power of independence, and the resulting outcomes as income. It is a place we imagine will buffer us from the buffeting winds and whimsy of a reckless and wreck-filled economy, sheltered because we take the time to question—and moderate our participation accordingly.

So it is that we homesteaders—whether in the country, suburbs, or city—begin to ponder whether to use accumulated knowledge, skills, and the homestead's resources simply to provide for our own needs or also to generate income. Quite often, the distilled question becomes whether to homestead or to farm. But at that point, one begins to wonder what the difference between homesteading and farming actually is. And why leap from one to the other?

In many ways, the difference is a question of scale and skill—not to mention an effort to exchange natural capital for our more common currency. Ultimately, I tend to think that it is wise for new farmers to bud from homesteaders, market gardeners to stem from home gardeners, and artisan producers to grow from kitchen experimenters. Even new cattle farmers might be wise to draft their management strategies from experience as ox teamsters, learning how animal behavior and handling techniques should blend. In all of these cases, risk is minimized, education is maximized, and occasional *Aha!* moments can supplant a torrent of *Oh no!* scenarios.

Scale and skill can be crafted on the homestead, incrementally and strategically. Ideally, a homestead is a playful place, an anchorage where ideas are tested and the results are harvested. It's a place to temper theory in the forge of reality, with a minimal risk of getting burned too badly. If we were more assiduous in testing, documenting, and sharing our individual homestead experiments, homesteads could perhaps play a much more effective role in helping us push against the edges of several exciting frontiers—in farming, renewable energy, home economics, and shelter design. In fact, the real frontiers that most need such playful experimentation are our suburbs and our cities. It's quite possible that the visibility of such experiments in those environments generates more conversation and collaboration than is the case for those of us out in the boonies.

Playfulness is seldom cited as the key virtue in homesteading, although authors like Rebecca Gould, Lynn Miller, and Gene Logsdon have acknowledged its importance in different ways. For me, it is the dreaming and the innocent experimentation on the homestead that leads not only to innovation, but also to a deep sense of self-satisfaction. Conjuring, conniving, concocting, confabulating, considering, constructing. Such innovation not only cultivates and satisfies an innate curiosity that we all have, but also spurs on the curiosity of others . . . neighbors, students, and, perhaps most important, our children. Ultimately, it generates an engaged, creative life.

While curiosity may be innate, it is also easily squelched. Often a somewhat latent trait once we enter school age, it can quickly dissolve into a recessive trait. In our middle- and upper-class circles, it is constantly suppressed by an economy that insists upon manufacturing and marketing a product that meets our every need and whim. It is certainly not sparked in cookie-cutter suburbs or box-cutter inner-city neighborhoods. Even one homestead in either of these environments can transform a community filled with unwitting acceptance and ennui into an engaged group of inquirers and innovators, exchanging ideas, seeds, and recipes instead of just muted greetings.

I know of no better example of such a venture than that of Will Allen's Growing Power model, in which he and his collaborators work to establish food production centers featuring greenhouses chock-full of nutritious vegetables, fish production in large tanks, and vermiculture composting—all within inner-city districts "red-lined" by grocery chains that refuse to place their stores in these challenged areas. Such playful innovation is contagious and inspirational.[3]

Playfulness is, of course, tied to joy. A homestead can be a forlorn environment in which all joy is sacrificed to financial, ethical, or religious austerity. Or it can be a place where seeds, hammers, chickens, and solar panels tempt and tease and novelty is self-created. We humans are not at a point at which cultural and technological stasis is acceptable or even feasible, and it is doubtful that much of the critically needed innovation is going to occur in the labs, factories, or boardrooms of most profit-centered corporations, simply because profit and progress are too tightly aligned—both have to be too immediate to be far reaching in their beneficence.

One could argue that the level of skill and the intensity of scale needed on a homestead are perhaps less than what one might need to run a successful farming operation. Whether that gross generalization is true or not, it does seem true that homesteading can foster and accommodate genuine playfulness a bit more easily than farming can. Farming is serious business, one that I find both to be playful and to require playfulness—and yet the consequences of errors in judgment are much more significant than most mistakes that a person might make in homesteading. Not only are larger economic ramifications involved in farming, but the increase in scale also means that the environmental impacts of one's mistakes are often more serious . . . in nature.

A homestead's household economy—even if the budget is tight—is relatively elastic. Most choices do not involve particularly large sums of money or even substantial tracts of land. Small experiments may yield small errors but big lessons. In farming, even a small experiment can yield a large error, and the lesson can be overwhelming, if not numbing. The homestead is a place for experimentation, innovation, and discovery. The farm should also be a place for discovery, but it is often constrained by the economic implications of miscalculations and mishaps. Since a farm is often reliant upon infrastructure and a certain level of scale and skill, once a path is chosen it becomes much harder to deviate from it than when an idea is attempted on a homestead level.

Another advantage of pursuing a project as a homesteader first and perhaps as a farmer later is that one can safely dabble on the homestead, trying out new things to find out which ones fit the lifestyle, the landscape, market realities, the necessary learning curve, and of course the family budget. Just as playfulness is underrated as serious business on the homestead, so, too, is enjoyment often ignored by potential farmers. What is not enjoyed on the homestead will certainly not be enjoyed as a farming venture. But perhaps more subtly, what one enjoys on the homestead level may not be savored to the same degree by the more intense involvement required by farming.

We've learned several lessons in this regard on our homestead. After experimenting with our first small flock of chickens, rescued from their moat of variegated glass, we discovered a love of keeping a colorful array of rare-breed layers. Over the years, we've grown our flock and our customers to the point that we regularly keep fifty to seventy-five layers in a mobile coop, providing eggs for Mach's General Store in town and fertilizer for converting our woodland edges into pasture. At first, a previous owner of the store had no interest in carrying our eggs, but after we convinced him to allow us a trial run, he quickly converted his negative inclination into entrepreneurial enthusiasm: The eggs began to sell out nearly as fast as we could deliver them. Before long, we'd driven the Organic Valley eggs off the shelves during the laying season, and the old-timers were buying them almost as quickly as the newcomers.

"You the guy with those runaway chickens?" one regular at Mach's once asked me as I went back to the cooler with a crate of eggs.

"Yeah, we're the ones with the free-range eggs," I smiled, gently correcting him.

"Yup, they're just like the eggs I grew up on. Only difference is we didn't call those chickens 'free-runnin'—we called 'em 'fox food.'"

In contrast, I have always loved goats—or at least I thought I did. Maybe it was the frequent sight of a farmer in the Alps going high up into the mountains with his goats, drawing in the whole herd with a simple call, regularly offering them grain out of a leather pouch tied to his belt as bait. Regardless of my imagined love, it warranted some experimentation, so when we were offered two free goats soon after I'd finished building the barn, we took them with no hesitation. Within a week, we had two new members of the homestead—Heidi, an Alpine, and Stubby, a near-earless LaMancha. Within a few months, the areas too brushy for Pet and Troll to appreciate were in obvious retreat, thanks to the complementary diets of the grazers and the browsers.

Nonetheless, I quickly made an unsettling discovery: Heidi and Stubby apparently knew more about fencing than I did. And they seemed to understand that our little solar-powered electric fence didn't have adequate zap much of the time, but particularly in the morning after a night of declining battery power. Several cloudy days in a row meant that they had full reign of the place, so I reverted to the earlier colonial method of worrying less about fencing animals in and concentrating instead on fencing them out. The fence around the garden grew to include a fence around the new orchard, and then I needed to build a fence around the cabin and its array of flowers and tender ornamentals.

Heidi and Stubby certainly expanded the perimeter of our clearing, and they did provide ample entertainment, accompanying us on hikes up the nearby mountaintops and climbing atop any object they could find that would increase their stature to the level that they deemed appropriate. After several years of inciting certain moments of marital discord due to their utter disregard for fences and their love for carefully tended plants, they both eventually died timely—and natural—deaths.

I was discovering a new appreciation for animals less intelligent than myself (on a good day) and a low tolerance for critters that needed more strands of fence than I had fingers on one hand. Single-strand bovines increasingly seemed to fit my view of the perfect livestock, although I wasn't sure that the constant training and working of oxen quite fit our hectic lifestyle at the time. Milk cows were certainly no less work than oxen, but the gratification was more immediate and, in our case, the utility began to seem higher.

NINE

The End of Petrol

Since acquiring Pet and Troll when they were a few weeks old, I had added my graduate studies to the bulk of my responsibilities, and I was feeling the burden. Meanwhile, Pet and Troll had added substantially to their own bulk—to the tune of about a ton apiece. Their gain in weight was, unfortunately, not commensurate with their gain in utility, other than their ability to open up and fertilize our meager pastures. Their inefficiency was directly correlated to my lack of time in training them, and Troll eventually began to take his name seriously, perhaps because the crimping of his testicular cords hadn't sufficiently halted the flow of testosterone to his body or his head. He bulked up much faster than Pet, and he became headstrong in a way that was unsettling for a skinny guy less than one-tenth his size. After I narrowly escaped becoming a wall ornament in his stall as a result of our disagreement about who was actually boss and who was merely *Bos* (in today's economy, capitalization often matters), I decided that it was time for him to go.

Of course, he was never more docile and in control than in our last walk down Tunket Road together. I didn't even have to hold the halter. He paid attention to the gentle direction of my goad, and as tears streamed down my face, I couldn't decide whether he was opting for a grand finale that would make me eternally regret my decision to send him to slaughter or whether he was playing upon my sympathy, in the hope that we would reverse course.

We got to the bottom of the road, and Troll stood calmly beside me, chewing his cud, ears twitching and head occasionally dipping and shaking to get rid of the flies that had appeared as we neared the Waites' barn and the hot sun. As I stroked him and brushed away the flies, I couldn't reconcile my mixed emotions. There was a sense of relief in finally having made what I was sure was the right decision, given how temperamental he was becoming, not just with me but also with Erin. Yet there was a sense that I had somehow failed him and my dream—

the dream team. To make it worse, I could hear Pet bellowing from the barn, where I'd left him hooked to prevent him from following us down the road.

After about ten minutes of choking back tears, I heard the jarring metal clangs signaling the arrival of a diesel truck pulling a livestock trailer. I tried to dismantle my emotions and put on a wizened farmer's expression, stoic and experienced in the realities of pragmatic choices.

The driver saw me standing by the mailbox, Troll's razor-straight back even with my shoulders. I saw him shake his head a bit and smile ever so slightly—knowingly, perhaps. I was sure he had delivered hard choices to their quick conclusion more times than I could imagine.

He pulled just past us and then backed up partway up Tunket Road, to a narrow point in the road that provided a confined entrance into this trailer once both rear doors were opened.

He got out, looked at Troll with a suspicious eye probably born of experience. "Nice-lookin' animal you got there. Think he'll load okay?"

"Yeah, I think so. He's pretty well behaved—except when he's not. That's why he's going with you."

"I see." He tossed in a few flakes of alfalfa-filled hay that I'd dropped off at the loading spot earlier with the intention of using them for bait to encourage Troll into the trailer. "How 'bout you trying to load him first by yourself, without me upsetting him. If that doesn't work, we'll both get him on."

"Makes sense to me." I was still doing my best to hold the tears. "Troll, get up."

Troll stepped forward, a model of discipline, tempting me to call it all a mistake and walk him back up the hill. But there had been too many close calls in his challenging both me and Erin, so I knew it was the right but hard decision. *Right hard, all right,* I thought, checking the tension of the rope on his nose, in case I needed to pull him into the trailer.

Troll walked straight up to the trailer, put his right front foot up, then heaved his heft with the left and got it in. Before I knew it, he had leapt up and in with his back legs, and he proceeded into the trailer, with me in tow, holding on to the halter. He stopped as he got toward the front of the trailer. He ducked his head to let me remove the halter and looked at me questioningly, but with a hint of defiance.

I gave him a last loving stroke under the chin and on his brisket and jumped out of the trailer.

The driver shook his head. "I don't think I've ever seen it go that easy. You must have him really well trained."

"Not well enough. That's why he's going with you." I looked down, hoping the emotion wouldn't seep through. I kicked a rock out of the crown of the road. "Or maybe it's me that's not trained well enough. I dunno."

"Well, better takin' him out of here in this"—thumping on the side of the trailer to emphasize his point—"than takin' you out of here in an ambulance."

"I guess you're right." At best, I was only half convinced.

Noting my lack of conviction, the driver decided it was best to go before I changed my mind. He walked to the cab of a truck and tore a perforated sheet of paper off his clipboard. "Here's your receipt. We appreciate your business. You should be getting a check for him in a week or two."

"Thanks." I wondered if the check would pay for the hay I needed to get Pet through the next winter.

Troll started banging around in the hollowness of the long trailer, making the trailer sway back and forth with his shifting weight. He would stop the barreling around every few moments, arching his head upward to sniff the air outside the horizontal slats high above him. Then he would let out a full-bodied bellow.

"Well, I need to go pick up some more company for him. I'd better get going."

"I appreciate your help—drive safe."

"Yup, driving's the safest part of my job most days. Okay, bye now." The driver gave a quick Vermont farmer's wave, hand going straight up and then right back down, not like the long, drawn-out waves I'd grown up with down South.

I walked the mile back up Tunket Road, shedding some simple dreams in the shape of tears. *Don't ever name them what you don't want them to be,* I thought.

From up the hill, I could hear another series of lonesome bellows. "Okay, Pet, I'm comin' . . . I'm comin'."

After Troll's unfortunate exile, Pet started to set records in the lawn ornament category. He grew to the point where his back was within 2 inches of the top of my head. He was as gentle as we could have hoped for, and he was adept at responding readily to *gee, haw, whoa,* and *back up.* But he had absolutely no interest in dealing with the uncomfortable waggle of the heavy single yoke I'd gotten from our friend Herb or the leather straps going along his sides and back behind him that I'd contrived as a harness from the parts I'd gotten from an Amish harness maker. Finally, given Pet's unwillingness to convert to new ways or to my frantic schedule, I moved toward the seemingly inevitable decision, one hastened by a $600 hay bill with not much to show for it—except one enormous and loving creature. In addition, our homestead was growing in other ways. Our first son, Asa, was born on June 27, 2002.

In the meantime, some friends had given us Molly, an old Belgian draft horse, to try out on our homestead. Pet quickly befriended Molly and, as best I could tell, enjoyed her company much more than Troll's bullying nature. Erin had worked Molly until the pregnancy had become too much of a concern, hooking Molly to a cart and going out for occasional jaunts, as often as she was able between all of the chores and the preparations for the coming baby.

Pet and Molly seemed the perfect oddball companions. One would have thought that Pet would have been the dominant one of the pair, with his girth and horns. However, Molly would simply stamp one of her huge rear feet and shake the ground all around, and Pet would concede to her every demand—whether it was letting her choose the hay she wanted or standing with his tail next to her head, swatting flies from her face with the arc of his powerful tail. She was occasionally kind enough to reciprocate with her tail, but Pet seemed more concerned with following orders than ensuring parity.

A few days before Asa was born, Pet found a break in the fence line, thanks to our local deer, and he was obviously suffering from the heat and the flies in the pasture. He did what any smart 1-ton ox would do—he saw the dining fly that Erin's mom Maggie had put up in the forest's edge, and he went to see if it fit his needs. It did—barely. After pushing aside the unnecessary objects, like the table, cooler, and chairs, Pet lay down, somehow conforming virtually his entire body to fit under the shade of the dining fly. By the time Maggie found him, Pet was in the height of his cud-chewing contentment, giving her a nonchalant look from underneath the nearly intact shelter, with only one corner pole having given way to his efforts to squeeze underneath. He had, of course, deposited a reminder of his satisfaction, just on the outer perimeter of the fly—on the verge of impoliteness, but not quite.

Maggie's shriek of "Oh my God!" and ensuing explosion into laughter alerted Erin and me to some unusual activity in the woods, so we ran—actually Erin roundly ambled—out to see what the commotion was all about. After a hearty collective laugh and a comical scolding of an ox with a misguided sense of humor, we haltered Pet and led him back through the obstacle-ridden woods and into the pasture. Erin and Maggie moved the dining fly to a spot where there were no "reminders" of Pet's brief sojourn in the shade.

However, Pet seemed to have relished his great escape, so a few days later he once again made his way through a hole in the fence, but this time he went deep into the woods. I was away running errands, so when Maggie saw Pet once again on the prowl, she went to get Erin. Erin put the halter on him, and Maggie wanted to lead him back to avoid any strain on Erin's very pregnant part. However, Pet responded better to Erin, so she led him through an obstacle course of difficult terrain back to the pasture.

Arriving home late that afternoon, I was served dinner and the story. Maggie was not pleased at the degree to which Erin had exerted herself. Erin seemed less concerned, but she wasn't feeling very comfortable, especially with the late-June heat. Erin did decide to go to sleep early that night, but it turned out to be a short night, thanks to the development of some back pain.

A few days later she went to Gifford Birthing Center in Randolph, Vermont, for a regularly scheduled appointment with her midwife, only to discover that her back pain was actually a sign of impending labor—six weeks earlier than we had expected. True to form, she was fully dilated but couldn't feel the contractions. No one at the birthing center could believe her pain threshold. Maggie and I weren't surprised.

Little Asa arrived later that night, soon after a series of fierce thunderstorms rammed their way across Vermont, finally ending our early summer heat wave. We'll never know whether the labor was ox-induced or not—Maggie swears that it was—but we didn't bother to share the adventure with the midwife for further speculation. Different professions and lifestyles breed divergent views of wisdom, although our midwife just so happened to be another off-grid homesteader.

We kept Pet through the summer, and he and Molly would perplex hikers who passed them on their way up Haystack—both enormous, beautiful creatures who seemed conflicted about their mutual affection.

By the time the pastures started to wane, however, I couldn't justify the enormous expense it was going to take to feed Pet through another winter . . . and there would be another, and yet another. Keeping him any longer was merely a means of assuaging my conscience rather than anticipating any real utility. Not only could Pet barely fit through the 4' × 7' barn door into his stall, but his massive size and weight were contributing to the pugging and compaction of our heavy clay soils.

As much as we hated to think about it, we knew we could always eat him, albeit only over an extensive period of time. Erin had been feeling the need for more protein and iron during the pregnancy, and, once Asa was born, the need seemed to intensify with the constant demands of breast-feeding. It was eventually her pragmatism that helped me make the decisive phone call.

A new slaughterhouse had opened up in our area. John Wing, the new owner, had designed and built it as a small, family-scale operation, with elements of the design reflecting Dr. Temple Grandin's recommendations for minimizing animal fear and making the animal's last moments as humane as possible. Dr. Grandin has built her career around utilizing her own autism and its associated sensations of light, heat, touch, and movement to help in designing animal facilities that reduce animal stress and suffering.[1] I had toured John's new facility with some other farmers and chefs earlier in the summer, and felt like, if I was going to send dear old Pet to his demise, I at least wanted to feel like it wouldn't be an unpleasant ending for him.

I called John, a former teamster himself, and he said that he would come himself to pick up Pet. He arrived at our scheduled time a few days later, and unlike my previous experience with Troll, I didn't need to pretend it was just a matter of course. John knew how attached I was to Pet—with a name like that and no Troll to complete the intended joke—and there was no sense trying to hide anything.

Pet rivaled Troll in his obedience. He walked right into the trailer, his head nearly touching the ceiling, and he lowered his head for me to get the rope halter off his horns. John watched the easy loading appreciatively.

"I know it's hard, Philip. I hate it for you. But you're probably making the right decision." He lit a cigarette. "I've been around this slaughter business ever since I was a little fella—but there are always some situations that rip your heart out."

I kicked at the gravel with the tip of my boot. "I know. It's the decision

I have to make. If I start feeling guilty about it, I can always remember that he got five more years than he would have. He was headed straight for the veal market when we got him."

"Well, and I know you're not ready to think about it yet . . ." He pointed inside the trailer with his cigarette and shook his head with a slight smile. ". . . but there's a helluva lot of burger coming your way. That is one huge steer!"

"Yeah, well, Erin's kind of glad to add a little bit of meat to our diet again. And I'm *really* glad. I usually want to know where it comes from, but I'm kind of bummed it had to get quite so personal this time."

"It's always personal," John replied. "At least on the animal's end of things."

"I guess so." I dug the toe of my boot deeper into the grit. "It's us humans who have the chance to remove ourselves from the situation—not the animals."

John and I kicked around a few more rocks and ideas and then he stubbed out the butt of his cigarette on the side of the trailer. "I'd better get going. Tomorrow's gonna be another busy day. I'll try to get him taken care of early so he won't be there when you come by for the legislative tour in the afternoon."

"All right." We shook hands. "Thanks, John. I'll see you tomorrow afternoon."

John cranked the diesel engine, and it quickly settled into a low, even idle. Pet hollered and stuck his nose up to the slatted window.

I could feel my vision getting blurry, but I looked up to see Pet's nose scouring the landscape for hints of the familiar. "See ya, bud. I'm sorry. I'm afraid you taught me more than I taught you this time around."

John looked in the side mirror to make sure I was out of the way and gave me a wave. He pulled onto the main road, and Pet bellowed and shifted his weight. The whole trailer shook.

It was sadder this time. But I was also more certain.

The next day, I went to the Wings' slaughterhouse to show our local legislators and agricultural officials all the environmental and humane components that the Wings had built in. Our region was short on slaughterhouses, and facilities such as the one where I had shipped Troll did not inspire confidence. A new slaughterhouse that promoted mortality composting, small-scale processing, low-stress handling, rotational grazing, and local marketing seemed like something to celebrate.

As a member of our local conservation district board that had helped fund some of the environmental practices for the facility, I arrived and shook hands with the diverse array of officials already gathered there. We all conversed casually, waiting for John to come out and lead the tour. I had a hard time with the small talk, as I kept wondering if I would recognize Pet as a split carcass—and what my reaction might be. Nonetheless, I chatted with folks whom I hadn't met previously, and John came out to greet us.

Needing to meet and greet the more important folks there, he just caught my eye and gave me a peculiar expression, raising both his eyebrows as some sort of signal that I couldn't interpret. Determined to think about the tour and not Pet's early-morning demise, I walked with the crowd as John pointed out various aspects of the facility. Having looked at the composting site, we rounded the corner of a building and came to the outer edge of the modest holding pen.

In an effort to keep myself in an upbeat mood, I told a joke to one of my colleagues—something about grave robbers unearthing Mozart, only to find him lying in his coffin with paper and an eraser . . . decomposing. As we both laughed, I heard a bellow.

No, I thought. *It can't be.* I looked to the nearby pen where I'd heard the noise, and sure enough, there was Pet. He'd heard my voice. I'd expected to see him in carcass form, not whole and bellowing. Pet let loose again, and the crowd turned to see who was making all the noise. "Geez, look at that fellow—he's *huge!*" one of the officials remarked.

John looked over at me and winced. "Okay, folks, let's head over to where we're raising the pigs." As he directed everyone that way, he moved around the edge of the crowd and came up to me.

"Philip, I'm really sorry. We just got so busy this morning trying to get the animals ahead of him done and then get cleaned up, I just couldn't get to him. And I just wasn't sure what you'd think seein' him hanging up anyway." He reached up and scratched his head just under the brim of his cap, grimacing empathetically. "He's the biggest animal we've had come through yet—by far—so I knew you'd recognize him right away when we brought this group into the coolers."

"It's okay, John. It just gives me one more chance to say good-bye, I guess."

"Well, I am sorry. But I'll take the group on over to the pigs, and you go over and visit with him, if you want."

I walked over to the pen where Pet was standing, the final corral before he walked up the chute. As I neared, he let out a gentle moo, unbecoming of a male his size, even if he was castrated.

I felt the tears coming. All I could was rub him under the chin, like I'd done for years. "You're a good boy, Pet," I whispered. I gave him a soft kiss on the muzzle. "This is more about me than it is about you."

I turned to rejoin the crowd. Pet's bellows followed me the whole way.

TEN

Plowshares into Swards: Grass Farming

Erin and I were slowly beginning to see Vermont through the eyes of our remarkably gracious dairy farmer neighbors, Donald and Joanne Waite. And I was learning a lot about Vermont agriculture from Donald— mostly about my own ignorance initially, but not because he ever made me feel ignorant. He would never tell me how to do something unless I asked, and he never told me when he thought I was doing something wrong. He would let me come to that conclusion myself, at which point I was lucky enough to have him as a resource to figure out how to do it right the second (or third) time. He could have saved me a lot of time by correcting me early on, but the resulting lessons tended to be vivid, although not always immediate.

I'd come to Vermont to start a college farm and to teach sustainable agriculture, but I didn't feel like I could do a good job teaching students about agriculture in Vermont if I didn't have a reasonable understanding of dairy farming. I had started out by teaching students how to raise organic vegetables in the modest college garden, but only a small subset of Vermont farmers were growing organic vegetables. Raising radicchio gets you only so much respect in Vermont, and chard doesn't get you much farther. Being ignorant about the biggest sector of Vermont agriculture didn't seem wise, but I couldn't teach what I didn't know. It seemed that the best place to start my education was at the back end of a cow.

Donald had a nice collection of such specimens. Besides, he'd always had a reason why Erin and I shouldn't pay for the milk we came to get for our calves, and eventually for ourselves, so we started helping with the easiest flatlander jobs in the barn—mucking out the manure and sawdust bedding from behind the cows in their tie stalls and tossing new sawdust under their front quarters. The tail-end detail was far from

irrelevant, but it demanded less discrimination on our parts than did the intake section on the front end.

I slowly began to realize the subtleties of what I originally perceived to be a relatively thoughtless job. There were verbal and nonverbal cues to give the cattle that I was coming up behind them, with certain taps to indicate whether they needed to step over or up. Most of them also liked knowing when the big shovel-load of sawdust was about to be strewn under their feet—the power of their kick and leap being directly correlated to their degree of surprise if I failed to give advance warning of my presence behind them.

Donald gently noted to me that it was best to get the sawdust under their front feet, as they would soon enough have it pushed back under the rest of their bodies simply by ducking their heads in and out of the manger. For a while, nothing made me feel more inept than my clumsy scattering of the huge shovelfuls of sawdust. Watching Donald and his son Doug scoop up a full shovel of sawdust and whip it perfectly underneath the cows was a study in rhythm and coordination, not to mention strength. Even though they made it look simple, just driving the big sawdust cart around the barn's tight corners took skill. I seemed particularly adept at having a wheel of the heavy cart end up in the gutter of the automated barn cleaner, earning a smile but never a comment from Donald.

I eventually started to notice the bright red drops of blood that occasionally appeared in the sawdust or under a cow's tail. "Bleeding off" meant that she had just completed a heat cycle. Donald had an excellent eye—and ear—for detecting cows in heat and getting the breeder to come and artificially inseminate them within the relatively tight estrus window. "Joanne, I guess you'd better 'call the bull' for me this morning," he'd say, casting a smile at us—a reference to a long-departed neighbor who had always gotten on the party line whenever he needed the breeder and would gruffly yell to anyone already on the line, "*Get off the phone—I gotta call the bull!*" Joanne would call the breeder, who would arrive within a few hours, see the yellow tag hanging above any cattle in heat, and render his artificial insemination services.

Between the separate feedings of grain, silage, and hay, and then again after all the rest of the chores were done, Donald would repeatedly fill his rustic corncob pipe with tobacco, light it once or twice with the ubiquitous pipe matches that he kept stashed in at least one pocket of every garment he wore, and gaze over his barn full of well-tended Holsteins, organized tidily into groups of milkers, dry cows, heifers, and calves.

It took me a while to understand that he wasn't smoking his pipe just out of satisfaction at having quieted the rowdy chorus (it's hard to complain with your mouth full) or at having completed chores. Rather, he was looking and listening for other signs of heat—cows dancing, bellowing, mounting, even staring wistfully into the distance—all subtle indicators that he needed to get the breeder there that day or mark the calendar to be ready to check that cow's heat cycle about three weeks later. He was also listening for coughs and snorts that indicated a calf might be fighting a respiratory infection, and he was looking across the length of the barn for any listless eaters who might be suffering from a digestive disorder.

I gradually realized that Donald's quiet demeanor paid off time and again in his management of the herd. Cows don't take well to hot tempers, but they are creatures of hierarchy and humans aren't exempt from the ranking. It was clear to everyone who was the boss of the barn, but Donald's reign was one of resoluteness and regular rhythm, not fear. Only the really obstinate or ornery animals earned his bark in an ordinarily quiet barn.

I came to love the framing of the day with the regularity and rhythm of chores. As we became familiar with the chores, the barn, the cattle, and even the Waite family's hierarchy in chore assignments, we assumed our tasks at the rear ends of the cattle, only making our way to the frontal portions of the bovines months later, after we began to understand which cattle got which rations and in what quantities.

Chores began with grain whipped into the central and side mangers from a wheelbarrow, with Donald's dexterity and precision unrivaled by anyone else in the family. He wielded the scoop with a pivoting wrist that arced the prescribed quantity of golden grain to the cattle in range, first to the left and then to the right—then he advanced the wheelbarrow forward a few feet. Cows would sway their huge heads in anticipation and occasionally lunge under the tie-stall rail in front of them, launching their tongues toward the wheelbarrow, in the hope of swiping an extra mouthful. Particularly bold advances earned a rap on the nose with the feed scoop.

Within about ten minutes of the grain feeding, it was time for the distribution of corn silage down all the mangers. The sweet fermented smell of silage permeated the barn as soon as it fell from the chopper up in the

top of the silo and through the vertical silo chute at the commencement of
chores. Loading the wheelbarrow with the silage fork was another art for
me to master, despite being someone who was quite accustomed to working for my own heaping servings at any feeding time. I'd watched Donald
push the wheelbarrow down the barn mangers, tipping the wheelbarrow
in quick, controlled jerks that delivered even increments of silage to each
cow, but I had no idea how difficult it was. I never saw Donald laugh
or smirk at my awkward tipping and uneven feedings, but eventually I
got the hang of it. My errors were erratic enough that no cows seemed to
suffer from obesity or emaciation due to my incompetence.

The cows adored their fermented corn salad and packed it away as
best they could, their huge tongues snaking out and over to their neighbors' piles, desperate to get anything extra that seemed in range, fairness
not being a prime component of any hierarchy. I'd never realized how
crafty or athletic cattle could be, with many of them performing "cow-
tortions" that seemed physically impossible, a few ending up inexplicably
under or over the tie-stall bars, often with no obvious method of arrival
and certainly not an easy return.

It was the time in between feeding silage and hay that I loved the
most. The pause wasn't long enough to warrant heading elsewhere to
knock out another task, so it tended to be the time of day when conversation wasn't an impediment to the day's progress. It was the time to pick
Donald's brain about cattle, local history, wildlife, politics, and anything
else that he was willing to share.

Manual labor breeds richer discussions than watercooler banter,
I think—perhaps because exertion makes trivial matters all the more
obvious. And trivial is different from mundane. *Mundane* literally means
"of the world," and it was in those long pauses between letting the cattle
finish their silage and then feeding them hay that Donald taught me
most of what I know about the world surrounding Tunket Road.

Even though I was in the midst of working on my graduate degree
in conservation biology, it became clear to me that I could design a host
of scientific studies to determine the ecological history and emerging
changes in the land around me and never capture the detailed and sophisticated understanding that Donald possessed as a result of his seasonal
orbits throughout the so-called North Pawlet Hills. He rode and roamed
the hills with the eye of farmer, hunter, forager, and forester. Developing
the lens for any one of those avocations meant looking for or inadver-

tently discovering a set of patterns among plants, animals, the landscape, and the seasons. I could describe a distinctive tree or another subtle landmark, and Donald would almost always know the spot I was describing. He knew the landscape intimately—with detail and affection.

He was especially patient as I pestered him with questions about wildlife and his grandfather's famous fermentation projects, all the while getting his take on whether the concepts that I was learning in classes and in my own research jibed with his sense of the human and ecological history of the area. He was intrigued by what I was learning about how to measure plant and wildlife populations and ecological shifts. He was less suspicious of the methodologies than of the notion that an ecologist—or an expert in any field, for that matter—could drop in on a territory for a quick survey and determine its history, particularities, ecological significance, and management needs. After all, his own assessments were steeped in chronology and daily redaction.

If a farmer's methodologies are crude, then a trained ecologist's methods are superficial. Together, the two can generate meaning and insight. I like to think of those conversations in the barn as a melding of two worlds that should be less disparate. They were also a good reminder that those of us who get paid to talk are the ones who really need to listen . . . and the quiet ones among us are not quiet because they don't have anything to say—it's just not clear that others are ready to listen. Donald always seems willing to abide a certain amount of ignorance, but he has no patience for arrogance.

Once the cows had finished most of their silage, Donald would head for the haymow and send down the proper number of hay bales—usually a mixture of first and second cut—for the various animals. Oftentimes, he would go into the haymow without a light, pulling down the types of bales by feel and memory. He would know precisely how much hay to throw down to satisfy the full barn of sixty to seventy cattle, and he would orchestrate which bales we should take and distribute to various groups. If he was going to rant about something—especially corrupt politicians—he usually did it in the frenzy and bluster of busting open hay bales and then throwing and shaking the flakes up and down the manger, with the cows' heads bobbing up and down in mock agreement—greedy to grab any handouts, just like the subjects of our discussion. Something about breaking up hay bales feels a little like giving a corrupt politician a good shake. It's therapeutic work, and maybe it even helped squelch a few farmer-led uprisings that perhaps should have happened in the past.

As a rule, Vermont farmers could never be characterized as nonjudgmental, and they certainly have their opinions, whether they choose to air them publicly or not. They don't have much patience with what they consider ill-founded notions. That didn't surprise me—it was in character with most of my experiences growing up in the South. But what did surprise me was the part of Vermont that I have come to love and that Donald represents for me.

Vermonters like Donald don't gladly suffer fools, but they do believe that even fools have their place. They would just as soon have that place be outside of Vermont, perhaps, but if not, so be it.

Donald explained it to us one night while we were waiting for the cows to finish their silage so we could spread out the hay bales. His was the perspective of a family that had been farming in Vermont since before the Revolutionary War, and he delivered it with a nod to Vermont's most famous farmer-soldier Ethan Allen and his Green Mountain Boys. "People around here didn't fight for things to be one way. They fought to let everybody live here the best way they each saw fit. Live and let live. That's the way it's always been around here. I hope it stays that way, but I don't know . . ."

With that, he invited us in to dinner, like he did on many of those nights. "We feed whoever shows up at the table, and we've got a big table . . . and Joanne keeps cookin' like we've still got five kids at home. We've got enough—c'mon up to the house."

We seldom refused. What we got from the conversations gave us as much to digest as what we heaped on our plates.

We filed through the barn door, with Donald taking a final look at the rows of black-and-white cattle easing into their nocturnal ruminations. He flipped the switch for the last of the barn lights and tugged the stubborn sliding door closed, pushing it the last few inches into its locking pocket.

"That's about as done as the day ever gets around here," he said, with a twinkle in his eye that I knew was there, even in the dark.

Our investigations into the nearly lost world of oxen had taken us to county fairs, draft animal events, living history museums, and Herb Troumbley's basement. Of all of those places, nothing amazed me more than Herb's basement—filled with beautiful hardwood yokes of all sizes, hickory bows with the bark still intact on the outside to prevent cracking, hand-forged bow pins from all over New England, and stories to go with each one.

But we had also encountered a bovine spectrum that undid Vermont's black-and-white Holstein stereotype. Wherever there were oxen, there were breeds of cattle that reflected nature's genetic imaginings and a human love of creative consistency: enormous white Chianias, Oreo-like Dutch Belteds, the once dominant Milking Shorthorns with their infinite colorings and patterns, the peculiarly striped and speckled Randall Lineback, the stunted-in-stature but big-bagged Irish Dexter, and of course the breed that built New England as we know it—the triple-purpose American Milking Devon.

Raising Pet and Troll had opened up a new world to us. I'd always loved cattle, albeit from a distance. Once we had Pet and Troll, I discovered that I did indeed savor the framing of the day with chores on either end, and the company of cattle was every bit the pleasure I had expected. As it turned out, our experiments with oxen were a bridge into the vast worlds of animal behavior, dairy animals, grazing dynamics, and rare breeds—and our guides and goads in finding our way were a cast of authentic New England characters, another waning breed whose disappearance would leave the landscape a little less colorful.

As I learned about New England agriculture and began teaching more sustainable agriculture classes, I once again felt the tug of old and new. Dairy farming as it had existed for about the past two generations in Vermont was under siege: low milk prices, high grain prices, rising real estate values, skyrocketing tax burdens, increasing environmental regulations, and fragmented farms and fields were all coalescing to cause Vermont's iconic black-and-white image to bleed red on balance sheets of all sizes.

At the same time, the grass was beginning to look greener to some farmers. Vermont may be a tough place to farm for a host of reasons, but its climate and terrain produce one crop even more reliably than tourists—grass. Coupled with the resurgent interest in grass farming (on the part of both humans and livestock) was a burgeoning movement among Vermont farmers, chefs, and savvy consumers for foods that are more artisanal than industrial—foods produced locally with craft (not Kraft) and care.

Farmers are often in the awkward position of having to be innovators on the one hand and stubborn traditionalists on the other. Both the ecological and the economic landscapes are extremely difficult to predict, and there is sometimes merit in hunkering down and doing things like they've always been done. Other times, it's wiser to try and read the subtle signs of change on the horizon and begin to innovate, unraveling the threads of a once comfortable paradigm and knitting together a new one. Both approaches have their merits as well as their dangers, and I'm not inclined to harshly judge either approach. They are both survival mechanisms.

Farmers who decide to put their heads down and weather the storms are often those whose entire infrastructure—farm layout, barn design, harvesting equipment, even breed of livestock—is geared to do one thing, one way, and do it quite efficiently. Significantly altering a system that cost hundreds of thousands of dollars to put into place during a period of economic uncertainty is generally considered foolhardy, not just by the farmers but also by their bankers.

As I traveled across the region with students and with Erin and I got to know farmers—both innovators and stalwarts—it wasn't hard to detect a growing interest in grass farming and its associated artisanal enterprises. I was still immersed in my graduate courses at the time, struggling to reconcile the enormous challenges presented by contemporary agriculture with the protection of the ecological integrity of our varied landscapes.

When I was with farmers, it was clear that they saw themselves as the primary stewards of the Vermont landscape. When I was with fellow conservation biology students, they tended to take a dimmer view of farmers' roles as conservationists. I couldn't help but believe that these worlds could coexist and that Vermont's dairy heritage could serve as a way forward. Wasn't there a way to combine ecological management with economic viability?

For me, the answer to that question came when I spent two weekends with someone many Americans encounter by name while traveling along our highways and interstates. The college sent me twice to Ohio to discuss funding possibilities for our strengthening agricultural focus with Bob Evans in Ohio, a friend of the college. Bob had built his restaurant chain out of his childhood farming experience and his early sausage-making enterprise, and anyone who met him in his later years discovered immediately that he had shifted from entrepreneur to evangelist. Grazing was his gospel, year-round grazing was the salvation, and a world filled with profitable family farms was his idea of heaven. "Grazin' is what's gonna save the family farm in this country" seemed to be his mantra.

Bob, his wife, Jewel, and his son Steve drove me through their majestic southeastern Ohio landscape, pointing out the modest building where Bob had begun his sausage-making business, the farms that he owned, the farms he had purchased for his faithful employees, the pastures he was managing with careful grazing, the cattle he was raising on forages, and the local livestock auction—a landscape tapestry that captured both the perils and the promise of farming in his region. Of course, each outing concluded with a meal at the original Bob Evans restaurant in Rio Grande, Ohio. He introduced me to Ed Vollburn and David Zartman, whose research and extension efforts at Ohio State University were focused on trying to find the path to 365 days of grazing in Ohio. Pragmatists with a zealot's backing, their research remains a critical beacon for farmers and researchers trying to wed dollars to ecological values.

Bob and Jewel were the kind of benefactors any region relishes—people who invest locally but are thinking globally. Bob spent his later years amassing information and networking related to forage-based livestock production from as far away as New Zealand, arguably the world capital of grass farming. He pushed people like me to climb out of our offices and clamber over the self-constructed walls of our paradigms—and he did it with unmatched graciousness and wit . . . and if that didn't work, he could add fire to the homily.

After my first visit with him, I decided I wanted to explore grass-based farming with rare breeds on our homestead. By the time I visited him a second time several years later, I had shifted my conservation biology research to grass farming, purchased eight American Milking Devon cattle, and started investing time and money into learning how to effectively graze some of the unused open land down the road from our wooded homestead. The goal was to see if we could combine rare-breed genetics and the principles of grass farming to create an economically viable farm that provided a centerpiece for our homestead.

The first order of business, however, was to work on feeding ourselves as much as seemed reasonable. Producing food for ourselves seemed primary. If creating a business still seemed like a good idea after we provided for our own needs and learned some important lessons, we could then take what we learned at the homestead scale and gradually translate it into a reasonable business plan for a possible farming venture that we could afford.

Farmers today can get so busy farming and producing such a narrow range of commodities that they often don't raise much of their own food. While I can understand how our beleaguered food and agricultural systems have created such a model, I find a certain wisdom in a homesteading approach to food, where feeding the family comes first, and producing food for income can follow.

Ultimately, although they were never great draft animals, Pet and Troll had nonetheless dragged me into their world, and Bob Evans had a new convert. It was time to turn plowshares into swards . . . of grass, that is.

ELEVEN

The Smallholder as Placeholder

I often feel torn between disparate worlds—homesteading and academia, smaller-scale farming and larger-scale farming, organic agriculture and conventional agriculture, environmental values and blue-collar realities. Amid all of it, I keep looking for the wisdom of the middle . . . and sometimes it seems like words just keep pushing people toward opposite sides.

Some of my friends and colleagues in the farming and business worlds occasionally use two terms that always get me agitated: *hobby farms* and *boutique farms*. Calling something a "hobby farm" tends to deny the seriousness and sweat involved in what is, hopefully, the playful and joyous work that takes place on a relatively small farm or homestead. Indeed, a small farm often requires off-farm income to get the operation up and running in the initial stages of development. My father once quipped that it's a good thing I have a job to support my farming habit. He was probably right—it takes a while to get any type of business to a point of economic viability, especially if one doesn't inherit the land or infrastructure.

I find *boutique farm* to be even more derogatory. It sounds like nobody's getting dirty or even breaking a sweat. It also often implies a disdain for certain moderate to high-end markets where unique foods and their cultural traditions can be conserved, and it concurrently risks denying a farmer's need to pay the bills, much less make a living. That said, we absolutely do need to increase accessibility to healthy food for persons of all economic backgrounds, while also finding ways to assess and charge for the true costs of food. If farmers choose to use the term *boutique* to describe their own operations, that's okay, in my view, but when the term is used to deny or minimize the relevance of any working farm, I get irritated.

By the same token, when I'm in the company of liberal-minded friends and students, I'm often equally frustrated by their problematic use of terms such as *industrial agriculture* and *large-scale farming*. The assumption seems to be that scale and mechanization are blanket indictments of the sustainability of an operation. Every farm or homestead warrants being judged on its own merits, not lumped into a category that rapidly disintegrates under careful scrutiny. For example, what is thought to be a large farm in Vermont would be considered a small to medium-sized farm in Iowa or California. And which is an industrial farm: a 2-acre pesticide-laden berry farm or a 200-acre organic orchard operation?

Regardless of how one might answer that question, it is important to recognize that the United States is clearly dependent upon farms of all scales, and scale does not immediately translate into positive ecological or ethical values. Terms like *family farming* and *corporate farming* also tend to break down in the light of day, as soon as one realizes that some of our largest and most "industrialized" farms in the US are, in fact, family-owned, even though the family may be absentee landowners. Furthermore, many small to medium-sized farms are incorporated so that the corporation can be used to protect the family's assets from lawsuits and bankruptcy, or to include all family members as decision makers in the operation and future of the farm.[1]

Terms of scale are not problematic when they are utilized merely as descriptors of size. It is when these terms become value-laden that they risk misrepresenting the actual realities on the farm. We are all guilty of this kind of "label lumping" that pejoratively portrays the "other" kind of farming with which we are unfamiliar or uncomfortable—regardless of how much we really know about it.

There is often a blurry line between what is considered to be a homestead versus a farm, and it's even more difficult to determine at what point a homestead becomes a farm. Although I think that a defining component of a homestead is that it produces something, I don't believe that homesteads necessarily have to involve any type of food production. For example, some homesteaders prefer to focus on producing their own power, shelter, heat, and hot water, or even products stemming from a cottage industry. However, the centrality of the table in the household certainly begs the question of whether a total lack of involvement in any type of food production is the wisest course for a homesteader, given how it connects us to nature, to our culture, and to one another. For that reason, most homesteaders tend to incorporate some aspect of gardening or farming into their lives, albeit on a small or even micro scale in most situations.

But are these micro- and small-scale agricultural endeavors on the homestead relevant beyond the homestead's boundaries? Is the filling of the pantry and the root cellar and the apartment balcony and the freezer simply a tightening of the ecological equation just for the household, or does the homesteader as gardener or farmer have an important role to play in the larger scheme of things? Are we merely living basic, utilitarian lives to fulfill our own needs and meet our own self-imposed expectations, or is there the possibility that homesteading ventures and experiments might be addressing some broader and less self-centered needs?

In other words, are we relevant in spite of our small scale . . . or, better yet, as a result of our small scale? I think the answer to both questions is *yes*—if we are willing to "live the questions."[2]

So much of our agricultural heritage—heirloom vegetables, "antique" fruit varieties, rare breeds of livestock, and the cultural and culinary traditions that are part and parcel of this agricultural biodiversity—all of these things stand little chance of survival if they are not folded into our daily lives. No matter how alluring our living history museums or complete our academic research and archiving or technologically sound our cryogenic preservation techniques, nothing supplants the security of having our country's diverse inheritance of agricultural tastes, traditions, and tasks safely conserved in the daily activities of the family and the homestead.

Perhaps there is no stronger argument in favor of conserving the small scale of the homestead than the fact that agricultural biodiversity is best protected at the scale at which it was born and nurtured. In fact, it is the massive scale of our current cultural default—entrusting the growing, processing, distribution, and cooking of food to a heartless and hearthless unnamed machine—that most directly threatens the biological and cultural foundations upon which our entire food system is based, even if these foundations are seldom seen or recognized by most Americans. These foundations are genetic, cultural, culinary, generational, and—lest we forget—ethical.

The lack of visibility of our endangered agricultural biodiversity and its link to a vast array of related cultural traditions in the United States is misleading. The importance of these genetic resources and their accompanying traditions is somewhat hidden, simply by virtue of their rarity, their intimate scale, and their broad geographic distribution. The magnitude of their importance remains obscured, until one recognizes the stark realities presented by the sum total of their absence. In fact, the smallholder is a placeholder for the future.

Soon after meeting Bob Evans for the first time and buying into his idea that grazing was a way to save the cherished American icon of the family farm, I invited Don Bixby, at that time the executive director of the American Livestock Breeds Conservancy, to speak at the college on the future of rare breeds. Don startled the audience by proposing that we could best save rare breeds by eating them. His argument became more complex, however, as he began to explain that rare breeds often fit into specific cultural and ecological niches, and their survival probably depends upon their ability to fit into associated economic niches. If the breeds can't pay their way on the farm, Don explained, they probably won't survive—or at least not in populations large enough to perpetuate adequately sized gene pools that will ensure the genetic diversity needed to avoid inbreeding or other potential problems.

After hearing Don's perspective, Erin and I felt the satisfying push of the puzzle pieces locking together. It all came together in one big, bulky question. Could we use our homestead to test the possibilities for integrating the conservation of a pastoral landscape, rare breeds of livestock, the rich dairy and culinary traditions from New England and the Alps, while at the same time using grass-based farming to reduce the use of fossil fuels in livestock agriculture? Perhaps there was a way, if we could afford it.

Despite having concerns about our own financial capacity to take on such a project, it struck me that if this kind of research were grant-funded or happened in an academic setting, then it risked not being replicable. But if we could make it work in the context of our homestead and our family budget, then some of the answers might make sense for ourselves and for others. Regardless of the outcome, it was a way of feeding ourselves in the process, while also weaving ourselves more tightly into the ecological, social, and economic fabric of our community. And it put me in the educational role that I much prefer—that of a student, not a professor.

Erin and I started exploring rare breeds of cattle. In late September, I'd invited Sarah Flack from the Vermont Grass Farmers' Association to give a pasture management workshop at the college. Sarah is a grazing and livestock specialist, as well as being a farmer herself. While we

were having lunch, she mentioned that Howard Mansfield, a breeder of American Milking Devon cattle, had suffered a heart attack and was working to sell a substantial portion of his herd before winter set in.

Erin and I immediately called up Howard and set up a time to go visit him and his wife, Marilee, outside Waterbury, Vermont, but when we pulled up to the farm, we wondered if we had the right place. There was a barn and a livestock trailer, but we saw only several intimidating emus—no cattle.

However, we knocked on the door of the house, and Howard stepped out smiling. "Emus just about scare you off?" He must have looked out the window and seen my skeptical glances in the direction of the pacing birds, clearly taller than I was. I'd never been so glad to see a chain-link fence between me and an animal.

"Their eggs make a helluvan omelet!" He walked over and warmly shook our hands. "But that's a waste of a valuable egg. You should see the size of the incubator we've got for those things."

Howard rapped a cigarette out of its pack and lit it up, apparently giving us a chance to acclimate a bit. "So, you folks interested in some Milking Devons?"

"We think so," I replied. "At least a couple . . ."

"We're still thinking about it," Erin interjected. She wasn't against it, but she wasn't about to commit that early in the visit.

Howard suggested that we all walk across the road to the far pasture to take a look at his herd. I looked across the road. "I don't see any cattle over there. Where do they hang out?"

He pointed up over the hill. "But I'll have 'em right up next to the fence here before you know it. Over here's my bait. I just stopped by the bakery this morning." Howard walked over to two 5-gallon buckets, brimming with doughnuts—glazed, chocolate, jelly, and crème-filled—and motioned for us to follow him.

Erin and I looked at each other and then hurried to catch up to him. "Doughnuts?" I asked, incredulously.

"Yup. Think about it—it's no different from grain with a bunch of molasses dumped on it . . . the only thing missing in the diet are the holes! And the doughnuts are free—left over from the day before."

I laughed, probably unconvincingly, not certain what we were getting into. The three of us walked across the road to the edge of a barbed-wire fence. "Now watch this," Howard said, setting down the buckets. He cupped his hands around his mouth and yelled the ancient call—stemming from the Latin word *Bos*—"Commmmme, Boss—come Boss! Get over here!"

If I thought the emus were intimidating, it was nothing compared with the sight of more than thirty brown, barrel-bodied, horned, and maybe horny Milking Devon cattle coming up and over the hill—charging full blast toward us and a few measly strands of barbed wire at the bottom of the hill.

Doughnuts started to fly, and the Devons started skidding to a halt just shy of the fence line, bellowing, jostling, and kicking up their heels, all scrambling for position between the fence and the apple trees in the pasture. I wasn't so sure I wanted any part of this. My vision of a mellow bunch of rare-breed cud chewers, basking quietly in the sun and ruminating on their good fortune of being saved by our philanthropic efforts—well, that notion was fading. And I didn't know what I'd do without a ready source of doughnuts to pacify them. I'd sort of assumed that some nice pastures courtesy of our neighbors would satisfy most of their needs. I wasn't prepared to start slinging doughnuts, although I did admire Howard's Yankee frugality, not to mention his ability to get his herd's immediate attention with a bunch of leftovers.

"Are they mellow enough to be milked?"

Howard looked at me with a deadpan expression. "It depends. How fast can you run with a milk bucket?" We both laughed, although my laugh was less convincing than his. "Sure, they're fine—you've just got to handle them a lot. I can sell you one that I've milked some. How many you want?"

"Well, we were thinking maybe just three . . ."

"Of different ages," Erin interjected. "Maybe a cow, a bred heifer, and a calf."

"Well, Pretty Girl here is a good one that I've milked some, depending on how much time I have." Pretty Girl had unusually delicate, curving horns, and she was as barrel-bodied as any cow I'd ever seen, with a long-hanging udder and fine-boned legs. She reminded me a little of the pictures of the now extinct wild aurochs, the ancestor of all of the cattle breeds. The last one was killed in Poland in 1627.

"You guys ever had any Devon milk?"

We both shook our heads.

"Well, there's nothing quite like it. Once you try it, you'll never want to go back to anything else, especially that watery stuff you get from a Holstein. Sometimes your spoon will just about stand up in the jar when you go to mix the Devon cream in with the rest of the milk."

"And they'll do okay just on grass and hay, right?" Erin asked.

"Oh, these Devons will survive on just about anything. But that doesn't mean you should be stupid about giving them just anything—they like to eat good like you and me . . . but they don't need to eat like a Holstein, trading you milk for grain. You give them good pasture, and they'll give you some of the best meat and milk you've ever had."

Before long, Howard had us convinced that Milking Devons were the way to go, and he suggested three of them as being good starters for us. He gave us a very fair price, noting that some people were only going to make rare breeds rarer by charging exorbitant prices for them: "They belong on farms—not estates."

We arranged for him to truck the three girls to us that weekend, so we hustled home to tell Donald the big news and to see if we could board them in his barn with his other heifers. He and Joanne had recently sold their milk herd due to low milk prices and a shortage of labor on their farm, so they were raising heifers for other farmers in the area. Donald readily agreed to add our cattle to his boarding operation until the next spring, when we could get them out on pasture on his farm.

I think we all questioned the wisdom of our decision when Howard and Marilee pulled up to Donald's barn with their livestock trailer and Howard started unloading the three cattle. He put the halter on Pretty Girl first, since she was the largest of the three. As it turned out, the halter didn't halt. Neither did Pretty Girl. She stalled at the edge of the trailer, with Howard beside her, but then she committed with a leap that could have put her over the moon, followed by an immediate martial-arts-style kick of her hind legs high into the air. Howard wisely let go of the rope. Fortunately, Donald had moved a few cattle around so that the front stalls nearest the main barn door were vacant. We were able to keep Pretty Girl in the general area of her home-to-be, and the bait of grain and good hay got her to the right location, although it probably would have been easier with doughnuts.

The next two girls weren't as big or as well decorated with horns, and Pretty Girl was clearly the boss, so they were relatively content to fall in beside her, albeit not too close, since she waved them away from her pile of grain with a quick shake of the head and a snort. Howard and Marilee stayed and chatted for a while before we wrote out the check and said good-bye, thinking that we might next see them the following spring or summer.

The cattle settled into their new home, clearly content with Donald's gracious rations, and we began pitching in with morning and evening chores in the barn as much as we could. Then, several weeks later in mid-October, Howard called me at the office and left a message for me to call him back. I got him on the phone late one afternoon and, after a few minutes of catching up on how the cattle were doing, he had a proposal.

"Philip, I need to get rid of more cattle before winter, and I like what you folks are trying to do and where you've got them. I wanted to know if you and Erin might like to buy a few more from us. You can pay us whenever you're able—I think you and Erin are good for it—I'm not worried about that. I just want to find a good home for them. You interested?"

I was shocked. We were planning to grow a herd over time, selling some beef and milking for ourselves while exploring making cheese, butter, and yogurt. Suddenly it seemed like we were falling into it instead of growing into it. I hesitated. I wasn't sure that we were ready to dive in quite that fast, and I knew better than to say yes without discussing it with Erin. I asked if he could give us a few days to mull it over and also to talk to Donald about it.

"I didn't think you'd say yes till you talked it over with Erin first. It's a big decision, and I only want you to do it if it's the right thing. But I wanted to give you first shot at them. They're fine cattle, and it's hard enough for me to see them go—I want to make sure they're going to the right place."

Howard had told us about one person to whom he'd sold a few cattle earlier. He'd gotten a call from the SPCA saying that they'd been informed of several starving cattle and, after investigating, they found out that he had been the previous owner. In utter despair, he drove out to the farm, and the cattle were indeed the ones he had sold earlier that year—hide-covered skeletons barely able to move. The buyer had left them to fend for themselves in a depleted pasture. Just because they survive on relatively low-quality forage doesn't mean they should be left to fend for themselves. Even the most versatile breeds are meant to thrive, not just survive. Howard loaded up the cattle and brought them back home. He cared about his animals, no matter where they were.

Erin and I discussed the idea before dinner, over dinner, and after dinner. Even though we were excited at the prospect of building a herd a bit faster than planned, we had some trepidations, most of them financial. Sustainable agriculture becomes much less theoretical when financial realities are involved.

I called my friend Ed Lewis, a local dairy farmer who was renowned in the region for his successes in breeding Holsteins. After reaching his seventies and going through three hip replacements, he'd finally relented and sold his milking herd since there was no one to take over his farm. I asked him if he'd be willing to come with me and help me decide which additional animals to buy from the Mansfields. I just didn't know enough about cattle, much less Milking Devons, to make an informed decision. Ed agreed to go with me the next week, following a meeting we had together in the northern part of the state. I wanted to get there as soon as we could to make sure that we got the best stock possible.

The next week, as Ed and I pulled up to the Mansfields' farm, I got to watch him have a similar reaction to ours regarding the emus. "Geez, look at those damn things! Now that'd be a drumstick you could work on for a week . . . if you could find a way to kill the darn thing before it ate you! I don't know much about Devons, but I really don't know much about prehistoric chickens! All the way back to the dinosaurs— he's taking this rare-breed thing a little far, ain't he?"

I just about spit out my last slug of coffee to keep from choking with laughter. No other Vermont farmer that I'd met could get me laughing faster than Ed, and his open-mindedness always surprised me. On the drive over, he'd been reflecting on his lifetime of farming. "You know, you live long enough like I have, and you see things go full circle. We used to farm the way you'd call organic now, and a fellow used to be able to get by milking ten or twenty cows, selling some fresh milk—*raw* doesn't seem like the right word to me. Hell, it's *fresh* milk—doesn't have to be cooked, in my opinion. Anyway, my family took our milk to East Poultney to the cheese factory that turned the milk into cheese and butter and shipped it to the cities before the flood of 1927 took out the cheese factory and most of the mills and buildings along the river. And we let the cows do most of their own harvesting without keeping them inside and bringing breakfast, lunch, and dinner to them like most farmers do now. Nope, there's not a lot that's good about getting old except that you start seeing that everything you used to know getting popular again and there's a certain satisfaction in knowing that it maybe made sense after all. Hell, we all got on the bandwagon that the government and the feed salesman brought right to our door, and everybody was so busy enjoying the ride that we forgot what we were leaving behind!"

But the Devons did give Ed reason to pause in his full-circle retreat. We walked in the barn where Howard had gathered all of the cattle for the coming winter, and Ed looked around, sort of chuckling lightly and scratching his head. He glanced over at Howard. "Well, they ain't Holsteins, are they?"

"No sir," Howard replied. "That's the whole idea."

I could see Ed's trained eye go from legs to back to udder, and then he'd make his way around to the front of each animal.

"Now, Philip, I can tell you what I'd look for if these were Holsteins, or maybe even Jerseys, but these animals are so different from anything I've worked with that I'm just guessing. I might not be shootin' in the *dark,* but it's about twilight!"

"Ed, there's more wisdom between you and Howard than there is between my ears, so you tell me what you think, Howard can give us his opinion, and we'll go from there."

"How many you want?"

"Depends on the price, but maybe as many as five."

"Okay, well, in that case, that's the best one in the whole barn, right there, according to my eye." He pointed to the biggest cow in the bunch.

Howard nodded. "That'd be Bonnie. And you're right. She is a beauty. In fact, I named her calf Beauty—her calf's right over there."

We looked over at a perfectly framed heifer calf a few cows over. "Take her, too," Ed noted without any hesitation. "You want to do anything with milk, then maybe my eye will help you a little, although I still don't trust myself. I'm just looking for dairy build—'sharp,' I call it. Some folks call it 'angular.' I'm looking for a frame that's got some points to it, not something heavy-boned and beefy . . . unless you're more interested in beef."

"Nope, the Devons seem to be proving themselves on the beef side of things. Erin and I want to find out what they can do with dairy—just with grazing and hay. That's pretty much what we want to figure out with these cows—and to find a way to have them pay their way."

"It's just a matter of figuring out what product makes the most sense,"

Howard interjected. "You're not going to get close to the kind of quantity of milk that you get from a Holstein or a Jersey, but it's a different kind of milk. I'm convinced of that. It might not be what farmers want to ship to market, but I think it's got promise for other markets. We looked into the Devonshire cream, but the regs make that seem impossible, at least for folks like us with no deep pockets."

I shook my head. "Well, we're gonna have to do something besides Devonshire cream. I can't make something I can't eat—and I just can't appreciate anything that seems like spoiled milk, even if it's a delicacy."

Ed laughed and continued looking around the barn. "Okay, now there's a sharp one . . . and she's got a real nice color to her."

"That's Annette. She's a good one. Her mother is one of my favorites."

"Take her." Ed nodded to me to write her name down with the others. "And over there's another one I think you should take. She's a really good-looking heifer."

"That'd be Lilly." Howard grinned at Ed. "You've got a good eye. She's also one of Bonnie's."

Modest as always, Ed brushed off the compliment and kept looking. "All right . . . well, if you want one more, I'd take that one." He pointed across the barn.

"That's Patsy."

"Well, Philip, that's five. You want any more?"

"I'm not sure I need five, Ed, but I kind of hate to pass up a good deal."

"Yup, I'd hate for you to pass up a good deal, too. Breeding and selling cattle always worked good for me, especially when milk prices or farm expenses were bad. I think you'll do okay, especially if you keep learning from Donald. Plus, if they don't work out on the dairy end, you can always get a line going for beef . . ."

"Or you can sell them for oxen," Howard added. "I do pretty good selling my bull calves to ox teamsters. And there's no better breed than Milking Devons for oxen, as long as you give them plenty of handling and start training them young. Devons are known for being smarter than most other breeds and even a lot of people. That can work for you or against you, depending on how good a job you do working with them. You just always want to work *with* them, not against them. You won't win that game unless they're in the freezer—and they still might be tough as hell!"

We all laughed and walked toward the barn door together, looking over the herd one more time to make sure we'd seen everything. "I think those should be your five, Philip," Ed concluded. "I'll let you guys negotiate while I go get another look at those dinosaur drumsticks . . . from a distance!"

With a mixture of excitement and trepidation, I walked out of the barn and toward the house with Howard. "Well, Howard, can we work out something for those five?"

"So let me write it down . . . okay—Bonnie, Beauty, Lilly, Patsy, and Annette." Howard put the names on a piece of paper. "Yup, we can make it work for both of us. That would make us happy. And your friend Ed has a damn good eye."

"I know. If you couldn't tell it from his cattle, you'd know by the wife he chose—she's great, too."

Howard chuckled and then gave me his prices. "You pay us when you can, as you're able. It'd be nice to get most of it in the next year, but you guys do what you need to in order to get things started."

I stuck out my hand. "We sure do appreciate it, Howard. I can't thank you enough."

"Well, you guys get into this thing, you'll start to realize, it's about a lot more than just you or me. It's the animals, it's the breed, it's trying to preserve something important that's going to be lost if we don't all stick our necks out a little. Who knows, we might be saving the future with a little piece of the past."

When you're trying to answer a question that you think is really important, whether it's in farming or physics, sometimes it pays to be richly steeped in experience, and sometimes it's better to come at the question with fresh and naive eyes. Experience can save you a lot of headaches and mistakes, but ignorance can help you avoid the constraints of an inflexible paradigm. Whether we liked it or not, we were in the latter category. As we plunged ahead into a new world of rare breeds, grazing, cattle care, and culinary experiments with dairy and beef products, we found increasing knowledge and support from pioneering groups like the Vermont Grass Farmers' Association, the American Livestock Breeds Conservancy, and Slow Food—as well as authors like Joel Salatin, Allan Nation, Paul Kindstedt, and Gary Nabhan.

But in the background was the quiet wisdom of Donald. Watching our new cattle in the barn and the pastures, he would offer his observations, but—as had always been the case—he seldom counseled unless we asked. His advice tempered our enthusiasm for many of the new ideas I brought to the barn from my contacts at the college or our books and magazines. Like Ed, he wasn't against new ideas. He, too, had seen and felt the cost of playing an unfair game in the dairy world, a game umpired by the financial winners who just processed the milk, not by the real players—the farmers.

When we were waiting our first calves to arrive the following spring, Erin teased that I was a nervous wreck, full of adrenaline and questions, much like a new father. Meanwhile, Donald patiently puffed on his pipe from the door of his barn, looking at the Devons and watching nature take its course, just as it had on his family's farm for well over two hundred years.

One day when we were both standing at the barn door, watching the cattle start on their evening hay, I asked him how many cows he thought he'd seen calve.

"I don't know." He scratched his beard and looked up with half a smile. "Almost enough."

I did a few rough calculations, given his lifetime of farming. "Seems like it'd have to be way over a thousand."

"Maybe. I guess that ought to be about enough." The brim of his hat didn't quite hide the humor or the seriousness in his eyes. He wasn't ready to be done quite yet.

I walked over and checked Pretty Girl's udder for increased swelling.

"She'll be all right until the morning, I think," Donald assured me. "The good thing is—they know more about being cows than we do. I doubt she'll have any problems."

Howard and Ed were right about Bonnie. She was a gorgeous cow, but at nine years of age she did not take kindly to a new residence or new owners. Donald put her by the main entrance of the barn, and it turned out to be a good thing. She was right by the silo, and since all of the other cattle in the barn got silage and grain, ours didn't want to be an exception. Whenever Donald started chores, Bonnie would bellow repeatedly until she got the first rations. Whenever I walked into the barn and past her—virtually without exception—she would wave her head and then snort with a single ferocious blow. More than once, she gave me full-velocity snot-shots, with a burst of phlegm exploding on my pants.

Pretty Girl had her calf right on time that spring, and Bonnie followed suit within a few days. I began my milking career with Pretty Girl. I still think it's the hardest thing I've ever done. If there was ever a smarter and more uncooperative cow, I'd hate to meet her. Even with Donald's expert help, within the first few days she developed mastitis, thanks in part to a plugged and slightly deformed teat in her hindquarter. Mastitis is a bacterial infection that causes swelling and extreme tenderness in the teats and can move into the udder and even become systemic if not adequately treated. Unfortunately, we had to call the vet, and she decided that the only solution was to slightly open the hole of the blocked teat with an incision. We sedated Pretty Girl, and within minutes the vet had made the incision and inserted a small catheter to help it drain.

While she was under the effects of the anesthesia, I milked her again, with a bit less trepidation. The sedation seemed to still her movements, for the most part, but it was quite obvious that her utter displeasure at my intentions of turning her into our family milk cow was still very much intact. I could still detect her suspicious gaze, despite her drooping eyelids.

As it turned out, we also had to sedate her for the next three milkings. I had tried to milk her alone without the sedation, but every zing in the bucket earned a well-placed kick to dislodge both me and the bucket. Donald couldn't hold her, and even with his son Doug holding her rear end and tailing her, it was hopeless. But we couldn't get rid of the mastitis if we couldn't get her milked out completely. The vet had guessed that we might have problems, so we went for the remaining doses of sedative that she'd left with us in case we had difficulties.

I was beginning to question my sanity. But after a few more painfully slow milkings, Pretty Girl seemed to have decided that it might not be worth the battle. She was still up for a spat, but she seemed less interested in a full-scale war of wills. We gradually developed a routine of mutual tolerance, although there was no guarantee that milking would yield any milk to take home—her aim was matched only by her timing, and she occasionally found ways to send the bucket and its contents flying into the muck right at the end of the process.

To whatever degree Pretty Girl was obstinate, Bonnie was equal in her malevolence. She made it perfectly clear that she did not like where she had ended up at this late point in her career, and given her violent thrashing of horns even at the gawking of any onlooker, I wasn't about to milk her. I was determined to keep my distance. We'd decided that we would get a few calves from her and then send her packing . . . or to be packed, whichever seemed like the best option. She was just too dangerous.

However, I walked into the barn one morning to find Pretty Girl's calf slightly tangled in his tie-stall chain. (All of the cow–calf pairs were separated by a single metal bar at about hip height.) I stepped into Pretty Girl's tie stall to pick up her calf's foot, only to feel a piercing blow catch me in the left side of my rib cage and pick me up off the ground and toss me about 4 feet over into the sawdust and manure right under Pretty Girl.

Bonnie had somehow gotten her neck and head under the adjacent tie-stall bar that separated her from Pretty Girl, and she had caught me with her horns from underneath the bar while I wasn't looking. Covered with about an inch of brown humiliation, I could barely breathe at first, much less move. However, Pretty Girl wasn't very excited having me on the barn floor next to her and her calf, so I rolled out of the way, unsure of how hurt I was. Bonnie had definitely cracked a few of my ribs and maybe broken one—I never bothered to get an X-ray to confirm what seemed obvious.

I struggled to get up out of the slippery mixture of manure and sawdust. Doubled over in pain, I looked up at Bonnie. Her piercing eyes weren't looking at me out of curiosity. She was still challenging me. Still stooping, I seethed. "I'll be eating Bonnie burgers before this is all over." I straightened up and scraped some of the manure off my pants and shirt. *This is a helluva way to get an education,* I winced.

I gradually recuperated, although every sneeze for the next few months reminded me of Bonnie. It was a good reminder that animals with horns—a breed standard for the American Milking Devons—require vigilance and peripheral vision, available head restraint, and a willingness to eliminate animals that can't be trusted. Keeping horned animals is a judgment call, and I respect the decision either to keep the horns or to have them removed at a young age. It depends on the farmer's perspective and needs. Horns are good protection against predators, and it's fascinating to see how many ways the animals can use them. In the long run, deciding to have horned animals requires a person to pay more careful attention to animal behavior—not necessarily a bad thing. Even then, accidents still happen.

Despite my struggles with Bonnie and Pretty Girl, I persevered, and the joys began to overcome the frustrations and occasional agonies, particularly once the cattle went out on pasture in early May. Despite all of my reading, research, and farm visits, it ended up taking me several years to figure out how to manage the grazing so that I could best satisfy the nutritional needs of a small herd of cattle. I experimented with various kinds of fencing and watering systems while also getting a feel for the variety and density of different grasses and legumes in different areas of the pastures.

Initially, I was limited in funds, expertise, equipment, and time, and I did a relatively poor job of managing the pastures to maximize the health of the animals and the vegetation. However, as I discovered new methods and equipment that helped me to provide the cattle with just enough forage for a twenty-four-hour period, I watched the cattle and the pastures begin to show the effects of good management. All the while, I was conscious of Joel Salatin's observation that cattle want to eat dessert first and save the rest for last, so good grazing management involves making sure they get both and eat both in each grazing period. As he noted, the mobility and versatility of portable electric fencing revolutionized the way we can manage pastures, since this kind of fencing provides both the steering and the brakes for livestock.[3]

However, it wasn't just about equipment. Ultimately, it was the gradual development of experience and a trained eye that allowed me to use the equipment wisely. I also needed to develop methods for building the fertility of the pastures through careful winter feeding of hay on the pastures—allowing the cattle to fertilize the pastures while working through their winter supply, with the unconsumed hay adding both seed and organic matter. The struggle was in determining how to distribute the hay relatively evenly across the pastures, with heavier accumulations in areas that I'd noted were lacking in fertility or desirable forage species—all without a tractor for the first several years. I used both square bales that I could place most anywhere I wanted with my truck and round bales that I had delivered to high ground so that I could simply roll them out from the top of the hill. Without a tractor, I found myself at a disadvantage, not just because I couldn't strategically place bales for careful winter feeding, but also because I couldn't clip the weeds in the pastures as needed, resulting in some weedy areas that took me a while to transform into good pasture. Fortunately, Donald and his family helped out with the mowing as they were able.

To complicate matters further, I needed to separate the herd at various points in time, mixing in or pulling out a bull, and, in later years, dividing the herd into various breeding groups with different bulls, while also isolating a few cows to experiment with artificial insemination using the genetics from bulls outside our closed herd.

Ultimately, it took me about six years of grazing and winter feeding to begin to get a handle on the best strategies for simultaneously managing cattle and pastures and to see a marked difference in the quality of our leased pastures. I was glad that our income was not dependent upon the cattle for the first few years, as I sorted my way through the ecological questions and strategies, balancing herbivores and a productive landscape. I was also working on the intersection of ecology and economics involved in grass farming by trying to graze as far into the winter as possible. I finally got to the point of being able to manage the cattle and the grass so that I could graze into early January most years, with little or no hay used up to that point.

A rule of thumb for most businesses is that it takes at least five years to reach economic viability, and farming is no different. If anything, farming is more difficult, since it is so tightly tied not just to the business climate, but also to the ecological climate—and the capital costs can be overwhelming. Although we've made plenty of mistakes in building our herd and experimenting with small-scale dairying, I am glad that we pursued our farming experiments in the context of a homestead, focusing first on increasing our own food production while learning how we might best scale up—strategically, incrementally, and in concert with the growth of our family. Our understanding of rare breeds, herd health, pasture ecology, dairy products, necessary homestead infrastructure, off-grid challenges and opportunities, and farm economics has grown tremendously—and we've eaten well in the process, as have some of our friends. And the balance sheet looks brighter every year.

TWELVE

Building a Future

Once again, we found ourselves debating whether to focus on shelter for ourselves or our livestock. Even with the addition of Asa and thoughts of another child, the cabin still fit us fine. Asa slept between us, allowing everyone to stay in bed for the nighttime nursings, and even once he started crawling, we had the advantage of being able to keep a close eye on him, since he was pretty much limited to a one-room range.

However, we were beginning to dream of things like a washing machine for dirty diapers and a sink with running water. Even the addition of a sink with a functioning drain in lieu of a bucket that had to be emptied several times a day seemed like a potential luxury. But a barn for storing hay and housing the cattle when necessary was a more immediate priority.

I'd been going down to the Waites' once or twice a day throughout the winter and spring to help take care of our cattle in their barn—not an easy task in winter, mud season, or the height of the semester at the college. I'd also realized that, although I liked using large round bales to feed the cattle in the fall and winter, the outer layers deteriorated too much by late winter and early spring to make them economical for use at that time of year. Any investment in hay storage was therefore a strategy toward long-term savings.

By this time, we'd lived "up Tunket" for five years, and we had identified a general area surrounding our first barn to establish our burgeoning homestead infrastructure. The area around this first barn was the driest spot that we could find—not an easy task in our water-rich environment—an area with ample southern exposure, proximity to our first barn and the existing road, and a nice view of the hills around us. It seemed to make sense to finalize the sites for a new barn and a prospective new house.

We were getting our finances back in order, having stretched our limits in 2000 by purchasing an additional 100 acres of woodland across

the road from our original 25 acres and adjacent to the existing properties being purchased and conserved by The Nature Conservancy. Although the entire parcel had been overlogged, to the point of having no marketable timber whatsoever, it was a magnificent piece of land that risked being developed into four separate 25-acre parcels. When we heard that the asking price had dropped to $59,000, we checked with The Nature Conservancy to see if they were interested in purchasing it. As it turned out, they had some interest in the portion of the property nearest their new preserve, but they needed to do an ecological assessment and an appraisal, as well as procure the needed funds, if in fact the assessment and appraisal fit their goals and budgets.

That process looked like it would take at least a year, and the results were uncertain. We suspected that the land would be purchased and developed before that process would unfold, so our Realtor friend Scott McChesney once again helped negotiate a purchase agreement with the landowners, allowing us to buy the land with a fairly risky balloon mortgage, with a low down payment and a somewhat high interest rate. If we couldn't find a way to pay the entire mortgage within ten years, either through a series of payments or a lump sum at the end, we would lose our entire investment.

In the end, we bought the parcel in the hope that The Nature Conservancy would decide to purchase at least a portion of it from us. Within several years of our purchase, the Conservancy did in fact buy about two-thirds of the property and purchased a conservation easement on the remaining acreage. We lost several thousand dollars in the sale because the appraisal came in lower than what we had paid, but we were delighted to have helped build the preserve. When we want to, we can usually find a way to afford to do the right thing.

Getting that second mortgage off our backs, we were then able to focus on making our own lives a bit more comfortable. So, once we got past mud season and into the early stages of summer, we called our excavator friend Leon Corey to get an estimate for putting in a concrete foundation for the new barn; this barn needed to be bigger and more stable than the first, given our need to store up to two thousand bales of hay for the winter. We were torn, though. Two of our nearby farming friends, Scout and Matt Proft, had impressed us with their efforts to do all of their building without concrete, so that if the farm infrastructure changed there would not be a disposal issue, as was the case with the concrete.

However, with the need to have a stable building that would hold more than 30 tons of hay, we were concerned that any option other than a solid concrete foundation risked a repeat of the foundation problems that we'd experienced with the cabin. Additionally, we needed to be absolutely sure that the barn floor would have excellent drainage and be perfectly dry for the animals. We knew that we didn't want a concrete floor—concrete is easy to clean, but it is hard on animals' hooves and legs.

We decided to install a sand floor, in an effort to use relatively sterile sand as bedding, under a layer of mulch hay. Although it is not as easy to clean up manure from a sand floor, we were optimistic that the addition of sand to our composted manure would create a compost that would at once incorporate sand, nutrients, and organic matter into our wet clay soils. Also, since our cattle were eating only hay and no grain or silage, their manure tended to be reasonably stiff and not too difficult to clean up off a sand floor. We also knew that cattle housed on concrete floors typically need their hooves trimmed several times a year, and we felt that the abrasion of the sand would relieve us of that unnecessary worry and expense. As it turned out, it was a good decision.

We didn't know it at the time, but there is in fact a new concern about concrete. It is one of the biggest sources of greenhouse gas emissions in the building industry, and the production and curing of concrete is estimated to be responsible for somewhere between 5 and 10 percent of global carbon dioxide emissions.[1]

In the end, we resolved that putting in a concrete foundation was the most pragmatic choice. We tried to make it a reasonable ecological choice as well by designing the barn to be multifunctional and versatile, so that it could easily be retrofitted for another homestead or cottage industry use. The versatility of the barn's design has already paid off, since we've already reconfigured the interior of the lower section for easier cleaning and feeding of the cows and their calves; plus, we've utilized portions of the hayloft and the rafters for drying and storing wood from the portable sawmill that we purchased just as we began construction of the newer barn.

Part of building the new barn involved diverting and capturing some of the water that sweeps down our hill from the top of the Fox Cobble, the ledgy ridge that rises up behind our homestead. There was one particularly wet spot between our cabin and our first barn—and not too far from where we were planning to site our new barn and house—that always appeared to want to be a swamp, not a pasture. In the end we decided that it actually wanted to be a pond.

When Leon came up early that summer to look at the proposed barn site and calculate the foundation costs, we showed him the potential site for a pond. It seemed like a good idea to have a fire pond—anything to mollify the insurance industry—and an even better idea to have somewhere to swim. Although the pond ended up being the best $1,500 I think I've ever spent (Erin's wedding ring was a family heirloom), for the first year it looked like the biggest hole I've ever dug for myself.

Erin and I just assumed that Leon would use his excavator to dig the pond. However, he said that he knew an easier way that would save us a lot of money. He was right . . . mostly. The first step was to wait until August, the driest part of the year in these parts. First we all agreed on the proposed outline of the pond, then we staked out the area. A few weeks later, Leon came back with his men and his equipment. While he excavated the site for the new barn, he put one of his men on a bulldozer for seven hours, going back and forth hundreds of times, pushing dirt lengthwise, then shoving the excess over to the dam side and packing it down by riding over it again and again. As it turned out, that entire summer was particularly dry—increasing our desire for a pond to dip into on the hottest of days.

The year prior had been one of the driest periods ever recorded in our region, with springs going dry that had always been reliable water sources for a lot of the old houses in the area. Like many other people in our region, we had decided then that we had to put in a well. We could do without a lot of things, but readily accessible water was not one of them. It was no longer a matter of just hauling in drinking water, as we'd done the first year. Now there were cattle to water and diapers to wash.

We had called a local family-owned well-drilling company. They were booked solid through the rest of the summer and into the fall due to the number of failed wells and springs. They finally drove up with their equipment just as winter seemed to be moving in, barely able to get their equipment where they needed it due to slippery terrain on our hill.

Before using their high-tech drilling equipment, Clarence and his son both walked over to one of our apple trees and each cut a forked dowsing stick. They began wandering in the general area that we said would be a suitable location for a well, given where we hoped to site the new house. Following the visible downward tug of their dowsing sticks, the two of them nearly ran into each other. They nodded in agreement at their point of intersection.

Clarence pointed down with the end of his stick. "There's a lot of water under here," He tapped his stick hard on the frozen ground. "I think there's a good vein about 60 or 70 feet down." His son nodded in agreement, so Erin and I concurred that the location they'd chosen would work for us. We watched as they set up the drill, and then we went back to the cabin to work. I went back out to check on progress a little while later. They'd just gotten to about 60 feet and Clarence was shaking his head, obviously agitated. I asked him if his estimate on the water depth was off.

"No, I got it right—dead on, actually. We hit more water than you could ever use at exactly 65 feet . . . but the rock down there is too crumbly. If we stop there and put your well at that depth, it's just gonna cave in. Might be a few months, maybe a few years—but it's not gonna last. We have to go till we find the next vein. I guess I'm just gonna lose money on this one. We're gonna be puttin' in a lot of casing—we'll be lucky if this is a break-even job."

Erin and I had opted to pay a flat fee for the well, no matter the depth, instead of paying a per-foot charge that could have saved us money if we hit water at a relatively shallow depth. Even though it looked like the deal was working out in our favor, I couldn't help but feel a little guilty. I did my best to apologize without inadvertently undoing the agreement.

"Oh, it's okay." Clarence rubbed his sandy beard. "This has been a pretty good year for making money. And if we finish up here fast enough, we'll get in another one this afternoon."

Within a few hours, they had installed a well with a hand pump that we had to special-order from out West. It was a good thing that we did install it, since we had another dry year the following summer, albeit not quite so bad. Even though it required nine hundred strokes twice a day to water the livestock, it still felt better than driving somewhere else to fill up huge barrels of water.

Leon and his crew had finished digging the pond in late August and had used the excess soil to level out some areas around the new barn site. That evening, with the roar of the dozer hushed and a huge 11-foot-deep gouge all too obvious outside our cabin window, Erin and I circumspectly walked the oval edge of the new hole, clambering over the pines we'd taken down along the upper edge of the pond. Then we went down into the muddy bottom, well below the roots that dangled from the uphill side, sheared off without any real forewarning.

We knew that a deep pond with steep sides is less prone to algal problems, but we couldn't help but wonder if we'd made an enormous mistake. The ecological cost seemed potentially much higher than the minimal financial outlay. If this hole in the ground turned out to be a big mistake, I didn't know how I was ever going to cover it up. The only thing we had to fill it with was water. I hoped that the water would come . . . and stay. And assuming it did come, I hoped the enormous dam on the downhill side would hold it.

The day after the big dig, I went over to Phil's Mill to pick up another load of lumber for the new barn. Leon and a friend of his would be pouring the foundation soon, and I wanted to stockpile the lumber for the first floor so that I could get the project going before winter moved in . . . again. Besides having excellent rough-cut lumber, Phil had become a critical resource for me. Whenever I needed a second opinion on any kind of construction, he had the best answers anywhere, as far as I was concerned. Anything he built or made was stout, elegantly simple, and well adapted to the Vermont landscape and seasons.

I'd already discussed the design of the pond with Phil a few weeks before. I wanted to know his thoughts on putting in an overflow pipe like we had in the pond at my grandparents' farm.

"Oh, geez, don't do that! A few years back, I built a pond on another farm, and we got a freak early-spring thunderstorm while the ice was still on the pond. Next thing you know, the level of the pond was going up by the minute, and the ice just picked up the top of the overflow pipe as it got pushed higher and higher . . . and before I knew it, the pipe was ripped out of there and the pond drained like a big bathtub, just about taking half the county with it!"

He looked down at the plank floor of his sawmill and kicked a small pile of sawdust, shaking his head as if he were trying to banish the memory. "No, just put in a simple outlet on one end and let it flow out somewhere away from the dam. That outlet pipe will cost you way more than the pond—probably twice over . . . the first time when you put it in and the second time when you have to clean up the mess it makes when it doesn't work. One more piece of overpriced technology just waitin' to fail!"

As usual, when I pulled up to Phil's Mill the day after we'd put the enormous gash in our landscape, Phil was again standing on the deck, pushing the carriage lever of the mill, allowing a perfectly shaped hemlock log to ride the carriage straight toward the enormous saw blade. The mill's diesel engine throbbed effortlessly, even when the blade met the tapered end of the log. Only the penetrating pitch of the blade changed, varying with the log's symphony of grain and knots.

Phil saw me coming and gave a tug of his cowboy hat and a flip of the wrist wave. Sawdust flew from the kerf, and the blade made its final high-pitched zing as it burst through the butt of the log. With the final zing came the solid thud of the rock-solid 2×8 as it fell away. Phil's helper carefully grabbed the fresh board, and Phil ambled over to me with a big handshake.

I told him about the progress on the pond, but confessed that I was getting nervous and wondered if he thought we'd done it the best way. "Well, that depends . . . did you get the dozer out before letting the water come in?"

I laughed. "Got that part right. But I hope it's not just going to be some big mudhole."

"I doubt that'll be a problem. You've got enough water up there to fill up half the town of Pawlet. Did you take out the keyline?"

"I don't know what it is, so I'm not sure if we did or not. If it went in the dump truck, I didn't notice it."

"It's a layer of gravel and real coarse stuff that you usually hit a few feet down—the layer where the water moves underground. It's especially important on the dam side, where it's probably going to leak the most. You guys just used a dozer, right?"

"Pretty much," I replied. "We used the backhoe a little to clean up the shape."

"The best way to take care of that keyline is just to get the backhoe and invert the layers of soil, just flip them right over on the dam side—that'll seal it up good and fast."

I knew that I should have come to pick up my lumber the day before.

At any rate, the pond did fill—almost too fast. It took two months just to get 2 feet of water in the bottom, thanks to the drought, but then it filled up in less than forty-eight hours after a snowmelt just before Christmas of that year. We were ecstatic, even if it was muddy water.

However, by the time winter had passed and the excess water level from the spring thaw had subsided, it became clear that there were some holes on the dam side that weren't filling very quickly. Our excitement level about our new pond vacillated with the water level.

By the time summer arrived, my optimism had dried up, and the crew of three that I'd hired to help me put up the hayloft walls and roof of the new barn had a bird's-eye perspective on my muddied ambitions. Having finished the first floor over the course of the fall and winter, I'd hired two college alums, Kurt and Mike, along with our carpenter neighbor John to raise the 12-foot walls on the second floor and to get the roof on before the summer's hay rolled in. The higher up we worked, the worse the mudhole looked. The silences and the long stretches of monotonous labor on most any construction site are filled with teasing, but seldom is the object of derision so evident. Whether I liked it or not, I was no longer alone in my doubt about the wisdom of putting in a pond.

By the end of July 2003, we were beginning the roof of the barn. Erin and I had also committed to a location for our new house, just above the new barn. Erin had been working on possible designs for several years. She was still unsure about all the details, but she did decide on a 24' × 36' foundation. Fortunately, our families had chipped in on some of the barn costs and part of the house foundation work so that we had some equity in the land with which to approach a mortgage banker for the balance of the construction costs.

We decided to go ahead and have the excavation and foundation work done so that we could cap the basement with floor joists and a subfloor before winter hit. We could then begin construction without delay the following spring. We hired Leon to prep the site for the foundation, and Erin had the rest of the winter to work out the architectural details. She put her art major to the test and made us both thankful that she'd shifted from drawing to sculpture, just to force her brain to function in a different way.

Dismayed by the leaking on the dam side of the pond and spurred on by Erin's dissatisfaction with a simple oval shape, we asked Leon to refine the pond while he was working on the house excavation. Erin had him add a bit more flair, giving it a larger kidney shape, while also working to compact the dam with the excavator. Within weeks, the pond was nearly full, and the jokes subsided as the walls and roof of the new barn began to block the pond from constant view. The August heat also made the muddy water seem all the more enticing, especially at midday after working on the heat of a roof.

By the following spring, the pond was filled with hundreds of frogs and thousands of tadpoles, and before long we had a blue heron and a few wild ducks stop in for a visit. Cattails appeared serendipitously, and salamanders migrated in as the water cleared. Now, several years later, the chorus of peepers, wood frogs, bullfrogs, and toads nearly drowns out our outdoor conversations in late spring and early summer, and nothing is more delightful than a moonlit swim among cattails and frogs.

The cows had a fine home, and so did the amphibians. Now it was our turn. Finally.

THIRTEEN

Crafting a Croft

Small matters. At least I thought they were small matters, albeit sensible ones. Off-grid power from photovoltaic panels and a small wind turbine, a solar hot-water system, wood heat, rugged full-dimension lumber milled locally, Erin as designer and me as builder—all in a beautiful setting adjacent to what was becoming one of The Nature Conservancy's most-visited preserves in Vermont. I confess that I didn't make mention of the composting toilets—well-dressed bankers just don't seem appreciative of that kind of regenerative wealth.

After several years of sketches, graph paper layouts, and even a few tabletop cardboard models of her different ideas for our new house, Erin homed in on a final design. Now that we knew what we were building, it was clear that we needed a mortgage. Leon had installed the house foundation and a septic tank the previous fall, right after we had finished building the second barn. Erin and I had pondered the best way forward throughout the winter of 2003–04, in anticipation of building as much of the house as possible the following summer.

We seemed to have two options. We could continue our tight-as-a-ship living space by building just what we could afford at the time and adding on later as needed, which certainly had its merits. More than one family in our area had opted to live in their capped basements for a few years, saving money to build the remainder of the house above them, so we knew that possibility wasn't out of the question. Our other option was to build the entire frame at once and to a scale that we knew would be sufficient not only for our long-term living space needs but also for a few cottage industry possibilities that we could fit on the same foundation and under the same roof as the rest of the house. Both approaches had economic and ecological merits—one followed the path of patient frugality while the other allowed for a fast-paced, entrepreneurial tack that was dependent upon outside financing.

We eventually opted to move ahead as quickly as possible, building a house that had ample living space for a growing family, as well as two potential guest rooms with a separate entrance, bath, and balcony. It was a model that we'd seen work well for the Bergbauern[1] in the Alps, with extra rooms providing the farm with supplemental income from tourists and allowing tourists a window into a life that was relatively foreign to them. It also seemed a reasonable source of potential retirement income, since we were investing all our extra money into the building of a homestead and farm that we hoped could endure climatic and economic storms for generations to come, through a design of buildings and income streams that would allow for flexibility, diversity, and frugality over time. We also designed a good portion of the basement to accommodate a cheesemaking operation or any other cottage industry enterprise that would fit well within the confines of the house, with appropriate plumbing, radiant heat, and natural light.

The most expensive parts of a house are generally the foundation and the roof, and keeping everything on a relatively tight 24' × 36' footprint gave us an array of long-term options while also allowing the entire structure to be heated with two woodstoves and supplemental radiant floor heat in the basement. By the time we finally moved into the house, our friends and family teased us about our leap in scale—going from a tiny cabin to four stories of living and working space. Nonetheless, we were happy to put all of our options under one roof and with a common energy infrastructure that still allowed us to maintain a relatively low-impact lifestyle.

As it turned out, the bankers didn't quite see it our way. It wasn't clear whether they considered us to be a backwoods joke or simply an implausible risk. We'd paid off both mortgages on our land well in advance of their due dates, our credit rating was excellent, and we already had the foundation poured and paid for (thanks in part to some help from our families). However, the bankers I visited clearly viewed our ideas of designing and building for energy independence and durability and doing it with the help of our friends and neighbors as risky at best, if not outright wacky. Besides, the bankers weren't interested in keeping their mortgages in-house—they admitted that they sold virtually all of them soon after they were acquired.

My first visit to a bank to discuss a mortgage made it clear what we were up against. I walked into the bank with which we'd been doing business ever since we'd arrived in Vermont. (Well, the same bank in the

sense that it was in the same building, though it had operated under three different names in a period of about seven years. I guess we'd been doing business with the very same building and a few of the same people for that period.) The branch manager was all too glad to discuss the possibility of reeling in another mortgage, until she started hearing phrases she didn't understand—*off-grid, photovoltaics, solar thermal*—and words she clearly understood—*owner-builder, wood heat, rough-cut lumber*. And there were a few unspoken terms—*composting toilets, lack of central heat,* among others.

"I'm sorry, Philip, but I'm afraid your idea of a house is too unconventional for us to take on as an investment—it's just too risky."

"What's risky about it?" I queried, relatively innocently at that point. Our credit was excellent, and we were talking about building a house that would have almost no utility bills.

"Well, we can't be convinced that other potential buyers might want to buy a house with solar and wind power, especially something that's so far off a main road. And heating with wood is a risk we don't really like—you need to have something that's dependable and safer, like oil or gas heat."

"I sort of like the idea of heating with what's right outside the door . . ." I smiled at her and thought better of continuing my line of thinking in that regard, namely that something that has to be imported from halfway around the world on a tanker seems more than a little risky to me.

"I know—but not everyone thinks it's practical to heat with wood. And what if you want to leave and go somewhere during the winter?"

The fact that the animals all have to be taken care of twice a day so someone always has to be there anyway didn't seem to sway her. And then we hit the owner-builder issue. "You know, I really don't mean to be disrespectful, but banks like to ensure that there's an architect and a professional contractor involved—people who do this kind of thing every day and know what they're doing. And we prefer graded lumber that we know is structurally sound."

I respectfully acknowledged her perspective but wasn't willing to concede. "I see your point, but it's hard to beat full-dimension hemlock lumber for strength and durability." I was sure that she had never been to a yellow pine plantation down South and seen the fast-growing twenty- or thirty-year-old trees they convert into "quality" lumber. I'll take a stout, full-dimension hemlock or northern-grown white pine any day. Slow-growing trees have a tighter grain and make a higher-quality wood than fast-growing plantation-raised trees.

I decided to try another tack. "You know, we're using a local sawmill and supporting a local businessperson who might even have his money invested here in your bank. I doubt Home Depot is doing your bank much good. Doesn't that count for something?"

"Well, since we sell our mortgages, the buyers don't really care much about that, even though we might. We're more concerned about it being built properly."

I couldn't convince her that we were inclined to do a better job building it than many builders might, since we were the ones who were going to be investing and living in it. And most other builders' ideas of good materials—OSB board, plywood, flimsy 2×4s, carpets and glue—certainly didn't jibe with our choice of materials. We were simply not interested in materials that off-gas and that don't last all that long except in the landfill—where they tend to end up in relatively short periods of time, in my experience.

Once it was clear that we were at an impasse, I decided to give up and head elsewhere. I thanked her for her time and wondered if I was getting a taste of things to come. She offered me a polite handshake. "I wish we could help you, Philip, but this is just too risky an investment for us to put in our portfolio."

That conversation pretty much repeated itself at the next two banks that I visited, albeit in shorter form. I was getting the message. *Risk* seemed to be the recurrent phrase from the bankers. Unsure what to do, I asked a local attorney who did a lot of real estate transactions what he would suggest. He told me that there were two independent banks left in the state, both of which he thought still kept all their mortgages in-house. "Try the First National Bank of Orwell up in Addison County," he suggested. "They seem to be great at working with farmers and people who want to build their own houses."

I called and made an appointment there with a banker that same week. Despite the fact that it was late January, I knew the construction season wasn't that far off, and we needed to be ready to go once the weather allowed us to begin transporting building materials up the road.

As it turned out, my appointment was with Tom Eddy, the vice president of the First National Bank of Orwell. I followed his directions to the bank, with no difficulty. Orwell is a town of about twelve hundred residents, and the village center consists primarily of the bank, the village green, the school, the general store, the main church, a library, and the post office, all located on the eastern shore of Lake Champlain near one of the most strategic sites on the lake during the Revolutionary War. I decided then that if I ever moved anywhere else in Vermont, it would have to be Orwell. My immediate aesthetic draw to the town was soon reinforced by an appreciation for what the bank stood for.

The smallest bank in Vermont, the First National Bank of Orwell dates back to 1832.[2] The simple but elegant Victorian Gothic style of the brick building provided a prelude for the unexpected decor of the interior. As I pushed open the heavy oak door at the entrance, the checkered pattern of the tiled floor pulled my eye toward the teller windows, where ornate brass bars protected the tellers from bandits old and new (in fact, the town was startled by an armed robbery of the bank later in 2006). Gilded chandeliers added an element of simple wealth and pride, without being ostentatious. I was shocked to see that the tellers still used the old wooden coin trays. But then again, it made sense, as I remembered how surprised I was to discover that the bank didn't have a Web site or an e-mail address that I could find when I was researching it. If the business was still going strong after 170 years, the bankers obviously knew what still worked and what didn't. I couldn't help but think that keeping the anonymity of the wired world at bay probably worked in their favor.

Tom Eddy's assistant called him out of his office to meet me, and he greeted me with a welcoming handshake and a gentle smile. He invited me into his simply furnished office, with a few wooden chairs surrounding a stout, handsome antique desk, a historic reminder that contrasted with the computer perched behind him.

"I really appreciate you taking the time to meet with me, Tom, and I don't want to waste any of your time, so why don't I just go ahead and tell you what we're trying to do and why three other banks have more or less laughed me out the door."

Tom raised his eyebrows a little and smiled slightly. "Okay—go ahead."

"So my wife Erin and I have paid off two mortgages, we have no debt, we've got good credit, we've poured a foundation that's capped and paid for, and we're trying to design and build an off-grid house ourselves— solar electric with a small wind turbine, solar hot water with a propane backup, primarily wood heat, and all rough-cut wood from a local mill and whatever wood I can find time to mill myself."

I looked up after ticking off all of the previously expressed concerns on my fingers, worried I might find the half-hidden smirk that I'd seen on the face of at least one of the previous bankers. Instead, Tom nodded.

He maintained a prudent banker's cautious conservatism, but he didn't look like he was inclined to halt the conversation. "Well, that sounds pretty much like how people have been doing things around here since our bank was founded . . . of course, the solar and wind stuff is new, but it's sensible. The off-grid power can affect the potential resale of the house, and that's something our board of directors has to think about. It doesn't mean that it won't sell—it just means that it might sell slower since you've really got to find the right buyer who's willing to live the way you are, plus it might lower the potential asking price of the house. Are you far off the beaten track?"

"You could say that."

"That's a good bit of what we have around Orwell, so that doesn't necessarily scare us, but it's something we'll need to think about. Again, it's more about resale value than anything else. Some people like to invest in their privacy, but they're probably a minority. So, do you have plans for the house that I can take a look at?"

I pulled out the eight pages of light green graph paper on which Erin had her scaled pencil drawings of the house elevations and floor plans.

"Did you do these?"

"No, Erin's come up with the entire design herself. She was an art major, and her dad's a civil engineer, so this is right up her alley. And I decided that if she designed it and I kept my mouth shut and just built it like she drew it, then our marriage should be able to survive the whole ordeal."

Tom laughed in agreement. "Probably wise. It looks beautiful. It's sort of got an Alpine style to it."

"There's a reason for that." I told him of our time in the South Tirol, where we were so impressed with the fact that houses were built to last for generations, and by the way in which balconies and terraces provided both outdoor living spaces and an attractive architectural flair that broke up otherwise monotonous lines and planes and added nooks and hideaways. Erin had long been an ardent fan of the book *Pattern Language,* and I loved Gaston Bachelard's *The Poetics of Space,* both of which advocated for the creation of unique spaces that could hold, in Bachelard's words, "compressed time."[3]

Tom continued to ask questions, and we went through each page of the plans. As it turns out, he'd built his own house as well and was sympathetic to the challenges involved. After about half an hour, he stopped asking questions and looked up.

"Okay, well, I definitely like the design of the house and how you want to build it and use it. The next step is for me to drive up to your homestead and see what you've got. Then—if things look okay—I'll take some photos, copies of Erin's drawings, and my recommendation to our board for consideration. You're just on the edge of our lending area, but I like what you're trying to do, so let's see how it all looks."

The next time I saw Tom, he was getting out of his old pickup truck, dressed in jeans and a flannel shirt, looking more like a neighbor than a banker. After a review of the capped foundation that we already had in place and a quick tour of the property, we invited him into our modest cabin and went through the remainder of his questions with the house plans and a detailed budget in front of us—on our table constructed out of an old countertop and recycled 2×4s. I'd used Erin's careful drawings to calculate every piece of lumber I thought we'd need in the house for every wall, floor, and rafter, as well as estimates of the rest of the necessary infrastructure . . . plus the purchase of some needed tools that I didn't yet have, most of them power tools that I hadn't been able to justify previously, given our lack of electricity other than a borrowed generator.

I'm not sure whether the bank considered us to be a safe risk or a worthy charitable cause, but within a few weeks we'd gotten word from Tom that the board supported our project and was willing to offer us a construction loan to complete the house. We could later decide whether to find another bank to take on the construction loan as a fixed-rate mortgage, or we could convert the construction loan into a mortgage with their bank. Besides making sure that they knew their clients and their projects, the Orwell bankers offer mortgages at a rate just slightly higher than the standard lending rate—generally within ½ to 1 percent of the national average—and the mortgage comes due every three years and is re-signed at that time, based on the current interest rate at the time. Obviously, a fixed mortgage at a low rate is ideal, but that three-year loan keeps the bank safe in the midst of huge market fluctuations over time.

In our view, it was a win–win. We were happy to invest in a bank that was willing to invest in people like us—and a bank that was literally so invested in the well-being of its community.

Spring was beginning its covert entry, with the road changing from rock-hard ice to slush to mud to clay-brick status. We could finally start bringing in loads of hemlock lumber fresh-cut from Phil's Mill in preparation for a summer of framing and roofing. In mid-April, I decided it was safe to pull the 30' × 40' heavy-duty tarp off the first-floor decking that had served as a roof for the basement foundation through the winter. The accumulated cold air surged out of the basement as I peeled the tarp away, the slightly musty scent dissipating into the April sunshine. The frogs that had just laid their stashes of eggs in the adjacent pond were basking spread-eagle on the surface, occasionally giving off vibrating grunts of approval for their new home. We were ready to be neighbors with them, as soon as we could.

On April 8, 2004, we laid out the first floor with a red chalk-line in the skilled hands of our neighbor John, an excellent carpenter whose ideals matched—and in some ways exceeded—our own. A self-employed bachelor, John built his own 24' × 24' house on a wooded hill, digging out his basement and the 5-foot-deep trench for the pipes from his well to his house with a pick and shovel. Through the use of materials salvaged on various carpentry and painting jobs, John incurred no debt in building his house, and he heats the tightly designed structure with less than two cords of wood a year. He gets his power from a small battery bank charged by running a generator one to two hours per day—while taking his shower and running the well-pump to fill his pressure tank. John takes on painting and carpentry jobs when the weather is conducive to it, saving his money to get through the rest of the year. He pays cash for everything, so he stays debt-free and liberated, spending his free months skiing and hiking the hills of the neighboring fields and forests. He's as healthy as anyone I know entering their sixties.

The next day, we signed the papers for the construction loan, and I started purchasing the tools we needed for the job: a contractor-grade gasoline generator that would later be the backup power for the solar and wind system, a reciprocating saw, a grinder, a handheld planer, and extra hand tools for friends and family, whom we hoped would be dropping in to help us throughout the project. As it turned out, we had plenty of time to shop around for tools, doors, windows, woodstoves, and other items thanks to the unbelievable record rains that started falling and ended up continuing through the rest of the summer. It was so bad in fact that a lot of farmers couldn't cut their first crop of hay that year until July or August—usually a task for May or June. By the end of May, we'd had more than 10 inches of rain in that month alone.

We also traveled to Worthington, Massachusetts, to meet with Steve Schulze, an electrical engineer and owner of New England Solar, a renewable energy sales and service company. Steve gave us a free consultation on designing our off-grid system to meet our needs and our budget, and we especially appreciated the sophistication of his understanding of the available technologies and his preference for sticking with proven technologies rather than immediately jumping on the bandwagon for every new cutting-edge device that had yet to prove its reliability and cost-effectiveness.

We left with a template for our needs, based on one of the "kits" he offered, essentially a photovoltaic package that fit our estimated consumption in the new house. Even with a kit, though, I felt the learning curve for installing the electrical system was beyond what I could handle while organizing the rest of the building project. We had to have the roof on by the end of the summer and the house sealed up by the beginning of winter. Otherwise, we were going to be in real trouble.

John and I worked on weekends in April and May as we could, and by the middle of May we were placing the main beams and joists for the second floor. In the meantime, I'd recruited our friend John Van Hoesen, affectionately known as JVH, to help with the summer construction and engineering projects. A geology professor with an insatiable curiosity, John is an adamant do-it-myselfer: It's no matter whether the magnitude of any DIY project is rational or not, John just has to try it (he's more recently taken on replacing boilers as a hobby).

John proved indispensable, not just in problem-solving but in problem-preventing, and we came to appreciate the fact that geologists apparently relish the physics of heavy lifting, whether it involves plate tectonics or heaving fresh-cut 6×8 hemlock beams milled the day before delivery—the kind of green lumber that spits back at you in retribution for putting a nail in it. He was also looking to pick up an eligible single woman, but our lucky streak continued and he didn't find his wife-to-be until the end of the summer, so our building project kept him distracted and minimized his frustrations in trying to find an eligible woman in small-town Vermont.

Even if the sun didn't want to shine that summer, fate did shine down on us the whole way through. The other regular member of the building team was Khanti Munro, a graduating senior who had designed his own major at the college to focus on renewable energy technologies. Luckily for us, he needed his first clients for a renewable energy installation project as badly as we needed his budding expertise. As soon as we all finished the semester in mid-May, Khanti moved into the loft studio of our barn—apparently not a bad place to lure curious eco-chicks—and he began planning our renewable energy system while also helping with the other grunt work on the homestead . . . framing the house. By the end of the summer, Khanti had also found his future spouse.

We evolved into an efficient team, with laughter clearly outweighing the occasional curses and inevitable frustrations. As soon as I could finish morning chores, I was generally running out to gather new materials while the other guys got started with the day's project. I gave Phil my lumber order in batches, usually a week or two in advance, and he would get it milled just as we were running out of the previously delivered materials and ready to move on to the next stage.

In the evenings and during the daily afternoon deluges, Khanti started to focus on his hybrid role as renewable energy systems consultant and marriage counselor. It's always hard to balance power concerns in a marriage, but when it involves actual watts, volts, and amps, there's a risk that new sparks can fly. Erin and I had to start thinking about life with electricity, but within the limits of our budget and our system's capacity. Determining which items were necessities and which items were luxuries wasn't quite as simple as we'd thought.

We'd lived for about seven years without electricity, so even just a few bare bulbs hanging from the ceiling seemed like an enormous step forward. We'd gone for a number of years using only kerosene lamps and LED headlights before finally hooking up our tiny six-LED light to a battery and hanging the little lamp over our kitchen table. I'm convinced that electricity brings no greater gift for ordinary life than safe, bright, and inexpensive light, and the evolution of LED lighting technology probably holds more promise for the developing world than any other advancement other than water purification. In our case, the next best electrical device was unquestionably the washing machine, especially given that diapers were involved. Having a washing machine inevitably involves installing a well pump and a pressure tank, and the well pump was going to be the biggest draw on our water system, so choosing the best design and components was critical.

The basis for most of our thinking in the design process was always that poop happens—a strong argument not only for a good toilet, but also for having a backup in place for any system that might go awry. For that reason, we ran gravity-fed springwater into the house for a primary source of tasty drinking water and a secondary source of water if the well pump failed. Our kitchen sink therefore boasts two spigots—one from the well, dependent upon electricity and other technologies, and one from the same spring line that feeds the rest of our homestead. Much to the chagrin of the well drillers, whom we brought back in to install our new electric well pump, we wanted to leave our cast-iron hand pump intact on the wellhead along with the electric version, just in case we needed it.

We also decided to run some DC wires to strategic spots in the house in case the inverter needed to be repaired or replaced at any point. The inverter shifts the direct current (DC) power that goes from the photovoltaic (solar electric) panels to the batteries into alternating current (AC). If we lost AC power coming into the house by way of the inverter, we could always have at least some DC power in key living areas for basic lighting needs.

While Erin and I haggled about what our immediate and future electrical needs might be—including the basic requirements for guest rooms and cheesemaking—Khanti worked on the energy and financial budgets for our potential system.[4] We were at an advantage in several ways. We were going from no electricity to what seemed like an abundance of power, which is probably easier than downsizing one's expectations and rethinking what aspects of electrical consumption are actual needs and which appliances are electron hogs.

We also had to buy new appliances, since we had none, so we bought the most efficient washer on the market at the time, in terms of both water and energy use. The Staber washer requires only 110 to 150 watt-hours of electricity and 15 gallons of water per load, compared with several hundred watts of power and up to 50 gallons for most older washers.[5] Saving water means saving electricity and potentially extending the capacity and life of a septic system. The Staber was a top-loading vertical washer that also came with an instructional manual and excellent customer support for taking it apart and repairing or even rebuilding it oneself—a boon for anyone aiming not just for efficiency but also increased self-reliance. We also chose a well pump that Steve recommended both for its efficiency and ease of service or replacement.

During a lunch break on one of our few sunny days that May, Khanti, Erin, and I were sitting at the picnic table outside our cabin watching Asa bang nails into a nearby scrap board with incredible precision for a two-year-old, while Khanti was quizzing us on probable electrical usage.

"So, will you guys be using a stereo several hours on a daily basis?"

"We don't have a stereo—just a battery-powered radio. But we'd like to recharge the batteries on occasion."

"Okay, how about a computer?"

"Don't count on it. You here me grumbling about e-mail all the time, so you know that it's the bane of my existence at the college, as far as I'm concerned. I'm not sure I want to bring that world into our lives here."

"You guys are way too radical, you know. I probably shouldn't have you as my first clients since the hardest part of a system designer's job is working with the homeowners to get their consumption down to a level that makes economic sense for the design of the system. You guys can't even decide what you want to use electricity for!"

"I guess we'd rather scale up as we go," Erin added, picking up a nail that flew under her feet from a rare miss of Asa's hammer. We'd decided it was better if he learned how to use the tools he was seeing us use while we were watching instead of telling him the tools were off-limits and then finding him hiding in a corner somewhere trying to use a banned tool on his own. To his credit, Asa only hit his thumb once the entire summer, and we've watched him evolve into quite a crafty engineer over the years—a fact that we attribute to growing up on a construction site.

"But you probably ought to plan for where you want to be, if you can," Khanti noted.

"Well, the other route is to build the system to a reasonable capacity, and then if we outgrow it, we'll expand it as we can afford it." I swatted at a deerfly about to bite Asa on the neck. "I don't think we can even afford a 1,000-watt system at this point. I've budgeted for Steve's 800-watt kit—let's just go for that, and we'll grow into it. Then, when you're a high-demand installer charging fifty bucks an hour, we'll find another desperate graduate who works cheap but needs a solid recommendation that'll land him or her a real job that pays better than we can."

"Hey, isn't this green-collar exploitation?" Khanti teased.

"Don't worry. I told you already—you're doing what I did. You're earning better than minimum wage learning what you need to learn at someone else's expense, and that gets you to the next level. Plus, there's a bonus for you at the end if you get it right. And who else can afford to support your ravenous appetites . . . eating us out of house and cabin and turning our barn into a love-shack!"

Despite our constant teasing, Khanti persevered, and he modified and upgraded Steve's kit to give us an 800-watt photovoltaic system, along with a small wind turbine that was virtually a break-even experiment for our sheltered location. State incentives that came in the form of rebates after the systems were installed covered much of the cost of the small turbine, the bulk of the cost for the solar thermal (hot-water) panels, and a small portion of the photovoltaic panels.

"This is definitely considered an undersized system for the Northeast," Khanti warned, "but I guess you guys are going to have to grow into it anyway. If you're being honest with me about your expected usage, then I think I've built in four to five days of autonomy for you."

"Autonomy? Can't you just use homesteading words I understand like *self-reliance*?" I joked.

"You know what I mean—I think the PV panels and the batteries will generally get you through four or five cloudy days, if you're conservative . . ."

"Do I look conservative to you, living out here like this! So how about winter? We gonna be okay?"

"Well, I know you don't want to hear it, but you're going to have to run that generator some. You have to take care of those batteries by getting them up to a full charge at least once a month, but I think you'd better do it a lot more often than that. And you don't ever want to get them below 30 percent capacity—even below 50 or 60 percent on a regular basis isn't great. They're deep-cycle batteries made to let you discharge them over and over, but the more you discharge and the more often you do it, the shorter their life. I'd like to see you get at least eight years out of them—maybe even ten, if you're really lucky."

"Me, too. I hate the thought of having to dispose of them."

"Yup. They're the armpit of the system—and it's an expensive armpit. It's easy to get romantic about off-grid living, but the batteries are definitely the downside to it all. That's where a grid-tie system has a real advantage—you're not using lead-acid batteries with a fairly limited life span, and you don't have the inefficiency, noise, smell, hassle, and costs of running a generator."

All of a sudden, every day started to feel like Christmas. Loads of lumber from Phil's Mill kept appearing as if on cue, the house frame was taking shape as we moved skyward, and appliances and renewable energy components started arriving by UPS and freight. Fortunately, we'd learned when we first arrived in Vermont that local hardware stores not only are reasonably competitive with box-store building supply companies, but also offer service, advice, and exchange policies that those box-store operations can never rival. Our local hardware store not only helped us problem-solve our way through numerous dilemmas, but the owners were also kind enough to take receipt of the delivery of our freight goods, since many of the items couldn't be delivered to a residential address. They already had our allegiance, but it was galvanized forever when they unloaded our shipments and held them until we could get to the store—and then used their staff and forklift to help us load it all on our truck.

By August 5, Khanti had the solar panels up on an enormous rack, with a 5-foot-deep hole filled with concrete to support the pole and its load of ten 80-watt panels. We had the future pantry roofed and ready for the installation of the inverter and main electrical components, and by the end of the next day, we were celebrating the harnessing of the sun. The construction site was quiet—the generator was immediately relegated to the basement—and John Van Hoesen plugged in his blender, brought over to celebrate the occasion. We made gallons of solar-powered smoothies with fresh summer fruits and hefty shots of "liquid volts" to toast the occasion.

Khanti and John Van Hoesen ended up sleeping on the second-story deck that night, and as Erin and I walked Asa back over to the cabin to go to bed, he looked up in the sky and said, "Listen to the moonlight."

The quiet power of building a new home was palpable to us all.

As summer drew to a close, I had to begin preparing for the upcoming semester. From that point on, I worked on the house as often as I could, squeezing in small projects between chores and my college schedule. With the help of our neighbor John and a host of friends and college students, we reached the goal of getting the house under a roof on September 18, although I'd once again been hit in the ribs by a cow a few weeks earlier, cracking the same ribs that I'd injured before. I was watering the animals and checking them for signs of heat at dusk when one cow goosed another in the rump with her horns. Unfortunately, I was in the flight path of the hasty exit and caught the tip of a horn during the younger cow's frantic escape from her superior.

Every move on the roof was painful, but every sheet of metal roofing we anchored down was a psychological relief as winter edged closer. We started putting up siding and finishing the trim and ridge caps of the roof. I was also gaining new respect for the rope and climbing skills of the college students and faculty members in our Adventure Recreation program. I confess that I was skeptical when our college began the first Adventure Recreation major offered in the United States, but my skepticism quickly turned to admiration and appreciation as I hired several students from the program to help with the last dangerous details of the roof and siding projects. For their part, they learned a new application of their skills, and it was a relief and a joy to witness their professionalism as they worked in teams to negotiate the high, steep angles of our roof.

By the first of December, friends and family had started showing up on weekends and holidays to help us finish the siding and install the windows and doors so that we could button up the house for winter, which was coming fast. The first week in January arrived, and we had yet to have any significant snow. We'd completed insulating the house and were finally ready to complete the installation of the two Metalbestos chimneys that ran from the two woodstoves on the first floor straight up to the roof on either side of the house. Making sure that I had a perfectly straight plumb line running 26 feet through three floors, right between two rafters and the surrounding purlins, was nerve-racking, since there was no room for error once we'd cut the holes through the floors and the roof.

For some reason, winter had hedged, and it looked like we had one more day of good weather before the roof was guaranteed to be icy, maybe until spring. Khanti and our friend Tim, another college alum, agreed to help install and flash the chimneys—not an easy task even in good weather, since the chimneys emerged near the apex of the roof. The forecast was for freezing rain.

We began installing the chimneys early the next morning, piecing together the 4-foot sections of insulated, stainless-steel pipe and following my plumb line up through each floor until we finally reached the attic and carefully cut a hole in the metal roof for each chimney. That part of the process went smoothly, albeit slower than anticipated, but by the time we were ready to send the final sections through the roof and flash them, it was four o'clock and nearly dark.

Then the light drizzle started. The temperature was 34 degrees. Tim and Khanti had also worked with the Adventure Recreation leadership program, so they were reasonably adept climbers. However, the training somehow skipped how best to traverse a 10/12 pitch on a metal roof with water droplets that were turning to ice—and then straddle a metal ridge cap for several hours in the dark using headlamps and trying to hold drills, metal self-tapping screws, and a caulk gun filled with sticky but cold, sluggish silicone.

In an act of unconscious retribution, Tim lost his grip on the portable drill and sent it tumbling to its death some 40 feet below, just missing my head, as I'd been peering up above the roof edge to pass materials to them while I was completing the installation down below. Somehow, they finished the job by 1 AM and led a very unhasty retreat down the roof—cramped, wet, and frozen. I have yet to repay them adequately and am not sure I'll ever be able to. Nor have they let me forget the entire ordeal.

But we finally had a roof, walls, windows, doors, and heat. Our first snow came two days later.

Khanti edged ahead in the ribbing that fall, as we learned that Erin was pregnant again. I couldn't accuse him of taking the whole farm fertility thing too far without him pointing at Erin's swelling midsection: "The contractor shouldn't have time for that kind of activity."

Our new son Ethan arrived on March 16, 2005, in an unanticipated rush. He was three weeks early, and we barely made it across the entire state to the birthing center in Randolph, where Asa had also been born, under the care of the same amazing crew of midwives. In both cases, the days we spent in the hospital's unique birthing center were like a vacation—great food thanks to a chef who cared about fresh, tasty menus; running hot water; and the gentle swirl of a caring staff who let the birthing experience evolve as we wished.

We returned home after several days, glad that we'd run power from our new house to a single outlet in the bedroom of the cabin, providing us with light to change diapers. All four of us somehow crammed into our bed, and the sight of the nearby house gave us hope that we would soon have ample space to stretch out.

About one month after Ethan was born, I was taking care of the evening milking, working to shift from hand-milking to using our new milking machine. The fatigue of doing chores, caring for the family, and trying to catch up on my work and classes at the college made the use of the milking machine seem all the more appealing. I'd been getting our cows used to the new sound of the humming machine in the barn and the sight of the shiny milk pail, as well as the feel of the machine. I was trying to break them into the new approach gradually.

I finally decided that it was time to shift, so I set the milk pail beside the first cow, Beauty, and reached under to put the teat cups on her. With her right rear leg, she impatiently swatted at the milking machine "claw" with its four dangling teat cups, knocking it to the ground. I brushed her to calm her down and went to put it on again. She seemed to be adjusting to the idea, and the milk started to flow through the clear tubing, when she suddenly erupted into a panicked fury. She lashed out with her right rear leg again, catching not only the claw but also my left knee. She hit my knee directly from the outside, pushing it inward with stunning force. I immediately tumbled to the ground and rolled out of the way as she gave the claw one final blow.

I knew it was bad—real bad. But I decided to try to stand up. As I did, I fell over—the lower half of my leg was useless. I grabbed a manure fork and a 2×4 and hobbled a couple hundred feet through the thawing terrain toward the cabin.

Pausing at one point to catch my breath and to ensure that someone knew what had happened, I yelled toward the cabin, steadied by my makeshift crutches. "Erin, I've got bad news!"

"What? What's wrong?" she asked, sticking her head out the kitchen window, where she was getting dinner ready.

"I think Beauty just broke my leg."

"No . . . no—are you sure? Are you okay—I mean, do you think you can you get inside?"

"I doubt it. I think I'll just get to the steps and sit there while you go get Donald to see if he can help. Then I'll drive myself to the hospital."

"You can't drive—you're crazy."

"Yeah, but you can't come—not with both kids. Who knows how long I'll be there."

"I'll just go get the Waites, and then we'll figure it out."

I spent the night in the emergency room with Peter, Donald, and Joanne's grandson. I left with a bound and immobilized leg, stuck until I could get a surgeon and a CAT scan. Fortunately, I got Dr. Melvin Boynton, the knee specialist for the US Ski Team.

After waiting more than a week and hobbling around on crutches during the height of mud season—with the crutches occasionally disappearing a foot or more into the mud and me tumbling to the ground while trying to keep my leg straight—I had surgery and began a long recuperation. If nothing else, it gave me a lot of time to bond with Ethan, since I was the perfect built-in babysitter. And I was quite relieved to have one outlet in the cabin, as it allowed me to plug in the bulky repetitive-motion machine that gave my leg the controlled full range of motion it needed to heal, several hours each day. Its gentle whirring motor put Ethan to sleep while I lay on the bed, pondering my predicament . . . and my good fortune.

It was a time to succumb to humility and to rethink the notion of self-reliance in homesteading. Not only did I have the time to think about it all on my own, but I was also in the midst of teaching my new course, A Homesteader's Ecology, for the first time. In class a few weeks before the accident, I had bemoaned the loss of an agrarian spirit of cooperation and mutual support in our culture. As I hobbled in two days after the accident, I had to rethink that critique in the company of my students, as I found myself dependent upon our neighbors who did our chores each morning and my college colleagues who helped Erin with chores every evening and brought us food every single night for almost a month straight.

The fragility of it all was readily apparent. Self-reliance and independence are perhaps reasonable targets, but not always appropriate ways of living. The expectation that one should live an autonomous life until some dramatic circumstance makes such an option impossible is problematic. It doesn't necessarily foster the careful crafting of community— a web that gives more structure and support than its elastic gossamer strands might suggest. While we may be trapped in an ecological web, we are also generally supported by the often unseen strands of community, whether we realize it or not.

Perhaps the homesteading tradition that we've inherited has either romanticized and exaggerated the realities of independence and self-reliance or inadvertently de-emphasized the importance of community in a homesteading venture. Or maybe our wired world and the demographic shifts to tighter living spaces have altered our cultural chemistry to expect connections instead of disconnects, whether those connections are earth-based or ether-based.

I suspect that the American homesteading tradition has, in fact, over-emphasized the notion of self-reliance and subsequently glossed over the importance of community in such ventures. Additionally, our twenty-first-century lives tend to be lived in closer proximity to one another than in the past, by virtue of demographics and technology.

It's clear that Thoreau's *Walden* and Helen and Scott Nearing's *The Good Life,* among other works in the American homesteading subgenre, do not adequately convey the expansiveness of *I* or *we* in the homesteading life. The predominance of first person singular and first person plural in most homesteading literature tends to mask or even ignore homesteading's dependence upon family, friends, a local community, and mentors from near and far. Any homestead is actually a culmination of influences and support from a host of players. The sooner we recognize that any type of homesteading venture—rural, suburban, or urban—is rooted in culture and community, the more likely it is that homesteading's best values and practices will find their way into our culture.

I propose that we start viewing homesteading as a means of connecting more deeply with our communities, another way of recognizing not only that we need one another, but that we need to think together and out loud. We can be individualists without touting misguided individualism. We can all be eclectic, experimental individuals without denying or denigrating our interdependence. Homesteading ventures create a stimulating commerce of ideas and experiments, ranging from shelter to renewable energy to education to food traditions. The resilience of a homestead comes only in part from the skills and determination of its habitants. The real resilience comes through its connection to others.

I hobbled around on crutches from April until August 2005, occasionally frustrated but generally warmed and humbled by the number of people who came to help finish the siding and basic infrastructure, while I did my best to coordinate both the hired and volunteer labor, along with the ordering and delivery of materials. One student apprentice, Ethan Waldo, stuck by us through thick and thin, helping take care of the daily tasks that I couldn't do, while climbing specialists like Kellen, Craig, and Tom helped with the tricky exterior siding in precarious places.

By the end of the summer, the house was getting to the point that it was nearly livable, at least in a rustic manner. With a toddler and an infant, we were finding ourselves constantly going back and forth between the cabin and the house, living in the cabin but spending most of the day and early evening working on the house. Once again, summer drew to a close, and I needed to shift my focus back to the college—a place that I viewed differently than before. I'd always appreciated the people there, but I now knew that it was much more a community than an institution.

The temptation was to work on the house as much as possible once I was liberated from my crutches, but I felt a need to give back as much as I could to the college community that had supported us through the birth of a child and the downfall of my independence. Progress on the house slowed dramatically, and Thanksgiving rolled around before we knew it. We began firing up the woodstoves several times a day to keep the water systems in the house from freezing, so when Erin's extended family came for Thanksgiving, we put them up in the house.

We had intended to live in the cabin at least until I had put down the floors and done some other basic work, but after spending a weekend virtually living in the house with Erin's family, we found ourselves reveling in having a wood cookstove, hot water, a washing machine, and ample lighting. The house was, in fact, the efficient home that we had long dreamed of and worked so hard to build. Plus, it seemed easier to live and build in one residence than to cart the kids back and forth between buildings.

On the spur of the moment, we decided it was time to move. So, an hour before Erin's family packed up to leave, we announced our decision, and everyone in her family graciously took our two sleds over to the cabin and began packing most of our meager belongings. The shift took less than an hour and only a few sled trips, thanks to a fresh coating of snow.

We left the cabin in disarray, stripped of its essentials and relegated to the category of "future project," and we entered a world of construction chaos. I had floorboards stacked around the edges of all the rooms of the house, stickered and drying out with the heat of the woodstoves and winter's low humidity. Rooms and trim were unfinished, but the relief of having abundant space and not trekking back and forth outweighed the occasional frustrations.

The kids both endured splinters from the subfloor for the next year, and sweeping upstairs simply resulted in more to sweep downstairs, with dirt and dust falling through the cracks. Despite the inconveniences, Asa reveled in his ability to drill holes and hammer nails most anywhere in the house without retribution. His biggest joy, though, was literally running continuous laps around the central stairwell, celebrating his release from the cabin's cramped quarters.

However, our hasty exit left us feeling like we'd parted ways with a cherished abode and a way of life to which we could never return. We had spent years crafting an elegant simplicity that had balanced economics and ecology by minimizing our expectations and heightening the rewards offered by the most basic of pleasures—eating, heating, bathing, and resting.

And yet, the growth of our family and the shrinking of our days meant that time had become more precious. For years, we had consciously rejected prevailing notions of efficiency, but now we needed to streamline some of our tasks. We were certain that we were entering a realm of increased compromises, but we were uncertain which efficiencies were compatible with our quest for *oikos*—a balance of household economics and ecology—and which ones risked leading us back to a life of unchecked consumption.

FOURTEEN

Technological Cascade

A solar panel should not be a scary thing. Particularly a compact 30-watt panel, comprising less than 3 square feet in surface area and perched atop a vertical piece of galvanized pipe pounded into the ground. In full sunlight, it doesn't provide even enough juice to equal the jolt of a cup of strong coffee. But Erin and I were leery nonetheless.

The first thing that Khanti did upon moving into our barn studio was to install a small solar array to provide him with enough power for a clock radio and a few compact fluorescent lightbulbs. Suddenly Erin and I felt like Luddites. It was so simple and sensible—the 30-watt panel used sunlight to create a flow of electrons that went through a charge controller to a standard 12-volt deep-cycle marine battery. The charge controller prevented both excessive charging of the battery and a reverse flow of electrons from the battery back to the solar panel at night. Khanti wired a small inverter off the battery to transform the battery's DC current to a more conventional source of AC energy. The whole setup cost less than $300—definitely less than we had spent on lamp oil over the previous seven years.

We looked out of our dark cabin bedroom window with mixed emotions that first night, nearly awed by the light of Khanti's two compact fluorescent bulbs filling the barn windows and spilling out onto the ground below, the cascade of light accompanied by a musical murmur drifting from his open windows. On the one hand, it seemed virtually miraculous—using photons to generate available electrons suitable for AC power. To our knowledge, it was the first time that such intense artificial light had shown from any windows up Tunket Road.

But we were worried. We suddenly felt adrift in uncertainty, feeling the hints of a hastening current that was pulling us toward what we feared was an impending technological cascade. Once we plugged back in, what was to stop us from simply importing a whole host of unnecessary electrical devices that risked undermining certain values that we had worked so hard to consider and develop over the past few years? To what degree would electricity become an ally as opposed to a culprit in continuing to craft a life that fit within our evolving values? I still remembered reading Chinua Achebe's novel *A Man of the People* in college. Achebe's description of how a person moving from poverty to comfort is unlikely to ever want to return to that more difficult plight had stuck with me for more than two decades: "A man who has just come in from the rain and dried his body and put on dry clothes is more reluctant to go out again than another who has been indoors the whole time."[1] Our economics hadn't really changed, but our daily comforts clearly had.

We certainly weren't the first to confront such decisions, and we were realizing that the responsibilities and time commitments involved in parenting had started to shift our perspectives on the defining line separating so-called necessities from luxuries. But it was Erin's interest in and understanding of the Amish—communities not so distant from her upbringing in central Pennsylvania—that provided a guiding tenet for many of our decisions. Unfortunately, most discussions of the Amish and their choice of appropriate technologies generally focus on the technologies that they eschew—not on their decision-making process about which technologies to accept as part of their lifestyle.

The Amish actually discuss which technologies to allow within their individual communities, based upon how a given technology will likely impact not just the quality of life for individuals within the community, but also the overall health and longevity of the community itself. How a technology might affect the spiritual life of the individuals and the community is clearly important for the Amish, but they also recognize that technologies can both foster and erode critical aspects of a tight-knit, supportive, and enduring community. Some communities or "orders" might allow a certain technology, while others might not deem it appropriate and therefore forbid its use.[2]

Regardless of whether those of us outside "intentional communities" such as the Amish agree with their ultimate decisions on the acceptability of specific technologies, we should take note that the Amish and other such groups at least take the time to consider their implications for the overall community. Unlike most of us, they do not blindly accept any new technology that comes their way. Seldom do most individuals, families, or communities in mainstream American society think seriously about

the long-term implications of any piece of technology. Most American households are overflowing with electronic whimsy and wizardry, with the excess bound for yard sales and, ultimately, landfills. We do little to consider how a specific technology is going to impact our relationships with others, much less with the natural world. Whenever a newfangled technology comes along, not only do we buy it, but we buy *into* it, generally without much discussion. Before we know it, these technological luxuries foster expectations that often evolve into "needs."

Over the years, friends have teased Erin and me for being backwoods ascetics. In college, my friends informally voted me "most likely to live in a cabin with a dirt floor." Upon hearing about how Vermonters use downhill runs of plastic pipelines to collect maple syrup in large containers at the base of the hill, my uncle once joked that I would probably try to find a way to run the lines uphill, just to add an element of challenge to the process.

But a reflective life is a rich life, and I'm convinced more than ever before that our greatest challenge in facing climate change, a growing population, increasing consumerism, and a loss of biodiversity is to find ways to *rewire the rewards*. Cutting-edge neuroscience research is demonstrating that our bodies are hardwired for anticipating short-term rewards, even those fleeting rewards that come from technological hits and consumptive habits. We are learning that shifting our behaviors is more than just a matter of changing how we go about things. Research is beginning to describe how our bodies secretly secrete physiological rewards for certain consumptive behaviors via a panoply of neurochemicals.[3]

Thus, the path toward reducing our vast appetite for gadgets and resources is probably not as simple as merely adopting the meager diet prescribed by consumptive asceticism. Studies indicate that dieting of any type seldom works over the long term, unless the rewards are quickly evident and sustained. Whether we like it or not, we humans operate at least in part on the basis of immediate mental, emotional, and physiological rewards, and our consumptive habits are no exception. Our best chance for changing our consumptive habits and our technological excesses is for us to find ways to rewire our rewards—to be cerebral and celebratory as we collaboratively craft a world that makes sense.

I reject the notion of homesteading as a search for simplicity. But I do believe that homesteading involves a rediscovery of simple pleasures:

hard work, good food, comforting shelter, meaningful values—and a covey of friends and family with whom to reflect and celebrate. The culmination of these pleasures ultimately results, in my mind, in an enduring sense of fulfillment.[4]

If it's all drudgery, we won't get very far. But if we help one another rediscover the rewards that come from simple pleasures—from savoring a peasant's hearty fare to relishing the beautiful symmetry of wind turbines in motion to building one's own small table—then we stand a chance of harnessing the energy from our human penchant for wild abandon and transforming it into a sustained determination to leave the world a better place.

Slow Food founder Carlo Petrini is fond of saying that "Pleasure is a universal right, and responsibility is a universal duty."[5] It's a concept that I think is worth savoring . . . perhaps over a pint of homebrew.

As a homesteader trying to do the right thing, it's fairly easy to become self-congratulatory or even self-righteous. In fact, it doesn't take long before homesteaders start vying against one another for the title of "Gaia Guru," but it's perhaps wiser to think more about our common human denominator—energy—than about the things that separate us one from another.

In a lecture about thermodynamics, mechanical energy, and carbon, Dr. Steven Chu—Nobel laureate and President Obama's Secretary of the US Department of Energy—paused to ruminate about the human need for energy and our search for reliable and renewable energy sources. He laid out the ground rules for our pursuit of mechanical energy, based on physics:

1. It's a game that you can't win.
2. You can't break even.
3. You can't quit the game.[6]

The fact is, we're locked into the game—a game governed principally by two physical realities, the first and second laws of thermodynamics. The first law states that energy cannot be created or destroyed; hence its other name, the law of conservation of energy. The law of entropy, the second law, follows suit, recognizing that energy cannot be created or destroyed, but it can be changed from one form to another. We are constantly transforming energy in our daily lives. The present quandary is how to transform as much energy as possible without releasing additional carbon . . . and how to use less energy overall, regardless of how green and clean it supposedly is.

As my former professor Tom Wessels of Antioch New England put it in his profoundly engaging and succinct book *The Myth of Progress: Toward a Sustainable Future*:

> Every environmental problem we face today is the result of entropy within the biosphere. If there is a foundation on which all environmental degradation rests, it is entropy generated by the ever-increasing transformation of energy by humans . . . Global climate change due to the build-up of carbon dioxide in the atmosphere from the burning of fossil fuels is a process of diffusion of carbon—entropy. Think of any environmental problem and you will see it is a process where complex systems are being simplified or concentrated materials are being diffused.[7]

Wessels goes on to consider the role of renewable energy systems in our search for a sustainable future:

> Our only solution to counter increasing biospheric entropy is to reduce global energy consumption. Renewable energy resources can definitely help, since they create a lot less entropy than nonrenewable forms of energy, but they have some entropic costs, too. How much entropy results from the mining, refining, and shipping of materials to build solar collectors, electrical wires, and batteries? How much then results from the manufacturing of these things, packing them for transport, the shipping to distribution centers, and finally to stores? Within each of these activities are numerous energy transformations. The wisest approach is to conserve energy as much as possible through the development of our most efficient technologies, and to reduce and eventually cease frivolous, unneeded energy consumption.[8]

If taken as a given rather than as a challenge, the reality of our current energy dilemma—based in the inescapable laws of physics—can lead to despair and apathy. However, if we do approach the dilemma as an energizing challenge, we start to view our future path and all of its accompanying choices as simultaneously intellectual and physical, solitary and communal, personal and cultural. In essence, our response requires us to use our heads, our hands, and our hearts to find our way forward, as Rob Hopkins describes in his provocative book *The Transition Handbook: From Oil Dependency to Resilience*.[9] Hopkins and his cohorts in the growing Transition Movement are focused on the twin issues of peak oil and climate change, two stark realities that will force us to recast our lives and our expectations in dramatic ways, particularly if the ramifications of the two coincide. They propose that communities come together to develop a response preemptively, instead of waiting until circumstances are palpably more dire than they seem to be—at least on the surface—at the present time.

In 1989, I was fortunate enough to receive a fellowship to attend San Francisco Theological Seminary in order to explore a career in religious studies. Perhaps the most important lesson I learned from that year of theological study came from my coursework with Jorge Lara-Braud of Mexico, a prominent Latin American liberation theologian. At the time, Central America was in the midst of various sorts of political turmoil and intense human suffering, much of it exacerbated by disastrous US foreign policy decisions, some public and some covert. Latin American liberation theologians—faced with death, economic oppression, and even opposition from their superiors in Rome—saw faith as a way to help their communities find their way out of seemingly impossible situations, predicaments without an obvious way out. This moment of doubt, confusion, and uncertainty is what liberation theologians would call *aporia,* an ancient Greek word meaning "without a door." *Aporia,* for the liberation theologians, became not the impasse but rather the beginning point for new vision and understanding—in essence, the point at which faith and hope would supersede the portal-less realities until a resolution could be found or created.

In the face of so many global challenges, I find the minuteness of any given homesteading venture to be much the same, as we humans work to navigate our way through some of the biggest challenges that we have ever posed for ourselves. We are groping for a door, trying to determine where to put our faith and, subsequently, our energies. As much as I love photovoltaic panels, solar thermal systems, and wind turbines, I still believe that our best chance of dismantling our current ecological *aporia* will come not so much from our ability to harness the wind, sun, and tides as from our willingness to harness our wants and whims . . . and to find joy not so much in simplicity as in simple pleasures.

Throughout the years in the cabin, our technological choices were circumscribed almost as much by economic realities as by ecological considerations. We didn't need much, but we couldn't afford much, either. We often passed the time while cooking or doing dishes, or even writing in our journals, thinking about how to balance the good life that we had with the desire for a few things that we thought might make life easier or more ecologically efficient. We weren't averse to physical labor, but we were feeling constrained by the time involved in many tasks. It was a challenge to find time to read, write, or do art projects, and our tiny kitchen and minimal food storage space made our food pursuits difficult and inefficient. *Small* and *simple* are staples of a homesteader's vocabulary, but neither guarantees human or ecological efficiency.

Our cumulative list of anticipated items for the future evolved over the years, as we planned for building a house. In rough order of priority, they included safe and efficient lighting, consistent refrigeration, a sink with running water and a drain to the outside, a washing machine, a reliable source of hot water, an indoor toilet for winter, a pantry, and a root cellar. Any discussion about communications technologies inevitably led to marital miscommunication, with me often feeling the need to connect with work and family while Erin savored the solace of a world without phones and computers.

Prior to having children, none of those items we coveted felt like a need as much as a luxury. After all, we were living healthy, contented lives—albeit busy ones. Yet, once the demands of parenting entered the equation, some of those items began to feel more like needs than luxuries. Questions of gender roles also began to emerge in new ways, driven both by the demands of breast-feeding and child care, along with the necessity of eking out a living.

We became more and more concerned about the safety of our oil lamps. We were increasingly prone to noticing the petroleum-burning smell, and as Asa increased his mobility, the potential hazards became more prominent. We avoided using flashlights for the most part until LED flashlights came on the market, simply because of the wastefulness of nonrechargeable batteries. Once we had the efficient LED lights, our guilt was mollified by using rechargeable batteries, but only to a degree. Our tiny six-LED table light had been a boost, but activity in the cabin began to spread beyond the dim radius of that light as Asa explored every corner of the two rooms. The cabin was tucked into a shady corner of our homestead, with no significant direct sun until the final hours of the day, so there was no real opportunity to install even a modest solar system, and the prospects for wind in our forested harbor were just as limited. Renewable energy options simply weren't viable in the cabin's location, so we selected the new house site based upon solar availability, access to our road and barns, and necessary drainage.

Perhaps no appliance gave us greater joy than our propane refrigerator. Immersing objects in cold springwater provided some refrigeration during the warmer months, but as water and ambient temperatures rose throughout the summer, keeping dairy products fresh became more difficult, and the trek into the woods before and after meals grew increasingly tedious. With reliable refrigeration, our menus grew, and we wasted much less food. And yet we were now locked into the use of propane, although the fridge's location outside in our mudroom meant that we used virtually no propane for about half the year. Our one consolation was that our Servel propane fridge was built for efficiency, with its thickly insulated walls far exceeding the standards of most ordinary fridges on the market. The refrigerator is generally the greediest standard appliance in the average American household.[10]

One might consider eliminating refrigerators and freezers entirely from a household, but a little research into nutrition would probably change a person's initial inclinations in that regard, as it ultimately did for us. I invited a nutritionist from SUNY-Buffalo, Dr. Peter Horvath, to give a lecture at Green Mountain College on "*Local* and *Organic:* Are They More Nutritious?" For better or worse, Peter robbed me of one of my most basic homesteading tenets, a gift from my grandmother: canning. Peter described the typical high-heat canning process and summed up the nutritional result as "good roughage with virtually no remaining vitamins." Freezing, on the other hand, tended to retain most of the vitamins and minerals within fresh foods. And, of course, there was also lacto-fermentation.

I was devastated. All of those beautiful jars lining the shelves of our new home's pantry and root cellar—colored roughage . . . and tasty, too!

It was, after all, part of what I most relished from my upbringing in the South, particularly at my grandmother's table. Then I began to consider the energy component. In the US food sector, home food preparation and preservation comprise more than 30 percent of the total energy consumption in our national food system.[11] Canning requires high heat, but freezing requires significant energy, too. Did one make more sense than the other from an energy perspective?

Two years after moving into our new house, we decided that a SunDanzer DC freezer was the appropriate technological compromise, allowing us to store fruits, vegetables, and meats in an incredibly efficient top-opening chest freezer. The SunDanzer's Danfoss DC compressor has a tiny piston that's about the size of a pencil eraser and consumes only the amount of energy produced by one of our ten 80-watt panels per day, thanks to its superior insulation and top-opening lid, not allowing the cold air to spill out every time it's opened. We placed the freezer in a portion of our basement that has no radiant floor heat to boost its efficiency, since that area ranges from 40 to 55 degrees throughout the year.

Not only does the freezer use minimal electricity, but its DC power comes directly from the batteries, reducing the energy conversion demands placed on our inverter. Every time there is an energy transformation, there is entropy (energy loss). Therefore, the DC-powered freezer saves one step in the process.

The PV panels transform photons into electrons, and those electrons are then stored in batteries. When the batteries are used for power, they lose and later regain electrons. If those electrons flow into the inverter for transformation from DC to AC power, there is some loss in efficiency, made noticeable in part by the heat given off by the inverter. In fact, the fan on the inverter runs fairly frequently in times of high electrical input or output. Minimizing the use of the inverter not only serves to extend the probable life of the relatively expensive (economically and ecologically) inverter, but it also means less is demanded of the batteries, thereby extending their expected life of eight to twelve years, if they are well maintained throughout that time period. Disposal of lead-acid batteries, even if they are recycled, leads to yet another entropic situation, so prolonging the life span of the batteries saves energy, as well as money. Bear in mind that the original manufacturing of the batteries also required significant energy, as did their distribution.

So what is the downside to a DC freezer or refrigerator? Initial cost.

Unfortunately, these refrigeration units are often two to three times as costly as their conventional AC counterparts, and they require a separate wiring run, assuming a form of DC energy is even available in one's house. Yet they are efficient, durable, and gratifying. And even though we still do some canning—habituated tastes are hard to give up—our SunDanzer freezer has helped us deal with energy and nutritional concerns. However, it's important to bear in mind it doesn't necessarily make sense to go out and buy a new freezer to replace an old one, since about one-half of an appliance's "energy footprint" comes from the embedded energy in its initial construction. According to Rebekah and Stephen Hren in their groundbreaking book *The Carbon-Free Home,* finding ways to make an appliance more efficient, such as adding insulation to a freezer's exterior, is ultimately less expensive and more energy-conscious than buying a brand-new freezer.[12]

The next practical step is for us to do more lacto-fermentation, a way of capturing natural forms of energy and nutrition, with a blending of historical and cultural traditions.[13] Regardless of whether one considers homesteading to be emblematic of progress or "progressive," it is definitely a gradual progression of learning and experimenting . . . and occasionally perfecting.

The human body is always in search of comfortable ambient temperatures, so it should come as no surprise that cooling and heating are two of the driving considerations in homesteading. One question that has permeated our thinking in our homesteading ventures has been how to efficiently capture heat for multiple purposes. The transformation of energy from one form to another always involves the "loss" of heat, and we wanted to capitalize upon our abundance of sunlight and wood (someday, we'd like to capture some of the methane released from the decomposition of cattle manure and bedding, too).

Although we'd been able to use our Jotul woodstove in the cabin for some stovetop heating and stovepipe baking, we'd always wanted a wood cookstove that would allow us to combine cooking and heating with better efficiency. We had long planned to purchase an Amish-made Pioneer Maid wood cookstove from Lehman's Hardware in Ohio—probably the most efficient American-made woodstove made for cooking and heating—but we ended up finding a beautiful used Heartland cookstove for about half the price in our local paper. Once we moved into the house, we began combining heating and cooking with the Heartland stove.

Tiroleans had told me that a wood cookstove was superior to a propane or electric model because wood heat cooks foods more evenly, both on the stovetop and in the oven. When I lived in the South Tirol, I used to walk to a guesthouse high in the mountains nearly every weekend, for the exercise as well as for a huge helping of *Kaiserschmarren*—literally "the emperor's mess," a sort of thickly chopped-egg crêpe topped with a sprinkle of confectioners' sugar and a side helping of *Preislberren,* tart berries preserved in juice. The family there at Gasthaus Longfall still cook Kaiserschmarren on their wood cookstove, and it wasn't until we started using our Heartland stove that I could begin to replicate— almost—the perfect browning of this hearty Tirolean dish.

As we stockpile our wood for the cookstove each winter now, I'm also reminded of the Tirolean wood stacks—*piles* would not be the most apt word, since the Tirolean sense of *Ordnung* seemingly forbids such indiscriminate storage. Wood is meant to be cut to a specific length and stacked in ways that capture the eye and enshrine the Teutonic sense of agrarian order. I think that the abundance of wood in the eastern United States has perhaps translated into a skewed sense of what firewood looks like. We envision either full rounds or split sections that tend to be at least as thick as a logger's arm, if not her thigh. However, one beauty of a wood cookstove is that small branches and even long-burning thick knots have a purpose. Such woodstoves burn most efficiently and cleanly when fed relatively small, dry wood—particularly bone-dry hardwood. Pieces typically ignored or discarded in most firewood-gathering expeditions suddenly take on a new value.

Burning a woodstove hot is important for two reasons. First, the hotter the stove burns, the less chance there is of creosote buildup that can lead to a chimney fire. Second, hotter fires using drier woods tend to release fewer particulates and greenhouse gases. While we worked to choose a second stove to serve as our primary source of wood heat, we thought long and hard about which type of stove to go with. Although we loved our green enamel Jotul, we'd tried to do the right thing by purchasing a stove with a state-of-the-art ceramic catalyst whose honeycomb structure was designed to intensify the heat during hot fires so as to burn more of the escaping particulates than an ordinary stove.[14] However, the catalyst was no longer effective after two winters, and its hefty price tag made it difficult for us to justify the cost of a new one, given the reports we were hearing about their short life span.

Besides Erin, the other hot object that I'd fallen in love with in the South Tirol and wanted to bring home was the Tirolean *Bauernofen,* or "farmer's oven." Virtually every farmhouse in the Tirol and most castles and guesthouses had a hefty masonry stove in at least one main living area. The traditional farmer's oven generally had approximately a 4' × 6' footprint, stood about 5 feet high, and was coated with a special white plaster. Consisting of several thousand pounds of thermal mass, these masonry stoves are designed with a series of channels wending their way to the exit flue, so that the masonry captures much of the heat from the smoke that is making its way to the outside chimney. The stove is designed to transform a quick, hot fire into an enduring radiant heat that can last for twelve or more hours. Using well-seasoned wood is imperative, given the danger of creosote buildup in the labyrinthine flue, but the hot fire creates more ash than creosote, while also resulting in a cleaner burn.

Wood of all sizes is used in a masonry stove, from bundled twigs to more substantial split logs. The downside, however, is that if all parts of a tree are coveted in an area with fairly high demographic pressures, such as the South Tirol, there may be little left of the tree to serve as critical biomass for the forest floor and, subsequently, the forest's regeneration. During one of my most recent visits to the South Tirol, I was hiking in a high-elevation valley with some friends, showing them the tidiness of the wood stacks, with stacks separated by diameter, including evenly sized bundles of twigs used as kindling to start the fires in the masonry stoves each morning.

As we admired one particularly beautiful stack, I looked across the road at the farm's adjacent woodlot. Even the forest floor was tidy. While I was struck by the aesthetic appeal of the carefully maintained wood-lot, I was reminded of how the European penchant for order, neatness, and even linearity translated into misguided introductions of agricultural crops and techniques in colonies across the globe, places where indigenous agricultural systems actually integrated various species in gardens and fields that seemed "messy," if not incoherent, to European sensibilities.

It's always an interesting challenge to consider both the advantages and the costs of imposing human order on an ecological system. I like to think of my inability to "clean up" all of the downed trees in our woodlot as contributing to nature's processes, with the cavity trees providing habitat for wildlife, the downed logs serving as critical detritus and biomass for the forest soils, and the toppled treetops helping forest regeneration by slowing down deer browse of the tree seedlings that are emerging under the relative protection of the tangled branches.

Despite our hopes of incorporating a masonry stove in our house from the beginning, the cost of such a stove and the lack of time to build it ourselves in the midst of so much other construction meant that we had to forgo the dream for a while. We did construct the floor in our main living area so that it would be strong enough to support a masonry stove, in the hope that someday we might cobble together the time, money, and expertise to build our own.[15]

We researched other wood-based heating options, including an outdoor wood boiler, which we finally decided we couldn't justify, despite the temptation to be able to burn wood of large size and minimal seasoning. Outdoor boilers have an overall poor reputation for particulate pollution, since they burn relatively cool and are often used for green wood and even trash. Some companies are working to maximize the efficiency of these units, but we also had to think about the small size of our solar system and the electrical draw needed to power the boiler's electric fan and water circulator extensively, day and night. The fan maintains a long and often smoldering burn, while the circulator is required to keep the hot water moving between the boiler and the house.

Ultimately, we settled instead for a Quadra-Fire woodstove, and as it turned out engineering the floor for a heavy masonry stove paid off. Weighing in at more than 500 pounds and with the capacity to accommodate several large logs at once, the stove enjoys consistently outstanding EPA emission ratings. Whereas an old-fashioned woodstove might release up to 80 grams of particulate matter per hour, our Quadra-Fire releases around 4 grams, if it is burning well-seasoned wood.[16] It actually has four burn zones, providing ample opportunity for the majority of the particulates to be incinerated before exiting into the chimney.

We also chose to install radiant floor heating in most of our basement, excluding the northeast corner, which we reserved as a cool area for the root cellar and an experimental area for aging cheeses. This heat source was meant to provide a comfortable floor in our cheesemaking and utility areas, while also boosting the warmth of the rest of the house, from the bottom up. We installed both a propane hot-water heater and solar thermal (hot-water) panels to provide for our domestic needs and as the sources of radiant heat. The trick in designing the system was to ensure that the circulator for the radiant floor, which we knew would run mostly at night, would not draw too much power from our limited photovoltaic system. We solved that problem and have kept our propane usage to a minimum by setting the thermostat for the radiant floor system at a temperature of 40 to 45 degrees during the cold winter months and cutting it off the rest of the year.

Even though electricity made much of our homestead life more efficient and safer, the renewable energy system that has most impressed us is our solar thermal system for producing hot water. From an energy-efficiency perspective, solar hot-water panels provide a much more efficient capture of solar energy than do photovoltaic panels—in terms of energy produced per square foot and in the speedy rate of return on one's economic investment.[17] Once again, it only makes sense, given the basics of entropy. Conversion of sunlight to heat energy involves less transformation than does the conversion from photons to excited electrons to DC electricity to AC electricity.

Not to begrudge photovoltaics in any way, but I will feel that our culture has finally come to grips with a fundamental understanding of the basic principles of renewable energy only when we start prioritizing and touting residential solar thermal systems over PV systems. Why are we burning coal, using nuclear reactors, and tapping fossil fuels to produce hot water when solar thermal systems can meet the majority of our domestic hot-water needs, even in a climate like Vermont's? I've seen my home's hot-water supply rise to more than 100 degrees on days when outdoor temperatures barely crested 0. The idea that any housing unit is using air-conditioning on a sunny day while simultaneously depending upon energy from the grid or fossil fuels to heat water strikes me as utterly absurd, if not unethical, given the fact that it is a blatant squandering of resources for coming generations.

But I don't think our culture will really appreciate the nuances of renewable energy systems until more people actually encounter these systems in their everyday lives. Once the systems become ordinary—not exotic or "alternative"—then the basics will filter into our culture, in terms of our acceptance and understanding of them. That's all the more reason for homesteads with renewable energy systems to flourish across the geographic spectrum, from rural getaways to urban ghettos. One could even make the argument that homesteaders and back-to-the-landers of all persuasions have been the one stable market for residential renewable energy systems in the United States up to this point—as well as the primary shareholders in the knowledge about the ins and outs of these systems.

Sure, such systems occasionally take a bit more work and understanding on the part of the homeowner, but is it necessarily a good thing that we neither understand nor do anything to earn our energy? One *New York Times* article actually focused on the efforts required to maintain a renewable energy system, citing as an example the fact that one needs to sweep the snow off PV panels.[18] I couldn't help but compare that minor task to all the work that we do to utilize our automobiles in the winter. It takes us far less time to sweep the snow off our PV panels than it does to clean the snow off of a single vehicle, and the sun on the PV panels does most of the work for us after a gentle brushing!

But before I begin to sound too evangreenical, let me confess that Erin and I are continually trying to find ways reduce the number of tasks that we have to do in a day—or at least reduce the onerous nature of some of these tasks. Despite our enjoyment of many of our outhouse experiences—watching calves frolic under an apple tree in full blossom might be my ultimate outhouse memory—I began to find the frequent emptying of our outhouse bucket more and more of an encumbrance on my time. I dreamed of the perfect composting toilet system. Had I paid more attention to the collective wisdom of authors on systems for humanure, liquid gold (urine capture), and graywater,[19] I might have come to the realization that it's all a trade-off. Every step forward in labor-saving technology almost always involves an increase in materials, energy, and potential breakdowns. In other words, we're back to the law of entropee and entropoop. A bucket is about as basic as you can get when it comes to collecting and dispensing or dispersing poop, pee, and graywater, but it seemed like we could improve on the efficiencies involved. So we opted to experiment and step up the technology . . . and the cost.

Despite its simplicity, the bucket had two primary drawbacks, in our view—the additional weight and the smell of the urine. The frequency of emptying the bucket became more of an encumbrance as parenting, homeschooling, and farming tasks increased, but there was also the issue of the weight of a full bucket and the smell and the splash as we dumped it into the compost pile. It was a task that was at times particularly difficult for Erin to handle when I was busy farming and teaching and as our parenting duties increased. Finally, in the seasons in which there was no splash due to freezing, the cumbersome nature of a frozen bucket of pee, poop, and sawdust created some frustrating logistical hurdles.

We also found ourselves needing to please our bankers—people (yes, people, and very good people, in this case) who were willing to help us in our unconventional dreams, but who also needed a secure investment in case the house was sold or foreclosed on at some point. We were also on the cusp of new septic regulations in Vermont, the first statewide effort at regulating residential wastewater systems. There was no question about whether or not we were going install a septic system, given the anticipated concerns of the bank and the regulators, but there was a question as to how we were going to utilize it. The statewide debate generated a shit-flinging fest that encouraged us to duck, with some developers pushing for approval of composting toilet systems so that they could develop areas now unsuitable for traditional septic systems and some environmental groups advocating for the elimination of such composting toilet loopholes in an effort to stem development in sensitive areas.

We were simply looking for a middle ground that would keep us fully funded and un-fined. We considered a few versions of the outhouse and in-house versions of composting toilets, but the efficacy of the outdoor units was questionable in winter, and the cost and space requirements of the indoor units seemed prohibitive. The large-scale composting storage units designed for basements meant that we would have to design much of the house based on the location of the toilets and the basement containment systems—and it didn't seem compatible with a basement cheesemaking scenario. We'd also not been impressed with the electrical power requirements or the ammonia smell associated with most of the "self-contained" composting toilets that we saw advertised in magazines and at conferences. And we certainly weren't going to use propane to incinerate our poop—that was just replicating the absurdity of the public sewage systems we were rebelling against. In frustration, Erin made a rare foray to the public library to surf the Internet. Once again, the Swedes showed just how enlightened they are . . . even if their engineering still isn't quite perfect.

Erin discovered the Swedish "Separett" toilet, available in both AC and DC versions. This composting toilet features a hatch that opens whenever one sits down. Below, a large bucket rests on a disk that rotates one notch every time one is seated, allowing for an even distribution of poop in the covered bucket. But the most innovative aspect of the Separett toilet is the fact that it diverts the urine away from the bucket and into a container of choice—be it a barrel below or a septic system. Diverting the urine from the feces minimizes the ammonia smell from the collected urine, and it means that the rotating bucket contains only feces and toilet paper. An exhaust fan contained in the toilet's plastic casing helps to carry away the odors, while also slowly drying out the feces. Without the urine, the bucket fills slowly and is not so messy to empty. Urine itself is relatively sterile, but when it is mixed with feces, it becomes a smelly vector for any potential pathogens, and high moisture levels in organic matter generally create an increased incidence of fly reproduction.

Since one has to sit in order to pee into the front of the Separett toilet and poop into the rear of the toilet—thereby separating the two—males don't find it as convenient as a conventional toilet. But the most popular item at our house for men when we serve lots of beer or iced tea has been a jaunt to our urinal, located next to the Separett toilet. Our geologist friend John—a natural john aficionado, I suppose—has always made sure that he could find the opportunity to use the urinal any time he's here, convinced that every house should have at least one.

All is not piss and bliss, however, as any toilet with a fan adds an extra electrical burden, and a fairly substantial one, as it turns out. We ordered an AC and a DC toilet for our two bathrooms, just so we could determine which unit was best. Anything that runs constantly in an off-grid house with a battery bank creates a substantial drain on the batteries, even if the load is relatively small, with the end result being a shortened life for the battery bank. We've been cautious in adopting any technology that runs constantly, but in the end we hoped that these toilets might be worth the energy trade-off, since we were significantly extending the capacity and life of our septic system while not using fresh water to eliminate human waste from the house.

DC fans tend to use only one-quarter to one-half of the power required for AC fans, and this particular DC muffin fan is also much quieter than its AC cylinder-fan counterpart.[20] We hooked up the AC unit first, simply because it didn't involve any additional wiring, but we could never quite come to terms with the energy consumption or the constant hum of the fan in a world of peace and quiet.

However, there was a bigger unexpected issue lurking that led to our pulling the plug on these nifty toilets, at least for interior use. After approximately four years of use, we found the clog in our pipedream. It's not that the shit hit the fan—rather, it was the urine that made the mess. For almost four years, we had struggled with the buildup of urine salts in the small pipes exiting from the toilet and the urinal, despite the fact that we rinsed the urinal and the toilet with several cups of water after each use and planned to tie the drain from the bathroom sink into the waste pipes so that the sink's graywater would help to wash the salts into the larger 3-inch PVC piping going to the septic system. (Our hope was that at some point, we would begin collecting and using the urine and graywater for irrigation and fertilization, but that was set aside as a project for later, when the kids would be bigger and we would perhaps have more time.)

Two to three times each year, the 1- and 2-inch pipes exiting the Separett toilet clogged with urine salts, and I had to disassemble and clean all of the piping going from the toilet and urinal to the main 3-inch stack that went straight down to the basement and then out to the septic. There is no way to romanticize that task. Emptying a bucket of sawdust, poop, and pee is not that offensive to the olfactory system, in my view, but cleaning out urine salts and releasing the ammonia smells while scraping away at the interiors of pipes and joints . . . well, that's about as thankless a job as anyone could have. Yet the infrequency of that onerous task seemed a worthwhile trade for not having to empty the 5-gallon bucket from our original outhouse toilet almost on a daily basis, particularly with two growing boys and another child in the making.

Ultimately, we thought that we'd made our last compromise in this system by sending the urine to the septic, but that all changed one fateful summer day in 2009 when we discovered that the issue of urine salts went far beyond what we—or even Dennis, our local plumber friend—thought possible. I'd cleaned out all of the 1- and 2-inch pipes, as I always did, and reassembled the entire system for the composting toilet and the urinal. However, when I tested the drainage on both units, I couldn't detect a difference in performance before and after the cleaning. The water simply wouldn't exit the toilet or the urinal. In a fit of frustration and fear, I once again took apart all of the pipes and got to the completely vertical 3-inch pipe. I couldn't believe it—that pipe, despite the fact that it ran straight down to the basement, appeared to be clogged.

I called Dennis to see if he could come by with his pipe snake and hopefully dismiss my worst fear. Later that afternoon, Dennis appeared with his heavy-gauge snake, and we tested it. "I don't believe it," Dennis said from the top of the ladder, burying his nose in his shirtsleeve to thwart off some of the ammonia smell drifting from the 3-inch pipe. "This pipe is almost completely full of urine salts. There's barely an inch of space left in this vertical pipe for the water to go down to the basement. I've never seen anything like it."

As it turns out, urine salts are not soluble in water, even warm water. According to Dennis, a toilet functions not just by eliminating wastes diluted in water but also by creating a swirling, scouring action, and this swirling action continues through much of the piping as the wastes are moved toward their final exit from a house. Funny what they don't tell you in a composting toilet user's manual—at least not the degree to which you can create an enormous problem and expense for yourself if you don't engineer the right disposal method for urine salts.

"You're lucky we discovered this when we did." Dennis was standing on the ladder sending the snake down the pipe. I had rigged a hose that reached from our solar hot-water tank up to where he was on the ladder so that we could scrape and scour the pipe before it clogged entirely. "If this entire pipe had gotten clogged, we'd be ripping out walls and maybe even concrete to pull it out and replace it." Dennis was working hard to break the crystallized salts off the pipe walls, and he was uncertain whether we would actually be able to break it all loose without clogging the pipe farther down in the basement.

By the time it was all over, we had made one more compromise, bigger than any other, we felt. We replaced the Swedish toilet with a low-flush toilet, hoping to build another outhouse for three-season use, with a pipe going directly from the toilet's urine bowl into a urine collection tank and with a PV panel to power the DC fan during sunny periods. And, of course, there will be a urinal. So we boosted the load on our septic system and subsequently dramatically reduced the twenty-four-hour draw from the fan on our power system, thereby increasing the life of our batteries and decreasing the capacity and autonomy of our septic system. Erin says that it's easier for bachelors and people with no children to avoid compromises.

Nonetheless, it's not a compromise to which we've completely resigned ourselves. It seems to be part of the evolution of a homestead, with the constant tension between good ideas and admirable ideals. An important part of the value of the entire process is, in fact, the pioneering experimentation involved. We are all in search of new ways of living and accompanying technologies that can support our ideals. Part of the pioneering involves failure, or at least setbacks, but these forays into frustration are an important part of the process, particularly if they are shared and not obscured. The obvious risk in all of this pioneering and dissemination is, of course, the possibility that we begin trading indictments of breaches of integrity and developing self-enhancing scales of purity and wholesomeness. The point is to experiment, share the failures and frustrations, and move on collectively and with mutual respect for one another's efforts. It's about the power of sharing knowledge . . . and the sharing of knowledge about power.

Electricity's greatest power is perhaps not its ability to make life more efficient—personally or ecologically—but rather its capacity to transform luxuries into needs. This transformation of desires into expectations is a product of our relatively uncritical mode of consumption. Our collective disregard for where we are headed is pushing us to the brink of national—if not planetary—crisis. A national or international debate on our collective need to reduce consumption has little meaning if we are neither accounting nor accountable for our own household consumption of resources.

Tracing the ever-shifting line between need and luxury should probably be one of the first points of household discussion. The Pew Research Center has examined data tracking American perceptions of household necessities and luxuries back to 1973. They recently discovered a significant increase in the number of items that Americans consider necessities in the decade between 1996 and 2006. Those items that were considered necessities by more than half of the survey respondents in 2006 included, in ranked order: a car, a clothes washer, a clothes dryer, home air-conditioning, a microwave, a TV set, car air-conditioning, and a home computer. A cell phone nearly reaches the top half but falls short at 49 percent.[21]

Interestingly, a more detailed analysis of the Pew Research Center data reveals that the higher one's income, the more likely one will be to consider certain items as needs rather than luxuries. Furthermore, rural residents consider fewer items to be necessities than do inhabitants of cities and suburbs. But what surprises and disturbs me the most is that the trend of shifting more and more luxuries into the needs category has endured for more than three decades, to the point that the most basic modern necessities, such as lighting, refrigeration, and running water, are automatically assumed to be needs, and thus have completely disappeared from the list.

Every time an item on the list of necessities becomes a given and disappears from the list altogether, we up our culture's base level of consumption. Not only that, but technological privileges can quickly become expectations, and the potential for thoughtful dialogue and debate about technology and consumption is greatly diminished. We are faced with the peculiar task of simultaneously reinventing necessity and reclaiming contentment.

According to the World Values Survey data, American happiness is not increasing at a rate commensurate with our increase in technological "necessities."[22] It is also not clear that we are healthier as a society, given the dramatic rise in national rates of obesity. One might even make the argument that all of our labor-saving devices are forcing us to work more, as more Americans are working more than forty-nine hours per week while fewer persons are working just forty hours per week.[23] And, of course, it seems inevitable that we exercise less as a result.

In the end, we can (and should) debate what these data really tell us about what we're doing to ourselves. Up to this point, homesteading in the American tradition has primarily been an individual response to a perceived misguided cultural trajectory. In other words, homesteading has been, in some ways, an individual-centered SOS—Save One's Self.

What is clear and different now—in contrast with Thoreau, the Nearings, and others in the American homesteading tradition—is that the homesteading movement's greatest potential contribution to society is no longer the salvation of the individual by means of rural exile. Rather, homesteading ventures and values need to focus on cultural and civic engagement—with a keen eye on energy—and not just in rural areas but also in comfortable suburbs and even the most difficult urban environments. First person singular has been the pronoun guiding the American homesteading tradition up to this point. But first person plural is the pronoun a good ecologist simply must use.

So we find ourselves in a world with ever-clearer ecological limits, a dilemma framed by the constraints of the law of entropy. Our likely sense of *aporia,* of having "no way out," is the sum total of our collective wild abandon, perpetuated by generations but intensifying in the hastening currents of our contemporary technological cascade.

If the homestead still has a place in the changing American cultural landscape, then it must be a place where we can actively ask questions . . . and try to better understand the incompleteness of our carefully lived answers. What we will probably find is that we can indeed control our technological cascade—collectively—much better than we can control its ecological consequences.

It's daunting, to be sure. But I have faith. There is a door, if we choose to open it. I'm reminded of it whenever I hear our college motto *Lux fiat:* Let there be light. The motto was undoubtedly meant to be a testament to the power of education. I subscribe to that belief, but, for me, it is also a reminder of a much-neglected gift.

According to the US Department of Energy, enough light hits the surface of the earth in a single minute to meet the current energy consumption of our entire human population for a year.[24] We can idly sit back and let government and industry capture that energy for us. Or we can stand up, spurred on by a basic understanding of entropy, and begin to lay claim to that light ourselves—with gardens, forests, livestock, and renewable energy technologies.

Despite the small scale of rural, urban, and suburban homesteads, we have entropy on our side. Entropy is, in large part, a function of distance and the energy transformations required to provide our necessities. So harvesting the light and transforming it into useful energy to power and warm our daily lives can best be done right at home . . . or, perhaps better yet, in the neighborhood.

It's all about wise choices and smart technologies—in that order.

FIFTEEN

The Clock, the Wallet, and the Hand

March 13, 2002. We were looking out of the cabin's bedroom windows at the night sky, filled with constellations and planets that we'd hardly bothered to notice until we moved up Tunket. Undoubtedly, artificial light had dimmed our view of the cast of characters who plied the night sky, swapping shifts and seasons while we modern mortals lost track of time, increasingly ignorant of the celestial calendar writ large between horizons.

"You know, the best feeling in the world is knowing that you're going to be home all day the next day," Erin mused.

I certainly didn't disagree. The question of "time" was an honored theme in our little cabin. As I was writing in my journal on the New Year's Eve just a few months prior, I'd reflected on years of travel and living abroad, finally reaching the point at which I wanted "an adventure in which I can just stay home." We'd made plenty of allowances for such an adventure. Some days in the cabin would melt into evenings of thankfulness, like after a nap with infant Asa sleeping on my chest one November day later that year. "Moments are more momentous, minutes are less like minutiae, and the hours seem more like ours," I'd written that night, thankful for a day of quiet, simple pleasures with my family.

But then there were—and still are—times that left me feeling like I was more apart from our homestead than a part of it. The struggle to make a living that would support our homesteading and farming habits has always been a challenge. The fortunate thing for me is that I chose not just a profession but also a very special college that allows me to integrate my job and my homestead, at least to some degree. It wasn't all fortuitous happenstance—integrating a homestead and any profession takes some careful consideration and strategic planning, and sometimes at least part of it works out. But I'm also lucky to have a spouse who relishes most every day spent at home. When we were both working outside the homestead, with Erin balancing three jobs at one point, we quickly discovered that the homestead dreams and realities begin to drift without an anchor. Erin is that anchor.

We trade frustrations on occasion, each of us thinking that the other has the more idyllic life. I leave, running, and enter another world full of stimulation and companionship—and often return spent, unable to fully appreciate what I missed that day or to rapidly reenter the mind-set of what needs to be done at home. Erin stays, laying claim to the quiet but bustling rhythm of the homestead, generally working with the weather and the seasons, although sometimes in direct conflict with them.

Some days, she's able to capture the best of what the place has to offer, spending the day in the garden or on a wooded walk with the children. Other times, she feels confined to the kitchen and the kids, wedded to our quest for wholesome food and homeschooling. With the birth of our daughter, Addy, in the fall of 2009, the balancing act became a bit more challenging, but the time with three children of different ages and genders is a joy and a privilege seldom questioned. Ultimately, each of our chosen roles suits our individual personalities well, but the best days are undoubtedly those in which we are all home together, with work and play mostly intermingled, if not indistinguishable. And of course, there are also days in which work and play seem to be in direct conflict.

The portrayal of the American homestead as idyllic and stress-free is mythic, and perhaps somewhat misinformed. I was relieved to encounter Jeffrey Jacob's sociological study of homesteaders in his book *New Pioneers*. Jacob's extensive surveying and interviewing of homesteaders reveals one of the most common and frustrating dilemmas facing homesteaders—the time–money dilemma. The search for balance between time and money—and the subsequent question of efficiencies—seems nearly universal and virtually unending, with homesteaders attempting a variety of approaches toward funding, building, and maintaining their homesteads.

Some homesteaders try to generate their income on the homestead, while others find it necessary to work elsewhere to support their homesteading efforts. The number of approaches is as diverse as the multitude of reasons that people pursue a homesteading life. First-generation homesteads seem particularly prone to the tense pull between homestead aspirations and economic constraints, often leading to a frustrating feeling of building a remote dream remotely, with too little time spent on-site. A mortgage is typically the limiting factor, leading me to believe that the greatest gift we might bequeath our children—if they want it and are willing to work for it—is the liberation of a mortgage-free homestead.

There are certainly ways to try to build a mortgage-free homestead, but such an approach doesn't necessarily fit everyone's circumstances or choices.[1] The size of a mortgage does have serious consequences, because size in the finance world is equivalent to time in the homesteading world—typically time that must be spent away from homestead projects and beholden to a bank. It's nice to be able to expend the energy of one's youth on the building of a homestead instead of saving the building and the pleasures for a time in life when one may be less fit or able to realize the dreams.

A mortgage also locks homesteaders into a world of responsibilities and legalities that may not jibe with their aspirations. We discovered just how intertwined we were with worlds that we were trying to avoid when we opted to build a house that required a mortgage. We ultimately decided that building a house incrementally, as we could afford it, wasn't the route we wanted to go. Having one child and preparing for at least one more made us anxious to have running water, stored hot water, a washing machine, and more efficient food storage and preparation facili-ties. It felt less stressful to build as much of our house as possible at one time, particularly with the growing pressures and time constraints of maintaining a larger herd of cattle and hoping later on to use a portion of our house as an "income center," with two off-grid farmhouse guest rooms and a basement cheesemaking facility. Besides, having tasted the sweet pleasure of living debt-free, we never intended to carry the mort-gage for the entirety of its twenty-year duration.

But we did discover that a mortgage meant house insurance . . . which in turn required reliable road access for emergency vehicles . . . which meant a tractor to maintain and clear our mile of road. (The tractor, of course, would also serve us well in much of our farmwork, particularly in placing round hay bales in pastures with poorer fertility, where we outwintered our cows, thereby using these bales for feed, seed, and fertil-izer. I suppose in some ways we've also used hydraulics to substitute for a large labor force.)

Our realization of the interconnectedness of the mortgage, septic, insurance, emergency vehicle access, and road maintenance was the moment at which we first felt that we had opened the gate to the outside.

The Clock, the Wallet, and the Hand

Prior to that, our homestead had been a bastion against many of the outside influences that we had consciously eschewed, but our mortgage shifted that reality, at least to some degree. Nonetheless, it was a trade-off—one that we didn't altogether embrace, but one that we decided to accept.

The American homesteading tradition is filled with purists, at least on paper. We probably need those purists to guide us forward and to force us to stretch hard to reach our goals. But it's important that the purists tell the full truth about their experiences, with humility and humor. I can't quantify it, but I tend to believe that most of the authentic purists whose writings have been influential to many of us have either been single or couples without small children—and not all of them have been open in discussing their compromises.

I'm afraid that I'm not a purist . . . and certainly not a Puritan. Less in my own defense and more in the defense of life as a constant interplay between learning and values, I would offer up the story of a much-admired campus pastor I came to know in college. The Reverend Bob Martin was a Cajun Presbyterian, a storytelling soothsayer who mindfully wandered about the college dining hall, looking for students like myself who needed to incubate a story, generally for our own edification, albeit seldom instant.

Bob caught me one day in some sort of egotistical bluster, lamenting someone else's poor choices. "Philip, you've heard a few of my stories about my Cajun grandmother, right?"

"Absolutely—she seems like a 'bijou of the bayou,' Bob!" I was hoping I impressed him with my French.

"Well, of all the things she ever told me, here's the most important. You listenin'?"

"Always."

"'Sometimes' would be more apt in your case, based on my experience." He winked at me. We both knew he was right. He decided it was worth trying again. "She told me that you can judge the character of a person based on the integrity of his or her compromises."

Compromise is not a word that sets well with homesteaders. It implies caving in—losing sight of one's values. But if a good portion of homesteading is learning more about ourselves, the natural world, our culture, and basic practical skills, then it only makes sense that we adjust our values to our changing understandings. It seems nearly certain that our understanding of the world is deepened and enriched by the homesteading experience. It follows that if the best values are those that are well considered and not merely inherited, then those values subjected to a homesteading venture will reflect accumulated knowledge and experience. Therefore, it only makes sense that we allow our values some flexibility. Adjusting them to fit our own growth as individuals and families is to connect theory and praxis, experience and values. Evolving values do not necessarily represent an abandonment of principles or a dilution of high standards.

Perhaps no term used on the homestead is more value-laden than *efficiency,* and it's probably because the word encompasses three of the most precious resources on the typical homestead: time, money, and natural capital. As we struggle with time and money, we are simultaneously trying to understand and structure our role in the natural world. I've nearly given up on believing that we're going to find consensus on how to best define *efficiency.* Instead, I think it wise for us to agree that it is the discussion of efficiency that is ultimately important, not a penultimate definition. Any conclusive definition is at best the starting point of a new debate.

A neoclassical economist's definition is going to comprise several basic elements: time, money, materials, and profits. An environmental economist's definition is going to add in environmental costs, benefits, and changes. An ecological economist will consider all these elements while also trying to think about efficiencies in the context of our entire complex ecological system. A homesteader may include the degree to which physical labor or organically produced foods will contribute to the family's health. A Zen master may discount all the other variables and simply focus on the degree to which a task elevates or lowers one's spiritual awareness.

In order to gain some clarity on how to approach the whole question of efficiency on the homestead, it makes sense to mull over the Latin root of the word, *efficere,* meaning "to make or carry out." In effect, then, efficiency is determined by what one intends to be the end result. If it's money, so be it. If it's the production of healthy food, that's great. If the idea is to combine the raising of healthy food with the generation of profit for the producer, then the determination of efficiency becomes a bit more complex. If the hope is to do all of these things while building a healthier soil and maintaining wildlife habitat, then still more head-work is necessary to establish a metric for efficiency. Finally, add a requisite element of

spiritual satisfaction for the grower, and the answer becomes even more difficult to determine, but no less important or relevant.

In the end, efficiency relates back to *intent*. If homesteading has any defining component, it is conscious and conscientious intent. But what drives that intent tends to vary a great deal. It's hard to determine the efficiency of any task or project until one is clear on the ultimate intent. Our own level of ambiguity will always exist, and we will probably never be able to measure efficiency from an ecological perspective with 100 percent accuracy. But nature is constantly tallying the cumulative results. We may not see the final score sheet, but at some point we begin to get a sense of whether or not we're on the winning team. Mother Nature not only has the home court advantage, but she controls the scoreboard, too.

Homesteaders are seemingly always looking for "how-to" methods, and that's important. However, not fully understanding or articulating *why* one is doing something a certain way creates a real bugaboo when one starts to face issues surrounding efficiency. The key to addressing the efficiency question is knowing which goals are primary.

I don't think I've met a homesteader yet who hasn't grappled with the time–money dilemma, a quandary that quickly brings the efficiency question into the picture, over and over again. Technology issues and environmental questions follow suit, and the spiritual nature of work often emerges, too. Knowing *why* one is doing something may well drive the choices as to *how* one does it.

Efficiency is in the eye of the smallholder.

"Jesus Christ! There's another splinter! Give me those damn pliers, Philip."

"Just another splinter from the cross you bear as our carpenter, John."

John grabbed the pliers from me and grunted as he pulled. "Remind me again—why did you think it would be such a good idea to use this damn rough-cut lumber? We could've had the roof on this house by now if you'd just bought dimensional lumber like everybody else. The studs would all be cut to length, and all we'd have to do is pop them up. And we sure as hell wouldn't be spending all of this time having to deal with studs and plates that vary in width and thickness . . . and I wouldn't be getting these splinters all the damn time!"

John was right, in some ways. The whole summer that we'd been framing our house, we were watching several other houses on our road go up in rapid fashion. The lumberyard trucks roared in and out of those building sites, unloading uniform materials with a hydraulic hoist, with the carpenters waiting with their chalk-lines and compressed-air nail guns.

Not one to stop after a full dose of morning coffee, John kept going. "Rough cut's fine for a barn, but why do you want to use it for your house? Just wait till we start putting in the horizontal nailers and prepping the interior walls for whatever you decide to use as wall boards— then you might regret it."

"I know it's a pain, John, but I never said I wanted to do everything like everybody else." I knew that when we were done, however long that was going to take, at least we would have a rock-solid house that wasn't going to be off-gassing formaldehyde from all the glues in the plywood and the other wood-composite materials.

"Well, this hemlock is definitely stout . . . ," John conceded.

". . . and reasonably rot-resistant, too," I added, "at least compared with all of that yellow pine everybody else is using."

I bent over to pick up a rough-cut hemlock stud and a scrap piece of yellow pine 2×4 that Erin had salvaged from another construction site for use as temporary post braces on our structure. The growth rings in the yellow pine were broad, whereas they were dense and tight in the hemlock board. I didn't dislike all aspects of the yellow pine—it grew straight and fast in the southern tree plantations. We'd used it to build our cabin on my grandparents' farm, but it was no match for the hemlock, in my mind. Hemlock was tougher and more rot-resistant than yellow pine, chiefly because of where and how it grows.

Hemlock usually lives in a shady and cool environment, in large part because it starts to dominate as a species in many of the forests where it gains a strong foothold. It tends to outcompete many other species of trees because it's relatively shade-tolerant, it covers the forest floor with its acidic needles, and it tolerates acidic soils. It definitely takes a while to mature, but its relatively slow growth gives it a tight, rugged grain.

"So where is Phil getting all of it for his mill?"

"Within about a 50 mile radius, he said."

"Well, you're definitely keeping Phil in business this summer."

"And a bunch of loggers," I added.

"You're responsible for raping the forests here, you know!"

"I'm hoping that these loggers are doing a good job. Actually, my biggest concern is the hemlock woolly adelgid—it's an insect that's attacking the hemlocks in states south of us. The hemlock is Pennsylvania's state tree, and they're losing entire forests down there. Everybody's on the lookout for it here in the Northeast. I sure hope it doesn't make it in."

Either John's caffeine was wearing off or I was wearing him down in his aversion to what I considered our best local framing lumber. "Well, I do love hemlock forests, and I guess the lumber's not that bad, as long as we're dealing with it while it's green."

We were framing the entire house with hemlock, nailing the boards up while they were still green, using 16- and 20-penny nails to lock them into place. "When this stuff dries, John, it's gonna be tighter than your wallet!"

I started telling John about Japanese carpenters and how they can boast of having the oldest standing wooden buildings in the world. Before they cut the trees for those temples, the carpenters marked which direction they were facing. So the side of the tree facing the north was placed in the temple facing north. That way, each side of the tree was exposed to the same elements—sun, shade, moisture conditions—that it faced when it was standing in the forest. Supposedly, that meant less twisting and adjusting as it dried. It made for a more stable structure that endured everything from storms to earthquakes for more than two thousand years.[2]

"More work initially, John, but less work fixing problems in the long run. That's what I'm after. My kids will tell us whether this was all a good idea or not. But that's why we hired you—we needed a craftsman, not a Home Depot hack."

John's loud laugh rippled off the deck of the second floor. "You just have to decide if your wallet is as patient as you are." He got back to his craft.

"You bought a bread machine? I mean, *you* bought a bread machine! You, who worships the Amish, spent money on a bread machine? I don't believe it."

Erin looked at me with a sheepish expression. "Ten bucks. Gotta love that kind of bargain!"

"Well, yeah, good price, but what's it gonna cost us in terms of energy? You know as well as I do that our solar system hates anything that uses resistance to create heat from electricity—it's just too energy-intensive."

"Philip, give me a break. You know I know that. But we keep wasting all our homegrown power on sunny summer days. The charge controller is shutting the system down because the batteries are full . . ."

I could barely squeeze in a nod of consent before she had me completely cornered.

". . . and I feel like I've got enough to do around here. There's no reason I should feel guilty about having a machine bake bread for me. Otherwise, I'm not going to get to it, and we're gonna be eating that crappy bread from the store that costs more than it's worth, with less nutritional value than my recipe."

I felt like a unicyclist with blinders, trying to backpedal. "Okay, okay, I guess it makes sense. It just seems like one more machine, taking up space even if it's not taking up energy."

"Space isn't a problem for us anymore. Time still is." She was right. And we both hated baking in the oven in the summer since it just makes the kitchen that much hotter. "And time I save in the kitchen is time I can be in the garden."

"Okay, okay, you win. It makes sense. So why was this woman getting rid of it anyway?"

"She said she was too busy to use it."

"Now, wait—I don't get it . . . too busy to use a labor-saving device?"

"She had a day care, and she just couldn't find the time to make bread anymore. She said she used to love it but decided to get rid of it after not using it for a long time."

"Hmmm. Better than the landfill, I suppose."

As if she hadn't already defeated me with her off-grid logic, Erin added the coup de grâce by calculating that it probably took less energy to heat up the tiny space in the bread machine than the oversized space in the oven just for one or two loaves. And, of course, she noted all of the embedded energy already invested in making the bread machine. "Somebody might as well use it," she concluded.

"Okay, you win! I'm done, defeated . . . you'd better pop in the ingredients in and get out to your garden."

She went to the pantry for the bread flour but stopped and did a quick pivot to catch me before I could escape. "And now I'm on the lookout for a Crock-Pot, for all the same reasons. Tell me if you see one for sale in the paper."

We had lots of good loaves from there on out, until two-year-old

Ethan put a rock in the bread machine to see what would happen. He probably should have gotten his buns toasted.

The used Crock-Pot still works, though. And Maggie got us a new bread machine the next Christmas. Oh well.

Most of my days start pretty much the same. I'm late, and I'm running. The pattern is pretty ingrained at this point.

Get up. Look out the windows southward down the yawning Mettowee Valley and across our little valley up to the peak of Haystack. Scratch. Bathroom. Dressed. Check the outdoor temperature. Make coffee. Light the main woodstove if it's cold. Light the wood cookstove if it's really cold. Eat a quick bite . . . or a slow one. Find other ways to get distracted.

Finally, grab the milk bucket and head to the barn to get ready to bring in whatever cow or cows are available and ready to get milked. Sometimes I've got an apprentice there to help with morning chores. Sometimes not.

My mother finally told me when I was forty that, ever since I was five, I'd gotten up every morning thinking I'd do more than any human possibly could in a day. I'd never quite realized that that trait was so much a part of my personality, although I suppose my first inkling of that tendency hit me when I was eight. I had invited all the neighborhood kids over to my house one afternoon to help me dig a swimming pool in the backyard. I was distressed that, by the time they all had to head home for dinner, we'd only gotten about a foot deep, even though it was a pretty big rectangular hole. My father, on the other hand, was furious at our progress. It might have been a different matter if the backyard had been ours. But we were living in the church manse . . . it sure took a long time to fill it back in all alone.

Anyway, the rhythmic zing of milk hitting the stainless-steel milk pail is almost always an upbeat sound, and the contentment of a cow eating fragrant hay in the morning helps to buffer the caffeine load. I milk by hand. The milking machine uses a ½-horsepower electric motor—too much draw on the solar system to warrant using it for one or two cows. Plus, it's a lot easier cleaning just a milk pail than it is a milking machine, and I tend to think hand-milking can be a little better for the cow, although the milk isn't necessarily as clean as it is when done by machine.

I take the milk inside to filter and refrigerate it, and, by that time, the family is usually beginning to stir. I go back out and let out the geese from their house and the chickens from their two coops, giving them all feed and water. I also give them the "chicken bucket," filled with leftover scraps and the rinsings from our pots and plates. Rinsing our plates into a bucket adds nutrients to the poultry water while helping to maximize the capacity and life of our septic system. Finally, I get the cow or cows out to pasture, feed any calves that might be in the barn, and head out to feed and water the rest of the herd.

Is it worth it, I sometimes wonder, all that work just for a few gallons of milk? After all, I've given up time early and late in the day that I once used for running or cycling. Is it making us all healthier, or is the minimal aerobic exercise and the day filled to capacity taking its toll on me?

Different days I have different answers. Probably not a good thing to say, coming from a guy who's supposed to be teaching this stuff. But it depends upon how I construct the equation, and sometimes I can clearly document inputs and outputs—hay, chores, breeding investments—while on other days I'm not so willing to dismiss the intangibles. Like having Asa and Ethan play in the barn, climbing over railings, caring for calves, sitting in my lap to milk a few hard-earned squirts from the nearest teats. The fact that I'm out in every conceivable kind of weather, getting fresh air and some exercise. The joys of having fresh milk in my cereal, dense cream in my coffee, roadside raspberries in Erin's delicious yogurt. And then there's the beef in the freezer, the huge pile of compost, the five kinds of cheeses aging in the root cellar, the sale of breeding stock, and what I hope is an ever-improving herd of grass-fed American Milking Devons for the next generation.

Everything counts for something.

I love my Kubota tractor. And I love not using it. That's one of the joys of grass farming—it requires more cow power than horsepower and more walking than riding.

I also love being the Candyman. The cows like to go where I go because they know that most every time I open a gate for them to enter a new area, there's cow-candy waiting for them. We just like each other's company, I guess. We keep each other fat and happy.

The efficiency of grass farming is not so much about avoiding work as it is about working within natural cycles and existing environments, and using the best-adapted livestock to do so. The better suited the soils, the vegetation, and the livestock, the better the chances of success for the animals and the farmer. But most of it hinges on the experienced eye and listening ear of the grass farmer. The efficiencies aren't shortcuts. Rather, they are a managed mimicry of natural cycles and systems, adapted to meet the human desire for meat, milk, and fiber without degrading the natural ecosystem.

Now that carbon counts and methane matters, grass-farming efficiencies are all the more important. Grass-farming does not require tillage; it encourages carbon sequestration; it promotes taking livestock to the feed instead of feed to the livestock; it utilizes "marginal" land less suitable for other types of food production; it can minimize soil erosion and nutrient runoff; it maintains perennial polycultures; and it uses livestock to convert sunlight directly into food and fiber.

We graze about 40 acres of land, graciously provided by neighbors. In exchange, our cattle manicure their pastures, supplemented by one or two mowings per year to keep the less edible "weeds" from becoming dominant over time. As a result, my family spends a lot of time putting up and taking down portable fencing in various fields, almost always along the edges between fields and forests.

Ecologists have long known the value of these ecosystem "edges" for maintaining biodiversity. The combination of habitats provides diverse types of food and cover for wildlife—a phenomenon known as the "edge effect"—and our hours spent walking along these edges confirm just how rich these environments are, not just for the wildlife, but also for our own education and pleasure.

There are certainly days when I wish that we owned some of those fields so that we could put in permanent infrastructure such as fencing, watering sources, and even some shelter for inclement weather, but such a scenario would require costs other than my time and possibly make our farming venture financially unviable. But my extensive walking of those fence lines also means that I get the chance to exercise and to observe things more closely than I would from a tractor seat. Even more important, our children would not make the same discoveries they've made while tromping through such different habitats, observing not just cattle but also red-tailed hawks, ravens, red-winged blackbirds, barred owls, turkeys, peregrine falcons, indigo buntings, scarlet tanagers, Baltimore orioles, porcupines, skunks, woodchucks, crawdads, caddis flies, foxes, and fawns.

And thanks to our wildcrafting friends Les Hook and Nova Kim,[3] I watch our kids make a meal out of most of their walks, eating a host of wild foods: violets, wood sorrel, trout lily leaves, raspberries, blackberries, gooseberries, blueberries, currants, fox grapes, apples, wild strawberries, oxeye daisies, barberries, dandelion greens, red clover nectaries, leeks, and mints to clean the palate. And they bring home young stinging nettles and tender milkweed for us to cook. Never would I have suspected that such young children could begin to identify so many plants—much less forage their way through field and forest with such zeal.

Surely there's an efficiency to learning things at such a young age. And a tragic absurdity at learning them too late in life . . . if at all.

SIXTEEN

Rewired Rewards

I'd lived in the Italian Alps and worked in a vineyard long enough to know that food produced in one valley could taste different from the same food raised in another nearby valley. In fact, I could taste the difference between grapes grown in the upper edges of Brunnenburg vineyard, just below the castle's plummeting walls, and the grapes of the same variety grown in poorer, drier soils farther down in the vineyard. I could see and taste the distinct differences between cheeses and butter from different alpine pasturages separated only by a hard day's hike. And it's never been a secret to anyone in the wine world that the same type of wine, produced in different vineyards and aged in different cellars, can vary dramatically. In Europe, I was learning firsthand in just how many ways the quality of most any food was correlated with the care with which it was produced.

But I didn't really grasp the whole picture. *Terroir*—that was a concept that required a gastronomist's palate and an ecologist's field notebook, with a farmer's careful cultivation of tradition somewhere in between. I confess that it took me more than a decade to begin really putting the pieces together.[1]

My South Tirolean friends Stefan and Christine had invited me to Stefan's family restaurant, the Wiedenplatzkeller (a name I could phonetically slither my way through only after a few glasses of wine), for a special meal featuring foods from our local valley, the Vinschgau. This broad valley swoops southeastward from the borders of Switzerland and Austria, carrying with it the infamous *Vinschgerwind*, a fierce and frequent wind that wicks the moisture from the air and soil, making the Vinschgau one of the driest spots in the Alps.

The length of the valley boasts orchards, vineyards, broad fields of grains and vegetables, and mountainside dairies. The history of agriculture stretches as far and wide as the valley itself. The Romans placed a statue of Maia, the goddess of spring, near the present-day city of Meran, in tribute to the region's hospitable climes. And Ötzi, the, famously preserved prehistoric Iceman, apparently ran up from the Vinschgau in frantic flight before his unsettling death some fifty-two hundred years ago, high in the mountains to the north of the valley (he was even carrying sloeberries purportedly from the valley—apparently a Neolithic form of Slow Food).

The purpose of the meal at Wiedenplatzkeller was to celebrate the Vinschgau's cornucopia of foods and accompanying traditions, exploring the nuances of taste and history that were giving way to the cultural homogenization of the area.

I was the prime example of the homogenization—an American working in a local vineyard and teaching students the history and culture of the region. But as I learned more about the purpose of the meal, I felt a little like the guy who is invited to dinner with cannibals, only to discover that he is in fact the entrée . . . with no exit in sight.

Opening the entryway door for me, Stefan provided the first hint of my destiny: "Philip, you are our special guest tonight. . . ."

"Yes, you're our token American," interjected Christine. She never passed up an opportunity to initiate a verbal jousting match with me.

I gave her my best endearing smirk. "Okay, I'm used to being your token *Auslander*[2]. So what faux pas would you like me to commit tonight to entertain you?" Christine was always letting me know if I'd been *unhöflich*[3], particularly whenever I failed to open a door for her or help her take off a jacket—things previous American girlfriends had chided me for doing. But when in Rome . . . succumb.

"Just having your American passport is enough tonight," she prodded. "This is a Slow Food dinner. Do you know what that is?"

"It doesn't sound very American to me . . ."

"Anti-American actually," Stefan and Christine both laughed, while I felt the water getting hotter. "Have you heard of the new Slow Food movement here in Italy?"

I hadn't. It was the early 1990s, and the idea of Slow Food was just emerging in Italy. Journalist Carlo Petrini and a band of food-loving compatriots had decided to take on the rapid influx of fast food into their country, seeing it as a threat not only to the Italian palate but also to the Italian way of life—the food, the landscape, the farming traditions, and of course the economy. And they were right to do so. Had they not formed their organization of food anarchists, the Modern Machine might have mowed Italy's food traditions right down. Instead, Italy is now the epicenter of the most important food fight ever invented. There's a parable of efficiency in the story somewhere: How can a country move so slow but be so far ahead?

Little did I realize that evening just what an important role Slow Food would soon play on the world stage, much less in my own life. It took a while to digest it all. In fact, the meal lasted from 8 PM until well after 2 the next morning. It wasn't a raucous Bacchanalian fest, although we did taste wines from a host of villages and a range of elevations. The cheeses came from several different high pastures and were made in various seasons, with the variation in forages standing out as subtle points of distinction. Grains like millet and buckwheat that were once a staple of previous poorer generations reappeared on the table before us, along with *Eigenbau* (home-raised and homemade) meats and aperitifs. Traditional breads of varying textures, grains, and shapes soaked up Tuscan olive oil and the regional spirits. My appetite was sated, but my curiosity was whetted. This was *terroir*—the experience of "tasting" soil and sun in foods prepared by the capable hands of artisan producers and farmers. Yet as the new European Union regulations were beginning to appear, in the guise of well-heeled and shiny-toed inspectors, these capable hands were being portrayed as culpable hands. It was clearly time for a modern peasant revolt.

The next day, as I shared the sensational and sensory experience with my American friends, I felt a certain tension about what I had encountered that I couldn't quite explain to anyone else. It was the sense that I had experienced something extraordinarily special . . . but was it something elitist? Certainly, we had all spent a fair amount of money that night—albeit not that much, thanks to the generosity of Stefan's family in preparing such an amazing meal. Also, a good portion of the money was going to the farmers who produced the food, not to a distributor. But we were essentially eating the traditional foods of peasants. Not downtrodden, poverty-stricken peasants stuck in medieval serfdom. After all, the Tirolean farmers were enduringly famous for their spirited independence—they had even addressed the Hapsburg rulers using the informal *Du* pronoun for "you," not the formal *Sie* form.

Something was astir here. Somewhat affluent tastes were recognizing and celebrating the pleasure of a peasant's fare, albeit in quantities probably seldom seen all at one time on the mountain farmers' austere tables. The Slow Food dinner was emblematic of the dream table of the American homestead. Wholesome, nutritious, tasty, crafted with care, linked to the land, and tied to tradition.

Is it elitist to celebrate the most basic pleasures of life, pleasures created without harm or exploitation—food produced with what most of us would consider appropriate values, skills, and technologies? It was a question that would haunt me for the next fifteen years . . . and perhaps longer yet. And while it might not have been a question that haunted Carlo Petrini and others in the early stages of the rapidly growing Slow Food movement, they later countered the question head-on, much to their credit.

Pleasure. It's an odd word in a way. To our American ear, it seems to generate dueling responses. There is the initial, knee-jerk Puritanical response that treats the word with suspicion, looking for the shadows of avarice, malice, and indolence. Then there is the Las Vegas bells-and-whistles reaction—frivolous wild abandon . . . rosin up the bow and let the city burn.

Maybe the concept that feels more appropriate to us is contentment, deep and abiding contentment. Satisfaction.

But in a world wired for instant winners, immediate gratification, and constant stimuli touting rewards, will mere contentment get us where we need to be in responding to the intertwined nature of our social and ecological dilemmas? I'm not so sure.

If pleasures are rooted in things we find meaningful—like food—and our bodies are in fact hardwired for rewards, then perhaps we should explore and share how the values, skills, and technologies of homesteading can impart pleasure. Perhaps the result is that we are bowing to the basest of human desires. On the other hand, perhaps it's simply a biological given, one that we need to accept and utilize. I remain uncertain.

But I do know that I see a lot more people headed to festivals and carnivals than to monasteries (this coming from one who tends to like monasteries). I've seen thousands of people swayed in the direction of renewable energy from attending our region's weekend-long Solarfest event in tiny Tinmouth, Vermont—a festival dedicated to renewable energy, music, and the arts—many more than the handfuls of people I've seen in cloistered classrooms and libraries for free lectures or workshops on the topic.[4]

There's something about sparking our cerebral interests with celebratory events. Granted, that spark is simply the ignition point. What fuels—indeed, sustains—that interest and propels us forward over the long term may well be something altogether different. Nonetheless, pleasure is a point of engagement, and it can be a source of continued—although not continual—inspiration.

I was fortunate enough to be a US delegate to Slow Food's audacious Terra Madre events in 2006 and again in 2008. Terra Madre is a convocation of farmers, fishers, food producers, chefs, academics, and food advocates from around the world. Filling the Winter Olympic facilities in Turin, Italy, more than six thousand of us gathered to share our common and disparate visions of a "good, clean, and fair" food system.

In my view, Slow Food has successfully eliminated any justifiable labels of elitism at these events. They have somehow found the financial and logistical means by which to bring together farmers and food advocates of all races, nationalities, and income levels from across the globe to a common site for four days of simultaneously translated discussions and celebration. Delegates from wealthier countries typically pay their own airfare to Italy (though even that is covered when needed and feasible), but Slow Food provides all of the delegates with ground transportation, housing, and food—food to die for. Such an event is probably as close to democracy as the politics of food will ever get.

In 2006, journalist and author Michael Pollan asked the audience to imagine "pleasure and politics co-habiting the same plate."[5] Still a bit skeptical of the need to wed pleasure with any call for food justice, Erin and I returned to Terra Madre in 2008 with an even larger and more diverse group of delegates, numbering more than seven thousand and representing 153 countries. The focus of the event was on bringing youth into the swelling call for "good, clean, and fair" food across the globe.[6]

In spite of the simultaneous translation services provided for all of us, the lingua franca for the 2008 event was music. Petrini and his cohorts had decided that if food could inspire us, music would captivate us. They were right. Musical groups from indigenous and peasant cultures across the world roused the audience time and again, with the closing ceremony concert being the most inspiring musical event I'd ever attended. Not only was the food at Terra Madre marinated with meaning, but the masterful mingling of musicians in traditional attire made for magic that I am sure endures . . . in ways and in places not yet noted.

If one were to survey homesteaders to ascertain what they found most rewarding about homesteading, many of them—myself included—

would probably respond that one of the most significant rewards is living close to nature. Rebecca Gould makes a strong case for this historical tradition in her excellent inquiry into the nature of American homesteading, *At Home in Nature*. I share her interest in looking back to find the threads of commonality in various homesteading ventures in order to understand where the tradition might be headed. In doing so, I'm particularly intrigued by the possibilities of finding what might be more neutral themes for the future of American homesteading, a future perhaps less dependent upon setting than has been the case in much of the American homesteading tradition, or at least as it appears in our literature. It seems that finding a "harmony with nature" might be—or at least appear to be—more elusive in some urban and suburban environments.

Financial security seems a reasonable place to begin. If done carefully and well, linking economic and ecological choices in making household decisions should provide for relative financial security, since both generally point toward minimized consumption. Of course, one could "eco-binge" and begin purchasing all new, and probably pricey, ecologically friendly household items instead of modifying either the belongings themselves or the way in which they are utilized. When faced with a consumption question, perhaps the best ecological and economic choice is "to choose not to." However, the notion of efficiency once again enters into the equation, in all its variable forms.

I doubt that many people would argue against the idea that a sense of financial liberation is a source of genuine pleasure, maybe even long-term contentment. Having twice achieved debt-free status and then heading into a mortgage for a third time only after long deliberations, Erin and I know firsthand the feeling of freedom and relief at being able to make choices directly related to our quality of life. That enduring sense of pleasure certainly spurs one on to find or reclaim financial independence.

The value that homesteaders generally place on various forms of independence cannot be overstated. Self-reliance implies a certain frugality, at least over time. It might require some initial investments—tools, books, even educational expenditures—but doing as much as one can by oneself (even if it occasionally involves other people!) can generate rewards that go beyond the financial savings. The satisfaction at completing a task on one's own is certainly a sensation to savor, and it often morphs into a confidence that provides other later benefits.

It's ironic that the notion of "metis," or manual intelligence, was such a critical component of what made the United States a world leader, given our lack of appreciation for such skills in recent times. Certainly the confluence of cultures and the relative isolation of numerous "homesteads" in the early colonial days contributed to the inventive and self-reliant spirit of so many Americans in earlier times. Even tools that were used by most cultures tended to vary in form, function, and materials, so the comparison of ideas between people of different cultures undoubtedly fostered imaginative engineering.

Unfortunately, the all-too-common segregation of the European newcomers from their Native American, African, and Asian counterparts meant that this manual intelligence was not always combined with what one might call "ecological intelligence," a way of thinking that was generally highly valued by these other cultures. The result was that we missed the opportunity to become apprentices of nature instead of posing as the masters of nature.

Finding our way back to an appreciation of manual intelligence and its accompanying pleasures is not going to be simple. In a culture that offshored the bulk of its manufacturing sector and subsequently did the same with its service sector, it is unclear what we consider to be our primary commodity as a nation, other than a collection of eager consumers. We have somehow built a culture that assumes making or fixing almost anything is somebody else's business. There may be relief in having someone else make, do, and fix most items in our households, but there is little long-term satisfaction in such an approach to life. We would also probably consume less (and therefore spend less) if we actually assumed more responsibility for our own goods and services, and we might rethink the disposable nature of so much of what we own. There is an inherent pleasure involved in beating the system and saving the planet by making something from scratch or diverting it from the waste stream. Such a practice can even become slightly competitive, adding to the sense of reward for a job well done.

Not only have we created a culture and an economy that too often devalue manual intelligence, but we have also created a monolithic educational system that typically trivializes ecological intelligence and relegates manual intelligence to a corner of our schools and colleges reserved for those who supposedly ain't so smart, or at least not in the fields of study that we tend to elevate above others. Basic trade-oriented skills that support our everyday lives are somehow viewed as inferior in a world that nonetheless depends upon them, not only to function as we live now, but also to find new ways of functioning in a world with more people, fewer natural resources, and less time to get it right.

As an example, consider the high school schism between students going into the college prep track versus those headed into vocational training. Not only is it tragic that these tracks tend to have a certain social and intellectual status and stigma associated with each of them, but it is also a shame that we see these worlds as divergent—not convergent. In my own experience, I experience a nearly addictive rush associated with understanding and solving a hands-on dilemma by utilizing knowledge from as many disciplines as possible. While vexing at times, it can also be pleasurable—even fun. Any puzzle fanatic knows that this kind of challenge offers a distinct emotive reward.

In sum, if we don't respect manual intelligence, much less embrace it, then we probably don't understand the pleasure that comes from the imaginative creation and repair of real, everyday objects, objects that can either magnify our consumption or minimize it. A cumulative lack of understanding of how real things work is a form of ignorance that does not allow us to ask the right questions about consumption, much less begin to discover the best answers.

One of the joys of installing and relying on a renewable energy system is that one is forced to start paying attention—to consumption, to daily weather, to seasonal climatic trends. The energy coming into the house is no longer a given, and it's not constant, as it is when "the grid" is one's sole source of power. Consumption, therefore, has to vary accordingly. Having at least a rudimentary understanding of how the system works becomes a necessity.

As our son Asa became enraptured with our indoor/outdoor thermometer, Erin and I laughed. He wanted to check the indoor and outdoor temperatures repeatedly throughout the day, to the point of driving us crazy at times. "Mama, what's the temperature outside now?" he would yell from across the house. "Papa, can you check to see how cold it got outside last night? I want to know if my plants in the greenhouse were okay."

Erin and I started to wonder about this new obsession . . . until we considered just how often we look at a little 5-inch-square box with a changing LED display, mounted prominently in our house. This

TriMetric meter measures our battery bank voltage, the number of amps being produced and consumed, and the battery bank's percentage of total capacity. Erin and I look at the TriMetric all the time, calibrating our anticipated storage and usage of electricity. It took about two years to get the calibration right, feeling out how much power we had to use in different kinds of weather and how much less power we could expect from the solar panels in winter than in summer, combined with the rough electrical usage of any device utilized for a given period of time. Asa was doing much the same thing as we were—calibrating abstract numbers with concrete realities. In his case, understanding temperatures began to help him guess which clothes to put on to go outside and be comfortable.

I daresay this calibration, trying to match available and expected resources with calculated needs, is kind of a game in our house. It's even more tangible with the solar hot-water system than with the PV system. Temperatures are less complex than volts and amps, and we often find ourselves running to the basement to see how hot the water is after a certain number of hours of sunlight, particularly on frigid days in the winter when the production of hot water seems so counterintuitive.

An energy diet is much like a food diet. You need some short-term rewards to achieve long-term reduction. Once again, there's a pleasure in beating the system by matching wits with Mother Nature—and the punishment for losing is the cost, noise, smell, and guilt of running the generator. Part of the resulting pleasure is cerebral, but it can also come in other forms. The kids know that a long sunny day in the summer means an excess of hot water, to the point that we often have to cover the solar thermal panels with a tarp around 1 or 2 PM. If the air is cool on those days or the kids are particularly dirty, we might opt instead to cool the solar hot water tank by emptying a portion of it to fill the plastic kiddy pool (salvaged from the dump and sealed with duct tape) with hot water for an afternoon splash or an evening bath. Sometimes Papa slips in, too, soaking in the luxury of nature's excesses. Few pleasures are so devoid of guilt . . . especially if they come after a day of hard physical labor.

For some, equating pleasure with physical labor is a hard sell and may even seem romanticized. Yet for more than two decades I have observed firsthand the transformation of young people's attitudes toward physical labor as many of them experience it for the first time. I've watched young people come to work on the farms at Brunnenburg Castle, Green Mountain College, and my own homestead, and many of them leave with a newfound respect and enthusiasm for hearty labor. They seem to revel in the playfulness and satisfaction of demanding tasks that yield tangible results.

Unfortunately, our urban and suburban environments are constructed on the premise of trading toil for ease, at least in life at home between the demands of job, school, and civic activities. Our skyrocketing obesity rates, the rise of energy-intensive modern conveniences, and a galaxy of sedentary entertainment options must have some correlation with how infrequently our young people encounter real physical labor. Yet I refuse to concede to cynicism about any generation's lack of understanding or appreciation for hard work. It's simply difficult to appreciate anything that one has seldom or never encountered—especially when the rewards haven't been made clear.

Giving any person unaccustomed to arduous labor an intense physical task and expecting much enthusiasm in return is probably misguided. The key, in my view, is to convey the pleasures beforehand and revisit them near the end of the task. Providing a hospitable setting for the work, a few unexpected midsession treats, and a celebratory ending are also critical.

As I managed the student workdays on the farm at Brunnenburg, then again at Green Mountain, and even now at our home, I have watched as neophytes to the world of hard labor discover a sense of accomplishment that they had seldom if ever encountered in their lives back home. The last part of a workday is a chance to revisit the end result with pride, with most everyone supported by the handle of a shovel or rake. The Alps always provided an important perspective on one's work from above, allowing the magnitude of a group's collective endeavor to settle in.

The meal at the end of the day is particularly important, since it is where pleasure, pride, and appreciation converge in an atmosphere of joviality. The intensity of the work remains as a topic of pride and joking banter, but the anguish has generally dissipated or disappeared. The rewards are real and relatively simple. None of this is a secret, nor is it just a desperate bribe for young people from an out-of-shape society. Much more austere societies have long utilized the bait and hook of collective physical labor with the promise of food and fellowship.

A common good, even a seemingly abstract one, can also propel physical-labor newcomers into the rewarding world of physically demanding work. On the farm at Green Mountain College, we've progressively

worked toward weaning the farm from petroleum energy inputs through the increased use of human energy, the power of draft animals, and renewable energy technologies. This "fossil-free agriculture" initiative—led by Dr. Kenneth Mulder, an ecological economist; Lucas Brown, a green architect; and myself—means that students engage in blending old-fashioned and cutting-edge technologies with a lot of sweat equity. In many ways, it is the students' collective sense that they are cultivating new ground in search of a more sustainable lifestyle that motivates them in haymaking with the college oxen or using hand tools for weed cultivation. When they seem a bit downtrodden, it never hurts to remind them of the comparative drudgery of writing papers. Physical labor, when linked to pleasure, is a method of fostering discovery that we have virtually abandoned in our educational system. In fact, we too often abandon discovery itself, and it is the pleasure of discovery that may well be the sustaining factor in one's decision to homestead, despite the challenges, year after year.

Discovery is addictive, in my view, whether one is the teacher or the student, or, better yet, a bit of both. It's addictive because the stimulus is novelty. Novelty engages the brain and begins to stimulate physiological reactions that tend to pique our interest. I reject the notion that novelty has to involve only our baser human appetites. New ideas can appeal to us, particularly when we recognize their value in the light of our individual and collective futures.

Is discovery more likely in a homestead environment than in many other household settings? I'm obviously biased, but I think so. In my view, homesteads are by nature dynamic. The interplay among evolving values, skills, and technologies means that life is neither rote nor static. Furthermore, although perfection in any aspect of homesteading is unlikely, the pursuit of perfection is an incessant enticement that can propel us forward year after year. Fortunately—as gardeners, cooks, and farmers know—the ebb and flow of the seasons helps to break the potential monotony and to bury the failures—all the while getting one excited and thinking about the next year's possibilities, often half a year or more in advance. The resulting pleasures may be sensory-based, or they can be rooted in the satisfaction—even euphoria—of a job well done.

Ironically, as I write these reflections on a magnificent spring day, I watch from the balcony of our new house as Asa and Ethan comb the edges of the pond for new discoveries. Within ten minutes, Asa comes up to the house with a dragonfly after nibbling on oxeye daisy leaves, eager to look at its wings and eyes with a hand lens. Meanwhile, Ethan has discovered a leopard frog, chased a sulfur butterfly, collected four goose feathers, properly identified a piece of shale, and questioned the unusual patterns in a piece of charcoal. Moments earlier, they were inventively testing different combinations of decorative spinning wheels mounted on tiny motors that they'd hooked to different-sized solar panels. Watching a four-year-old and a six-year-old play in this way assures me of the correctness of our family's decision to homestead and to home-school. Again, both decisions are, in the scheme of things, choices born of a certain luxury.

I think that access to a natural setting is an asset, but perhaps not requisite for important learning to occur on a homestead. The most important aspect needed for a child is the opportunity to cultivate the art of discovery, to begin peeling away the layers of the ordinary, until newness gleams and beckons. The most common impediment to enhancing the development of that discovery is the constancy of television and video games. The blank spaces in a child's day need to be filled with imagination and curiosity, not media programming. Both parent and child can reap the resulting rewards.

From a family perspective, perhaps homesteading should be more about discovery than anything else—discovery in the pursuit of a life that fits our ecological realities. There is pleasure and purpose in such a life, certainly enough to sustain the search.

The dilemma we face can be summarized in a seeming contradiction. We live in a culture of denial, but at the same time we do not live in a culture of denial. We habit a society continues to deny the ecological realities that are closing in on us because of our choices and our lifestyles. Yet we are a culture that has little interest in any lifestyle that embraces even a modicum of self-denial.

The best way to cross the threshold of this *aporia,* this place with no apparent exit, may be to rewire our thinking about rewards so that we will find pleasure—preferably deep and abiding contentment—in doing the right thing.

SEVENTEEN

To Gather Together

I was standing outside by the grill beside the pond, wiping my eyes from the applewood smoke that had just drifted my way. Asa and Ethan were poking around the cattails with their nets, running back and forth to a 5-gallon bucket filled with nearly equivalent volumes of water and spring amphibians. My mouth was watering—not so much from the thought of the burgers themselves as from the prospect of serving one up to Khanti.

It wasn't long before our dog barked and the geese squawked—Khanti and his wife, Kerri, had made the trek up Tunket Road with their son Kaiden in his backpack—a rocky and rutted memory lane from their first summer together. They got to the edge of the barn near the goose house and waved, wise enough to stand their ground until the geese made a reticent, hissing retreat back toward the lower edge of the pond.

Before the round of hugs was even complete, Khanti looked over at the southern facade of our new house and shaded his eyes with his hands, squinting. He feigned a look of disbelief and shook his head.

"Now, that's a sight I never thought I'd see on this homestead!"

"What's that? You're not checking to see if I've got the right summer angle on the solar panel array again, are you?"

"No—it's the satellite dish! What the hell is goin' on around here? You just didn't know when to stop once I got you power up here, did you!"

"Hey, things change. Either we're getting wiser, or we're fooling ourselves and just selling out. But remember, you'd better go easy on me—I'm about to serve up one of our grass-fed burgers to a reformed vegetarian, you know!"

"I know, I know . . . just couldn't resist the opportunity to push your buttons a little bit—since you've got so many of them up here now."

"So many what?"

"Things with buttons."

At first I resisted, but then I laughed. After all, he was right. And also partly responsible.

"So what made you guys do it? I can't believe you got satellite Internet! I thought you'd never bring that e-mail you hate so much up here . . . of course, you probably don't reply to all of those e-mails any better than before. You just wanted to have the pleasure of hitting the delete button in the comfort of your own home, didn't you?"

Khanti was right. Deciding whether or not to introduce the Internet directly into our home was a long and difficult debate for us. There were definitely technological traps that we had long since decided to avoid, items that we felt would diminish the quality of life of our family— there was nothing more prominent in that category than television. We'd conceded to occasional movies on an old television and VCR given to us by a friend, but seldom more than one every week or two and almost always educational videos for the kids.

But the Internet was a more complicated decision. It brought with it an onslaught of advertisers and potential diversions from our rooted lives, but more important it brought the most consuming part of my job home with me—e-mail. For years, we had lived without even a phone, much less a computer. And yet there were costs to not having Internet service. There were days that I was commuting almost exclusively in order to do e-mail or research in my office—16 miles each way. That was costly in pollutants and in dollars, not to mention family time and lost daylight hours for exercise and work. We were also beginning to market our cattle for breeding stock, with the Internet looking to be the best form of advertisement. And Erin was beginning her first year of home-schooling the children, and we'd seen how much curricular material and other resources were available online.

I'd tried to divert the conversation by feigning the need to flip the burgers and wipe the smoke from my eyes, but Khanti persisted. "So what was it that finally drove you to get the Internet up here?"

"Well, it was definitely a combination of things, but the decision that finally pushed us was the need to sell some of our cattle, and the Internet seemed like the best way to market them. I never would have guessed just how successful it was going to be—it's been nuts. I can't even keep up with the number of inquiries—people calling and e-mailing from as far away as Washington State, Iowa, Texas . . . some from South Carolina,

Virginia, and Pennsylvania. It's interesting, though, because a lot of it is being driven by the crazy gas and grain prices last summer. I guess it takes a crisis for people to see the value in rare breeds and thinking about letting a cow do what a cow's supposed to do—be outside eating grass and hay."

"I know. Being connected is definitely an asset. I see it every day now, teaching my online renewable energy classes for Solar Energy International. I've got students in the South Pacific, Antarctica, Africa, all over the United States—all learning how to install renewable energy systems without having to fly to some distant workshop site. A lot of them could never do it if they had to fly or take time off from work. And we've got a waiting list of several hundred interested people. Last summer's energy prices drove home the reality that renewable energy makes sense, even if you're on the grid. It's getting harder for you left-wing back-to-the-landers to argue that the Internet is evil!"

"I guess at this point I see it as a burden sometimes, but not evil. And I've gotten myself on so many boards lately that if I'm going to be effective, I've pretty much got to have e-mail and Internet access at home. Otherwise, I keep getting stuck staying at the college office all sorts of ungodly hours instead of being home with the family."

"So you're saying it's a good thing to have in the back-to-the-lander's toolbox?" Khanti's grin contorted just enough to let me know I was cornered.

"Of course it can be. I mean, I can't deny how helpful it's been for Erin to do homeschooling research—checking out the state standards and requirements, buying used curricula and books on e-Bay . . ."

"E-Bay—you guys are doing *e-Bay?*"

"Not me . . . just Erin." I was hoping the corner didn't start to feel any more confining than it already did. "But I guess it fits into the homesteading world. We're always looking for rather peculiar items and odd bits of knowledge, and so are other homesteaders. I don't know how else we'd all find one another so easily—or find one another's used stuff."

"Yeah, but then you've got the delivery of the stuff from place to place."

"I don't know about that—I guess it depends on the item. But isn't it better to put the stuff with all its embedded energy into the hands of someone who might use it instead of having them buy it new? That's got to be worth something."

"You're probably right."

"But you know what I think is most amazing about it all? It's the world that's opened up for Erin. You know we've never felt deprived to be up here—it's usually felt like a privilege to be in such a beautiful, relatively isolated spot. And nobody enjoys not having to go anywhere on a daily basis more than Erin. But she's actually felt affirmed in a way, just by connecting with other homesteaders, homeschooling parents, and online Vermont recyclers. She seems to appreciate knowing that other folks out there are thinking along the same lines she is, and most of them are like her—either they're not too anxious to run around finding one another, or else they don't have the time to do it. I have to confess, there's more to this online thing than I suspected."

"Better than your cell phone?"

"Different. The cell phone has just meant that we don't have to spend time, money, and gas running around trying to find somebody or something or take an hour or more to walk down to the Waites' to use their phone for important calls, like we used to. As far as I'm concerned, the best feature on the cell phone is the on button. And for Erin, it's still the off button. But she's right—there is a definite advantage in using a cell phone for calling out and not having calls come in."

"Except that you have to go to the outhouse or the pasture to get reception . . ."

"Yeah, but I've usually got to go to both of those places at least twice a day anyway!"

"I bet you miss that outhouse, don't you?" Khanti teased.

"Not in the winter—hey, these burgers are done, I think. Let's go in and have some dinner. I'm eager to watch you eat your words."

"Goes both ways," he reminded me.

"We're both older and wiser, Khanti . . . older and wiser."

For the record, he ate two burgers.

Sometimes it's just a matter of perspective. I wouldn't have guessed that a book of aerial photographs would be so enlightening, but Elizabeth Humstone's brilliant study of how regional planning—or lack thereof—can impact the evolution of our landscapes really took me by surprise. *Above and Beyond: Visualizing Change in Small Towns and Rural Areas* is a collection of aerial photographs taken across the country over time, showing the impacts of development on communities and natural resources. I was particularly disturbed by the photographs taken of Vermont over the years, many of them in towns close to us. The impacts of a lack of foresight and planning were tragically evident, as farmland and forests disappeared with increasing rapidity, frame after frame. Humstone used the photographs to show how our all-consuming appetites were constraining future choices and possibilities.[1]

It was 2002, and I'd recently joined the planning commission for our town of Pawlet. I was just beginning to see how complex this planning process was. As it turned out, others were already delving into the issue of supporting agriculture in the midst of increasing development. One of our alums, India Farmer, had recently begun working with the Rutland Regional Planning Commission, and she had introduced me to her new colleague Tara Kelly, a regional planner. We ended up at lunch together with Marli Rupe, the district manager for our local conservation district. I'd joined the conservation district board a few years earlier and was beginning to learn the challenges of supporting farming endeavors in our watershed while simultaneously working with a slew of new and controversial environmental regulations being developed statewide. I was quickly discovering the degree to which farmers were feeling targeted by well-intended regulations while also facing intense economic and development pressures.

As our lunch progressed and I shared some of my questions about the relationship between regional planning and agriculture, Tara and India noted that every town plan in our region called for protecting the viability of agriculture. It was a clear, common concern among all of our communities, but it was also one of the most perplexing. Marli astutely noted that, even if we were able to conserve a majority of the land, it wasn't clear who was going to farm it. Most of the farmers in our region were in their fifties and sixties, and there wasn't a lot of interest in the field—nor did there seem to be many obvious marketing opportunities for new farmers, especially if they wanted to produce something other than fluid milk for conventional markets.

I was gradually beginning to realize how complex and interrelated the issues were. And it wasn't clear to any of us which agency or group was going to tackle it. Trying to conserve a healthy agricultural landscape while also helping to rebuild a crumbling agricultural economy and supply it with savvy new farmers and markets—it all seemed incredibly complicated. In addition, given the way that organizations, municipalities, and government agencies are set up to handle a prescribed and often somewhat narrow set of responsibilities, it wasn't clear that any entity was going to take the bull by the horns, or the cow by the tail. As we investigated further, we were shocked to discover that there wasn't even a comprehensive database for all the farms, market gardens, and farm stands in our region. In essence, there was a pretty pessimistic mood in the region regarding the future of agriculture.

The amount of work that needed to be done to begin addressing these issues felt daunting to all of us, but we also sensed that, if there was one common desire that stretched across the region and across political lines, it was rebuilding the local food system and the regional pride that went with it.

The whole concept certainly fit with my homesteading values—conserving the landscape, producing healthy food, building markets for small producers, honing skills for new farmers and gardeners. But it was prying me away from an underlying assumption that our homestead was a retreat—a retreat from the forces and woes of a larger market economy that seemed to contradict our values. Instead, I was starting to realize that a homestead should be a retreat that offers rejuvenation in the face of a world that seems out of kilter, but it shouldn't necessarily be a place where retreating—disengaging—is a way of life.

Homesteaders are generally accustomed to hard work, but we may need to habituate ourselves to a different kind of sweat—one in which we work closely with others on social, economic, ecological, and political issues. If we hold our values and knowledge to be true, then there's little sense in harboring them in the isolation of a backwoods retreat.

An ecological life is, by nature, a civic life. It involves working hard, very hard, to understand our place, role, and impact in the world. And then we need to determine if we—all of us—can do better. If so, then the collective work continues.

We independently minded homesteader types should probably also bear in mind that mingling and exchanging ideas with others generally gets us closer to the truth—truth that will stick. Just as the homestead can be a shelter from the storm, it can also engender sheltered assumptions. Civic ecology certainly begins at home, but it seldom stops there, and I'm increasingly convinced that this is a good thing. The only thing worse than going up the proverbial creek without a paddle is going down the same creek with a bunch of individualists who do have paddles and are all facing different directions.

In that vein, Marli, Tara, India, and I decided it was time to broaden the discussion and our own understanding of the regional food system, so we put together a yearlong series of six guest lectures at the college for our community, including a presentation by Elizabeth Humstone. As the audience grew and interest developed over the course of the year, a fairly diverse core group of interested persons evolved. Before long, we decided to form an organization called the Rutland Area Farm & Food Link, generally known as RAFFL. Now a 501(c)(3) nonprofit, RAFFL annually distributes more than forty thousand copies of our *Local Buying Guide,* featuring farms, farm stands, restaurants, and food vendors and distributors. Plans are under way for a "food hub" with a commercial kitchen and flash-freeze operation to support small-scale processors and institutional purchasers, as well as storage and distribution for farmers, processors, and local and regional food banks. RAFFL is also working with the Vermont Land Trust to establish an incubator farm to support and train new farmers for the region by providing them with land, equipment, mentors, and access to markets, ideally all in a central location.[2]

Homesteaders like myself need the kind of illumination and integration that service in community organizations provides. Inevitably, we learn a tremendous amount about "the system" that we are in essence calling into question. In the best of all worlds, questions beget solutions, and solutions don't occur without people who are committed to finding the answers by working diligently together. Working toward inspired ideals and responding to community needs means that our communities become much less anonymous.

We homesteaders tend to talk a lot about "scale," but it is perhaps the scale of our cooperation, the scale of our engagement, that matters most. Otherwise, we risk becoming cloistered cynics. Cynicism is the armor of stasis. The modern tenets of homesteading—sustainability and resilience—are most likely to be found in the company of others.

In essence, I've come to the long, slow conclusion that it in fact makes little sense to retool our individual lifestyles if we are not just as committed to working toward retooling our communities. In teaching various aspects of the history of toolmaking to students over the years, I have often referred to the etymology of the word *tool,* stemming from the seldom-used English word *taw,* meaning "to prepare," historically a reference to the process of preparing a skin for leathermaking. We are, then, retooling our lives and our communities in order to prepare for changes, changes that are inevitable as a result of our collective overconsumption. While those changes are ecological in nature, they will also manifest themselves socially, economically, and politically.

As with any good toolmaker, a homesteader's first step in retooling is "to get a handle on things." That's where education enters the equation, in my view. Homesteading and education—particularly higher education—might seem like odd bedfellows. However, I think it is difficult for any of us to grasp the complexity of the ecological and social challenges that we face without the help of at least some expertise and interdisciplinary discourse. If we build our values—homesteading or otherwise—on a weak understanding of basic ecological and economic principles, then the values that arise from this flawed foundation will risk structural failure over time.

The problem with formalized education is that it seldom places ecological understanding as an educational centerpiece—and rarer yet is the educational program that allows students to explore the integration of values, practical skills, and appropriate technologies in a way that sets the stage for leading not only thoughtful but also practical lives. Many educational institutions pride themselves on preparing students to lead a life of inquiry, but few actually challenge and support students to embrace the ecological questions and immediately begin living the possible solutions—not later but in the midst of the educational experience itself. I'm certainly fortunate to teach at one of the few colleges that does just that.

But formalized education is not necessarily a possibility or even a good option for every person wishing to homestead. We should all engage our surrounding communities, one person at a time, looking for mentors who can help enrich our ecological understanding and show us a path to habiting the center of our questions in a way that integrates us with our community, the landscape, and the regional economic realities.

There are also new ways to think about how our penchant and passion for renewable energy can integrate into the community. Off-grid living has its romantic appeal and is, in cases like ours, the only reasonable economic option. However, off-grid living suffers from three problems that can be alleviated by becoming part of a community-based energy system: the maintenance, cost, dangers, and embedded energy of large battery banks; the cost, noise, and pollution of a backup generator; and the excess energy captured but not utilized on days when sun, wind, and water are more than adequate for one household.

Although it varies by state, homeowners with grid-tied systems can generally buy power as it is needed (for instance, after a string of cloudy or windless days or during times of peak consumption), as well as sell power to the utility company when it is produced in excess. Renewable energy systems that are tied to the grid often make the most economic and ecological sense, particularly in more densely populated suburban and urban areas.

Furthermore, an increasing number of grassroots-based community organizations are working toward "distributed generation systems," energy infrastructure systems in which relatively small amounts of energy—in comparison with our traditional coal, nuclear, and natural gas power plants—are produced and distributed locally. In fact, these systems are, in some cases, community-owned and -operated. Such systems utilize small generation plants that transform wood chips, bio-gas, sunlight, wind, tides, and other "renewable" resources into electrical and other forms of power for the locality or the region. In recent trips back to the South Tirol, I've seen villages building community-owned and -operated wood-chip plants to provide heat and hot water for village residents in close proximity to the village center, while also buffering residents from some of the vagaries and vacillations of external market forces.

Greg Pahl analyzes most of our renewable energy resources and their potential for community-based energy solutions in his book *The Citizen-Powered Energy Handbook: Community Solutions to a Global Crisis*. As well as explaining how the systems work, he also cites a number of examples in which communities and organizations around the world are finding new sources of power and empowerment in their pioneering energy efforts.[3] Thomas Friedman also highlights many of the possibilities in his book *Hot, Flat, and Crowded: Why We Need a Green Revolution—And How It Can Renew America*. Friedman even provides examples of how the US military in Iraq has been building distributed generation systems there in order to avoid reliance on an unstable grid, to reduce dependence on fuel-guzzling generators, and to increase security for Iraqi and US forces.[4] Rob Hopkins provides an actual guide for communities to "transition" in a world that is running out of oil and racing headlong into the throes of climate change. *The Transition Handbook* is inspired by Hopkins's permaculture and natural building experience and is inspiring in its optimistic and community-based approach to relocalization as a means of renaissance.[5]

If anything has back-to-the-land homesteaders like myself rethinking our original suppositions for settling into our reclusive retreats in the dawning light of climate change, resource depletion, and economic turbulence, it is distance from our places of work and our centers for community. Stephen and Rebekah Hren tell the story of their decision to move from their self-built off-grid passive solar cob house with a small garden and poultry in rural North Carolina, only to discover that running their automobile used the same amount of power as 350 100-watt lightbulbs. Each of their hour-long round-trip commutes to town consumed as much energy as they needed to power their home for more than a month. So they moved back to the city of Durham, North Carolina, retrofitted a house from the 1930s, and weaned their home almost completely from fossil fuel inputs—a story they tell in their fascinating book *The Carbon-Free Home*.[6] It is that kind of combined thought and action that I suspect will transform our traditional image of homesteading in the United States.

I struggle with the question of distance and isolation quite a bit, and yet I am precisely—and perhaps selfishly—where I have wanted to be for as long as I can remember . . . in a clearing amid the forest, nestled in among the mountains with a beautiful wife who is smarter than I am. (Tip: Always marry up.) My response is not to move, but rather to find ways to stay put more often.

My greatest dream is to be home with my family and cows as much as possible. We have been building incrementally and strategically toward that dream for years, trying to do what we can as we can afford it. We have been collecting knowledge, cheese equipment, furnishings for future guest quarters, and other infrastructure, trusting that there will be a time when our family can truly gather together most days. We know that it's what we love—we've often gone ten to twelve days without ever making it past our mailbox, spending time working and playing together. Ecologically, psychologically, individually, and collectively, that is when all of us in our family seem to know we are healthiest. These are also typically the times when we manage our small farm the best.

It seems far from lonely, probably because of the flow of present and former students and homestead apprentices, some of whom drop by for a visit and others who settle in for a few months as apprentices. They help us keep the dream fresh, honest, and in perspective. But the tug to participate in the reinventing of the world is simply too great for us to ignore, so we find ourselves stretching the integrity of our compromise a bit thin as we travel to learn and to share.

Homesteading is ultimately about choices. Not only do we choose our values, skills, and technologies, but we also choose our place in the world. Although they may not be choices for luxury, our choices are nonetheless luxurious. Most people in this world do not even have the power to choose.[7] Nor is it likely that coming generations will have the same stunning array of luxurious choices that we do.

Regardless of whether we ultimately call it "homesteading" or not, the way that we live our lives directly impacts the choices that others will have in places both near and far, tomorrow and in the distant future. Undoubtedly, there will be a gentle winnowing of our hopes and dreams, but some spilled grains of truth will certainly take root in the gentle pressing of our retreating footsteps.

If it was the conversation with my student Aviva that first began to unravel my predominantly back-to-the-land vision of homesteading, then it was the essay—complete with photos—that another student handed to me a year later, when I next taught my homesteading course, that forced me to rethink the likely trajectory of the American homesteading tradition.

Ruth took my assignment—to visit and document a place likely to be defined as a homestead—to great lengths. In a time-honored college tradition, she went to Florida for spring break. In fact, she went to the Florida Keys. However, that's where the traditional nature of her spring break ended and where her new life—and my broadened perspectives—began.

Ruth went to visit a family friend whom she had heard about for some time, a young man named Tim who had already packed a number of unique life experiences into a relatively short period of time. He had constructed a "home" entirely of recycled materials deep in the Arizona desert; he had built a highly ornate raft of recycled materials on which he had lived for several months rent-free, anchored right next to the high-end skyscrapers of Manhattan; and he was now living a life of minimal consumption in a motorless sailboat that he had purchased for $3,000. The sailboat was complete with a woodstove, for burning driftwood and scrap lumber, as well as a wind turbine, for generating electricity.

In her subsequent presentation to our class, Ruth maintained that Tim's life represented a form of homesteading, one that was arguably less consumptive than some of the other back-to-the-land models that we'd studied. As the class conversation orbited around the photos that Ruth shared with us, it became clear that if one were to strip away the ecological context, by pulling Tim from a marine environment and plopping him into the New England woods, he sure looked like a homesteader—except that he was eating fish caught from his boat instead of vegetables grown in his garden.

I confess that I was feeling a bit perplexed at this point, as were many of the students. The question of how we might begin to redefine homesteading—independent of setting—was one that has consumed me (and, I hope, my students) ever since. Ruth seemed just as intrigued by the question, so she pursued her interests further by joining Tim on his sailboat later that year. After living any mariner homesteader's ultimate sailing dream for a while, we heard that Ruth had given birth to their beautiful son Zeb on their zip-code-less floating homestead. Zeb's birth certificate lists the boat's GPS coordinates at the time of his birth, and was signed by a ferried midwife. Ruth, Tim, and Zeb all returned to our college soon thereafter for Ruth to finish her studies. They built a home of recycled and natural materials for themselves in a forest not far from campus, spending less than $2,500. They dubbed it "the fuzzy house," thanks to the hairy appearance of its living roof.

So the homesteading approach to life would appear to be adaptable and versatile, a creative interplay of appropriate values, skills, and technologies. While it does need to be informed by the ecological context in which it takes place, the choice of setting doesn't seem to unravel any of homesteading's traditional motifs. I would hope that our own story, told through the themes of the chapters of this book, has helped to reveal some of the basic homesteading principles and practices that can be applied to such a life in most any context: *bioregional literacy, place-based knowledge, historical understanding, apprenticing, practical skills, appropriate scale, efficiency, renewable energy systems, technological choices, the time–money dilemma, retooled pleasures,* and—hopefully—*community engagement.*

Opening up homesteading to a multitude of environments does not mean that we are abandoning our role as pioneers. In the end, homesteading is a pioneering of ideas more than of landscape. Defining the parameters of homesteading too tightly will simply squelch the possibilities and the participation of a much-needed diversity of players—likeminded people living very differently from one another, all working to find our way through this ecological *aporia,* the impasse that defines life in the twenty-first century.

In our rural areas, we face the significant ecological burden of distance in our commerce and connections, but we are blessed with resources. In our urban areas, we are challenged by minimized productive capacity due to a lack of space and available natural resources, but our tight demographics create certain ecological efficiencies. "Homesteaders" from both environments—and from every cultural context in between—need to begin "crafting common cause," not just by means of conservation, but also through conversation. In the end, it is only our collective impatience with the present that will propel us forward with enough velocity to penetrate the walls of our self-constructed *aporia.*

ACKNOWLEDGMENTS

This book is ultimately an acknowledgement of the people who have guided us and the places that have inspired us, and yet there have been many others who have helped in the creation of the book itself. Particular thanks goes to Margo Baldwin and Ben Watson of Chelsea Green for their belief in and support of the project from its initial stages. I am also indebted to the Green Mountain College Board of Trustees for granting me the privilege of a yearlong sabbatical to bring the project to fruition. None of the story would have happened without Tom Benson's encouragement to join the GMC community or without Shep Ogden's behind-the-scenes gardening guidance. And for the sharing of ideas and good times in a community that cares, I thank all of my friends at GMC, the college that could and decidedly did.

The writing itself would not have happened without Erin taking on the majority of the parenting duties, nor would the book be what it is without her masterful illustrations. It was her art that drew me to her . . . and my puns that nearly drove her away.

Special thanks to family members who read the initial drafts and offered suggestions, as well as to Ryan Dixon and Laird Christensen, two astute readers who helped shape the book in its formative stages. Thanks to Ryan for his superb research and constant philosophical challenges and to Laird for his sage advice on how to tell the story . . . not to mention his own pithy ditty about our adventures. Any shortcomings at this point are entirely my own.

Most any book stands on the shoulders of other authors who have forged the way forward, and I am particularly indebted to Rebecca Kneale Gould and Jeffrey Jacob for their keen insights on homesteading and the back-to-the-land movement.

Of course, thanks must be given to the students who have been our apprentices and homesteading compatriots, including Ollie, Joe, Nate, Matt, Jane, Chris, Adam, Ethan, and Khanti. Special thanks to Ollie for braving the elements so many mornings and doing my chores so that I could write before the rest of the family found their way downstairs to the woodstove.

Finally, numerous students and alumni helped us construct our dreams. Unfortunately, we recently lost one to a tragic avalanche. Kellen, the vestiges of your craftsmanship here remind us why it's so important to lead a spirited life among friends and amid nature's wonders, with a lurking chance of mischief hiding in the shadowed edges of any given moment.

ENDNOTES

Chapter 1: Once Upon a Tunket Time

1. For a fascinating discussion of forests, clearings, and cultures, including a discussion of Vico, see Robert Pogue Harrison, *Forests: The Shadow of Civilization* (Chicago: University of Chicago Press, 1993), 3–13.

2. Esther Monroe Swift, *Vermont Place Names: Footprints of History* (Rockland, ME: Picton Press, 1977), 705.

Chapter 2: Learning One's Place

1. Eliot Coleman, *The New Organic Grower: A Master's Manual of Tools and Techniques for the Home and Market Gardener* (White River Junction, VT: Chelsea Green, 1995), 56.

Chapter 3: When Time Was Made of Trees

1. Several New England locals have mentioned to me the possible link between *cours du roi* and *corduroy,* an explanation that I find more viable than any of the inconclusive etymologies one finds in various official etymological sources such as www.etymonline.com/index.php?term=corduroy.

2. Janet Vorwald Dohner, *The Encyclopedia of Historic and Endangered Livestock and Poultry Breeds* (New Haven, CT: Yale University Press, 2001), 266.

3. For more detail on the impacts of the colonists on the forests of New England, with numerous references to their often excessive land-clearing and firewood practices, see William Cronon, *Changes in the Land: Indians, Colonists, and the Ecology of New England* (New York: Hill and Wang, 1983). Another valuable reference is Howard S. Russell, *A Long, Deep Furrow: Three Centuries of Farming in New England* (Lebanon, NH: University Press of New England, 1982).

4. Cronon, *Changes in the Land,* 117–18.

5. www.clarksonny.org/html/historian.html.

6. Numerous sources review species introduced by the European colonists. I have utilized several, including: Elliot Rowland Downing, *A Source Book of Biological Nature-Study* (Chicago: University of Chicago Press, 1922), 261; http://wiki.monticello.org/mediawiki/index.php/Insects (accessed February 23, 2010); www.kingdomplantae.net/commonPlantain.php (accessed February 23, 2010); and www.oardc.ohio-state.edu/weedguide/singlerecord.asp?id=750.

7. For a comprehensive study of the impact of livestock on Native Americans and the eastern seaboard landscape, see Virginia Dejohn Anderson, *Creatures of Empire: How Domestic Animals Transformed Early America* (New York: Oxford University Press, 2005). Additional perspectives are offered by Cronon and Russell, cited above.

8. For an excellent primer to interpreting the history of the New England landscape, see Tom Wessels, *Reading the Forested Landscape: A Natural History of New England* (Woodstock, VT: Countryman, 2005). Tom was one of my graduate professors and one of the best teachers under whom I have ever studied. I owe him an enormous debt for my still-evolving understanding and appreciation of the New England landscape.

9. Hiel Hollister's *Pawlet for One Hundred Years,* originally published in 1867 and reprinted by the Pawlet Historical Society in 1976, seems to confirm current speculation as to the original forest composition in this region.

10. Charles C. Mann, "America, Found & Lost," *National Geographic,* May 2007, www.charlesmann.org/articles/NatGeo-Jamestown-05-07-1.htm.

Chapter 4: *Oikos:* A Household Economy and Ecology

1. Junichiro Tanizaki, *In Praise of Shadows* (Sedgwick, ME: Leetes Island Books, 1980), 4–5.

2. Joseph C. Jenkins, *The Humanure Handbook: A Guide to Composting Human Manure,* third edition (Grove City, PA: Jenkins Publishing, 2005).

Chapter 5: Looking Forward to Yesterday: Weaving Chronologies for the Future

1. David Pimental and Mario Giampietro, "Food, Land, Population, and the US Economy," http://dieoff.org/page40.htm (accessed February 23, 2010).

2. *Peasant,* as we tend to use the term culturally in the United States, often has a connotation of subservience; a person warranting pity. For the Tiroleans, on the other hand, mountain farmers were icons of independence, distant from cultural centers but not always far removed from politics and regional economies. As an example, Tirolean farmers often made up the bulk of local governing bodies, and during the time of the Hapsburg Empire, they were allowed to address the emperor using the informal *du* pronoun for "you." The pejorative sense of the word *peasant* is often an attitude that we convey in our usage and our lack of understanding of the other culture, not necessarily an accurate depiction of the condition or status of farmers in their own cultural contexts.

3. "Now you're a real Tirolean."

4. "Motorized scythe."

5. William H. Coaldrake, *The Way of the Carpenter: Tools and Japanese Architecture* (New York: Weatherhill, 1991), 8.

6. Dennis J. Werner and David F. Ritchie, "Peach Cultivars Introduced by the North Carolina Agricultural Research Service 1965 to 1981," State Bulletin 464 (North Carolina State University–Raleigh: Agricultural Research Service, April 1983), www.ces.ncsu.edu/depts/hort/consumer/agpubs/ag-464%20(reprint).pdf.

7. Letter from Ruth Clayton to Carlyle and Adelaide Clayton, September 8, 1949.

8. Letter from Robert Aycock (NCSU class of 1949) to Adelaide Clayton for Philip Ackerman-Leist, February 4, 2000.

9. Catharine Paddock, "Parkinson's Disease Linked to Pesticide Exposure," *Medical News Today,* March 28, 2008, www.medicalnewstoday.com/articles/102112.php (accessed February 23, 2010).

Chapter 6: The Simple Life: An Ecological Misnomer

1. Rebecca Kneale Gould, *At Home in Nature: Modern Homesteading and Spiritual Practice in America* (Berkeley: University of California Press, 2005).

2. Jeffrey Jacob, *New Pioneers: The Back-to-the-Land Movement and the Search for a Sustainable Future* (University Park: Pennsylvania State University Press, 1997).

3. For an overview of the ecological significance of old fields and their significance in the development of ecological theory, see *Old Fields: Dynamics and Restoration of Abandoned Farmland* (Washington, DC: Island Press, 2007).

4. I would like to make it clear here that I do not believe scientists were the first ecologists in the broad sense of the word that we often use. Native peoples, farmers, and even observant pedestrians were certainly ecologists who could challenge and complement the knowledge base of ecologists trained in the modern sciences. In this case, I am referring specifically to scientists trained in this discipline.

5. Donella Meadows, *Thinking in Systems: A Primer* (White River Junction, VT: Chelsea Green, 2008), 2.

6. *Old Fields,* 314–15.

Chapter 8: Of Scale and Skill: Homestead or Farm?

1. "Building Sewerless Cities," www.iatp.org/hogreport/sec3.html (accessed February 23, 2010).

2. "Industrial Fire (Food Processing Plant) Hamlet, NC, September 3, 1991," as appeared in "25 Die in Food Plant Fire" by Thomas J. Klem, *NFPA Journal* 86:1 (1992), 29–35, www.nfpa.org/assets/files/PDF/fihamlet.pdf.

3. Read a full description of Will Allen's projects in the cover story of the *New York Times Sunday Magazine* at www.nytimes.com/2009/07/05/magazine/05allen-t. html. Numerous online articles and videos also portray the contagious energy surrounding the renewal of communities through healthy foods and technological innovation.

Chapter 9: The End of Petrol

1. For more information on Dr. Temple Grandin's fascinating work, see www .grandin.com.

Chapter 11: The Smallholder as Placeholder

1. For the most thorough and balanced explanation that I know of regarding the complexities of terminology used to describe various sizes and types of farms, see Marty Strange, *Family Farming: A New Economic Vision,* new edition (Lincoln, NE: Bison Books, 2008).

2. *Living the questions* seems to be a phrase that many of us who have studied theology come back to, as it relates to the act of testing out one's beliefs and relying upon some sense of inner conviction in that process. I was surprised to realize that Gould and I were both using the phrase—she in her book and I in my classes— until I more carefully read her excellent overview of *lived religion* on page 6 in her introduction, in which she links the concept of lived religion with homesteading. As I reflected back upon my own theological studies and how they tie in to my homesteading views, I found her arguments increasingly compelling. I highly recommend reading the introduction and all the rest of her fine book.

3. Joel F. Salatin, *You Can Farm: The Entrepreneur's Guide to Start and Succeed in a Farming Enterprise* (Swoope, VA: Polyface, 1998).

Chapter 12: Building a Future

1. For a general introduction to the issue, see Henry Fountain, "Concrete Is Remixed with Environment in Mind," *New York Times,* March 30, 2009, www.nytimes .com/2009/03/31/science/earth/31conc.html, and also Charles Q. Choi, "Concrete Proposal to Cut Carbon Dioxide," January 29, 2007, www.livescience.com/ environment/070129_clean_concrete.html.

Chapter 13: Crafting a Croft

1. "Mountain farmers."

2. The First National Bank of Orwell has garnered significant attention since the 2008 financial crisis, given its financial solvency and growth in a time of crisis for the banking industry. For additional insights, see Katie Zezima, "Vermont Bank Thrives While Others Cut Back," *New York Times,* November 7, 2008, www .nytimes.com/2008/11/08/business/08bank.html?partner=rssnyt&emc=rss and other articles on the bank and its recent acclaim.

3. For further reading, see Christopher Alexander, *A Pattern Language: Towns, Buildings, Construction* (New York: Oxford University Press, 1977) and Gaston Bachelard, *The Poetics of Space* (Boston: Beacon Press, 1994).

4. For a more complete technical overview of our off-grid photovoltaic system and an excellent article on sizing and designing similar systems, see Khanti Munro's lead article "Design Your Own Off-Grid System: Plan Ahead to Power Your Independent Home" in the April/May 2010 issue of *Home Power* magazine (www .homepower.com/home/). The article is located on page 78. *Home Power* magazine and the associated Web site are superb resources for anyone interested in renewable energy systems.

5. www.staber.com/solarpower.

Chapter 14: Technological Cascade

1. Chinua Achebe, *A Man of the People* (Nairobi: East African Educational Publishing Ltd., 1966), 37.

2. For more information on the Amish, I highly recommend Donald B. Kraybill, *The Amish Struggle with Modernity* (Lebanon, NH: University Press of New England, 1994).

3. Nate Hagens, "Status and Curiosity: On the Origins of Oil Addiction," *The Oil Drum,* July 7, 2008, www.theoildrum.com/node/4240 (accessed June 7, 2009). I am indebted to Nate Hagens for sharing many of the concepts expressed in this posting as part of Green Mountain College's Family Farm Forum in spring 2009. His presentation helped to inspire my thinking for chapter 16 ("Rewired Rewards") of this book.

4. It is worth noting that *pleasure* is not a term necessarily embraced as something we should encourage others to pursue. For example, Tom Wessels contrasts the ephemeral nature of pleasure with the enduring nature of fulfillment. See Tom Wessels, *The Myth of Progress: Toward a Sustainable Future* (Lebanon, NH: University of Vermont Press, 2006), 95.

5. Sasha Chapman, "Gourmets Are Egotists and Pleasure Is a Right," *Globe and Mail,* May 6, 2009, www.theglobeandmail.com/life/article1139583.ece.

6. Steven Chu, "The Second Law and Energy," a lecture given at MIT on October 5, 2007, available in video version at http://mitworld.mit.edu/video/543.

7. Wessels, *The Myth of Progress,* 51–2.

8. Ibid., 57.

9. Rob Hopkins. *The Transition Handbook: From Oil Depedency to Resilience* (White River Junction, VT: Chelsea Green, 2008).

10. www.eia.doe.gov/emeu/reps/enduse/er01_us.html (accessed February 23, 2010).

11. http://css.snre.umich.edu/css_doc/CSS01-06.pdf (accessed June 7, 2009).

12. Stephen Hren and Rebekah Hren, *The Carbon-Free Home: 36 Remodeling Projects to Help Kick the Fossil-Fuel Habit* (White River Junction, VT: Chelsea Green, 2008).

13. Sandor Ellix Katz, *Wild Fermentation: The Flavor, Nutrition, and Craft of Live-Culture Foods* (White River Junction, VT: Chelsea Green, 2003).

14. Daniel D. Chiras, *The Homeowner's Guide to Renewable Energy: Achieving Energy Independence Through Solar, Wind, Biomass and Hydropower* (Gabriola Island, BC: New Society Publishers, 2006), 126.

15. David Lyle, *The Book of Masonry Stoves: Rediscovering an Old Way of Warming* (White River Junction, VT: Chelsea Green, 1998).

16. "Long-Term Performance of EPA-Certified Phase 2 Woodstoves, Klamath Falls and Portland Oregon: 1998–1999" (EPA-600/R-00-100, November 2000), www.epa.gov/appcdwww/ecpb/publications/EPA-600-R-00-100.pdf (accessed June 4, 2009).

17. Hren and Hren, *Carbon-Free Home*, 16.

18. Kate Galbraith, "Solar Meets Polar as Winter Curbs Clean Energy," *New York Times*, December 25, 2008, www.nytimes.com/2008/12/26/business/26winter.html.

19. Helpful texts in this regard include Art Ludwig's *The New Create an Oasis with Greywater: Choosing, Building and Using Greywater* and Carol Steinfeld's *Liquid Gold: The Lore and Logic of Using Urine to Grow Plants*.

20. For more information on the differences between DC and AC power, see Karen George's white paper "DC Power Production, Delivery, and Utilization" at http://mydocs.epri.com/docs/CorporateDocuments/WhitePapers/EPRI_DCpower_June2006.pdf.

21. "Luxury or Necessity? Things We Can't Live Without: The List Has Grown in the Past Decade," http://pewresearch.org/pubs/323/luxury-or-necessity (accessed June 7, 2009).

22. See www.worldvaluessurvey.org and proceed to "Findings," where the results of the long-term study "Happiness Trends in 24 Countries, 1946–2006" can be accessed.

23. US Department of Labor Bureau of Labor Statistics, "Issues in Labor Statistics: How Long Is the Work Week?," http://stats.bls.gov/opub/ils/pdf/opbils09.pdf (accessed June 4, 2009).

24. "US Department of Energy: Explanation of Solar Cells," www.youtube.com/watch?v=oeJAExKjELg (accessed June 6, 2009).

Chapter 15: The Clock, the Wallet, and the Hand

1. Robert L. Roy, *Mortgage Free!: Innovative Strategies for Debt-Free Home Ownership*, second edition (White River Junction, VT: Chelsea Green, 2008).

2. Coaldrake, *The Way of the Carpenter: Tools and Japanese Architecture*, 25–6.

3. For more information on Nova Kim and Les Hook and their fascinating work as wildcrafters, see www.wildgourmetfood.com.

Chapter 16: Rewired Rewards

1. For the definitive overview of *terroir* in English, see Amy B. Trubek, *The Taste of Place: A Cultural Journey into Terroir* (Berkeley: University of California Press, 2009).

2. "Foreigner."

3. "Impolite."
4. Solarfest is an event not to miss if you're in Vermont in the summer. Visit www. solarfest.org.
5. Michael Pollan gave his speech to the Terra Madre gathering on October 26, 2006.
6. See Carlo Petrini's *Terra Madre: Forging a New Global Network of Sustainable Food Communities* (White River Junction, VT: Chelsea Green, 2010) for a complete overview.

Chapter 17: To Gather Together

1. Julie Campoli, Elizabeth Humstone, and Alex Maclean, *Above and Beyond: Visualizing Change in Small Towns and Rural Areas* (Chicago: American Planning Association, 2004).
2. For more information on the Rutland Area Farm and Food Link (RAFFL), see www.rutlandfarmandfood.org.
3. Greg Pahl, *The Citizen-Powered Energy Handbook: Community Solutions to a Global Crisis* (White River Junction, VT: Chelsea Green, 2007).
4. Thomas L. Friedman, *Hot, Flat, and Crowded: Why We Need a Green Revolution and How It Can Renew America* (New York: Farrar, Straus and Giroux, 2008), 318–21.
5. Hopkins. *The Transition Handbook: From Oil Dependency to Resilience.*
6. Hren and Hren, *Carbon-Free Home,* xvii–xviii.
7. A sincere thanks to my research assistant and friend Ryan Dixon for reminding me throughout the writing of this book that not all Americans have the power to choose where they live or even necessarily how—mere survival is the focus of their daily lives, and homesteading is, from their perspectives, a choice of privilege.

ABOUT THE AUTHOR

Philip Ackerman-Leist and his wife, Erin, farmed in the South Tirol region of the Alps and in North Carolina before beginning their ongoing homestead adventure in Pawlet, Vermont. Ackerman-Leist is a professor at Green Mountain College, where he established the college farm and sustainable agriculture curriculum and is currently Director of the Green Mountain College Farm & Food Project.

ABOUT THE ILLUSTRATOR

Erin Ackerman-Leist has a degree in art from Guilford College. She homesteads in Vermont with her husband, Philip, and homeschools their three children. She creates art in her hard-won spare time.

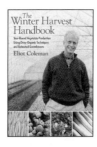

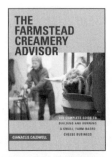